PENGUIN BOOKS

Words with Power

Northrop Frye was born in Sherbrooke, Quebec in 1912 and
spent his childhood in Moncton, New Brunswick. He was
educated at the University of Toronto and at Oxford
University. He returned to Canada in 1939 to teach at the
University of Toronto, becoming the principal (1959) and then
Chancellor of Victoria College (1978). He earned
international acclaim for his works of literary theory, which
include among others, *Fearful Symmetry: A Study of William
Blake, The Educated Imagination,* and *The Great Code.* One
of the world's most respected scholars, he lectured at universi-
ties in the United States, Canada, Great Britain, Ireland,
Scandinavia, Japan, New Zealand, Italy, Israel, Australia, and
the Soviet Union, and taught at Harvard, Columbia, Princeton,
Berkeley, Oxford, and others. Among a wealth of awards and
honours, Northrop Frye won the Royal Society of Canada's
Lorne Pierce Medal, the Canada Council Medal, the Toronto
Arts Lifetime Achievement Award, the 1987 Governor
General's Literary Award for Nonfiction for *Northrop Frye on
Shakespeare,* as well as numerous fellowships and honorary
degrees.

BOOKS BY NORTHROP FRYE

Fearful Symmetry: A Study of William Blake
Anatomy of Criticism: Four Essays
Fables of Identity
The Stubborn Structure
The Critical Path
Creation and Recreation
The Great Code: The Bible and Literature

Northrop Frye

WORDS
WITH
POWER

Being a Second Study of
"The Bible and Literature"

Penguin Books

PENGUIN BOOKS

Published by the Penguin Group

Penguin Books Canada Ltd, 10 Alcorn Avenue, Toronto,
Ontario, Canada M4V 3B2

Penguin Books Ltd, 27 Wrights Lane, London W8 5TZ,
England

Penguin Books USA Inc., 375 Hudson Street, New York,
New York 10014, U.S.A.

Penguin Books Australia Ltd, Ringwood, Victoria,
Australia

Penguin Books (NZ) Ltd, 182-190 Wairau Road, Auckland
10, New Zealand

Penguin Books Ltd, Registered Offices: Harmondsworth,
Middlesex, England

First published in Viking by Penguin Books Limited, 1990

Published in Penguin Books, 1992

1 3 5 7 9 10 8 6 4 2

Manufactured in Canada

Canadian Cataloguing in Publication Data
Frye, Northrop, 1912-
Words with power

Includes bibliographical references.
ISBN 0-14-012925-1

1. Bible and literature . 2. Literature and society.
3. Creation (Literary, artistic, etc.). I. Title.

PN56.B5F78 1991   809'.93522   C90-094279-7

to Jane

Contents

Acknowledgments

Three men and three women in particular have done much to make this book possible. Robert Denham of Roanoke College, A. C. Hamilton of Queen's University, and my research associate Michael Dolzani of Baldwin-Wallace College, have been of immense help in coordinating the criticism by and of me, and the last two have also read the whole manuscript and contributed most valuable suggestions for it. Helen Heller, my literary agent, assumed the task of styling and editing the manuscript; Jane Widdicombe, my secretary for twenty-two years, to whom the book is dedicated, has shown once more her unlimited patience and efficiency in coping with my revisions and the complex machinery of contemporary bookmaking; my wife Elizabeth has been essential in innumerable personal ways. I am also most grateful to the Social Sciences and Humanities Research Council of Canada for a grant that was of material assistance in processing the manuscript.

I am sorry for the near-obliteration of the footnotes; but trying to make them a useful and functional part of the book would have delayed its publication indefinitely.

N. F.

Introduction

This book continues the study begun in a book published some years ago called *The Great Code,* subtitled "The Bible and Literature." The significance of the "and" was that I was not attempting to isolate the literary features of the Bible, or deal with "The Bible as Literature." There were already many books on that subject. I wanted to suggest how the structure of the Bible, as revealed by its narrative and imagery, was related to the conventions and genres of Western literature. As a preliminary investigation of Biblical structure and typology alone took up a whole book, I promised a sequel. I then found that it was a mistake, at least for me, to think in terms of a sequel to a previous book, and the present one has been delayed by my poor judgment in not starting once again at square one. It does assume, however, the general position of *The Great Code,* and refers to some of its data. For those who have and want to use the earlier book, I have inserted "GC," with the page number, where such reference has occurred. But I hope and think that what follows is complete in itself. Readers primarily interested in the Bible may find it annoying that it takes three chapters to get to the Bible, but a shorter path would have been a much steeper one.

The Great Code was a very vulnerable book, and I regret
its deficiencies, but what mattered to me was the sympathetic
response of so many readers, who made up a much wider public
than I should have thought possible for such a book. It seemed
clear that, whatever its merits or lack of them, it had done
something to meet a genuine need. The present book puts more
emphasis on critical theory, and tries to re-examine the Bible
on a level that makes its connection with the literary tradition
more comprehensible. It is therefore something of a successor
also to the much earlier *Anatomy of Criticism* (1957). In fact, it
is to a considerable extent a summing up and restatement of
my critical views.

The repetition of themes from *The Great Code* here is inevitable; but at first it was a disappointment to find this book
beginning to sound like an initial (or a genuine) farewell tour.
However, other factors qualified the disappointment. First, the
context being different, a reader who has had difficulty with
my earlier books—and the appearance of Professor Denham's
bibliography makes it abundantly clear that there has been a
great deal of misunderstanding of them—may find it easier to
get his bearings in this one. For example, the sequence of verbal modes in the opening chapters covers much the same set
of phenomena as the Viconian sequence in *The Great Code,* but
may be simpler to follow in reading. Perhaps, of course, repetitiveness is merely the result—the flip side, so to speak—
of getting it right the first time.

Second, my general critical position, set out in *Anatomy of
Criticism* and other books, revolves around the identity of mythology and literature, and the way in which the structures of
myth, along with those of folktale, legend and related genres,
continue to form the structures of literature. *The Great Code*
owed a good deal to Vico, the first modern thinker to understand that all major verbal structures have descended historically from poetic and mythological ones. But even Vico had a
limited interest in the continuous social function of literature,
and he paid little attention to the principle that makes it insis-

tent. The same is true of Schelling, who began with similar postulates. In modern times, from Frazer on, there have been many remarkable essays on what Graves in *The White Goddess* calls a historical grammar of the language of poetic myth. These would include the works of Mircea Eliade, Joseph Campbell, and several Freudian, Jungian and other psychological studies. But as a rule these still show only a perfunctory interest in literature. Graves is an exception, but his personal attitude to his white goddess cult tends, in my view, to put his literary perspective considerably out of focus.

To summarize briefly my central thesis on this point: every human society possesses a mythology which is inherited, transmitted and diversified by literature. Comparative mythology is a fascinating subject, but it is quickly exhausted as a scholarly study if it remains simply a configuration of patterns. It is generally understood that it needs to be grounded in psychology or anthropology: it is much less understood that its central and most important extension is into the literature (along with the criticism of literature) which incarnates a mythology in a historical context. In the opposite direction, a literary criticism that cuts off its own cultural and historical roots in mythology becomes sterile even more quickly. Some forms of it stop with an analytic disintegrating of texts as an end in itself; others study literature as a historical or ideological phenomenon, and its works as documents illustrating something outside literature. But this leaves out the central structural principles that literature derives from myth, the principles that give literature its communicating power across the centuries through all ideological changes. Such structural principles are certainly conditioned by social and historical factors and do not transcend them, but they retain a continuity of form that points to an identity of the literary organism distinct from all its adaptations to its social environment.

To adopt the principle of the identity of mythology and literature means devoting a good deal of attention to the connections between literature and religion, literature being an aspect of culture that descends from a time when the word "religion" covered much more of the cultural area than it does now. In *Anatomy of Criticism* I gave a good deal of attention to separating the two: the reason was that religion has always been a close ally of literature, and because of that it can also be an insidious threat to its integrity. My present interest, both here and in *The Great Code,* is not in religion and literature, but in the Bible and Western literature. Between religion and literature, in every culture, there can be any number of "either-or" conflicts, dilemmas, or, to use the elegant term, aporias. Between Western literature and the Bible there are conflicts too, but what seemed more immediate to me was the common language in which they were written. The Bible's immense prestige as the source of the major religions of the Western world needs no further emphasizing. But, like the Emperor of Japan in the Shogunate period, its pre-eminence has remained largely theoretical: our actual sources of verbal authority have come to us in other linguistic forms. This is a close parallel to the traditional role of literature in relation to the ideologies that surround it in every age, where the very different linguistic structures of ideology and dialectic are normally regarded as superior and more trustworthy approaches to whatever words are supposed to do for us. The tendency to subordinate literary to other forms of language, though it has had its questioners, is essentially unchanged.

It is not always recognized that the strong prejudices to be encountered in this area are of linguistic origin. Traditionally, religious scholarship is the most anti-literary of all verbal disciplines. For Christian scholars since New Testament times, and *mutatis mutandis* for Jewish ones, poetry and fables were what other religions had: they had the "truth," and while truth might be conveyed in descriptive or conceptual or rhetorical language, it could never be conveyed in literary language. This assumption persisted in the face of the fact that the Bible is, with unimportant exceptions, written in the literary language of myth and metaphor: it is, in short, a work of literature plus. The present book attempts to explain once more what that "plus" is, why the beginning of the response to the Bible must be a literary response, and why, within the Bible itself, all the values connected with the term "truth" can be reached only by passing through myth and metaphor. This is a motif that has to be repeated in different contexts throughout. When I first began to think about a book on the literary context of the Bible, anti-literary prejudices were all around me, in various forms. In religion there was a fundamentalist response that simply denied the existence of myth and metaphor in the Bible, so far as such a denial was possible, and asserted that the truth of the Bible was expressed in historical and doctrinal language. There was an institutional response that admitted the poetic nature of much of the Bible, and drew the conclusion that the doctrinal commentaries of priestly and rabbinical traditions formed the real basis of religion. There was also a view which accepted, more or less, the mythical quality of Biblical language, but regarded it as a contamination of its real statement or *kerygma* (a word I retained in *The Great Code,* for reasons that are expanded in this book). The view I have, I think, consistently advanced is one that can be expressed in the phrase "literary literalism," a jingle so hideous that it may be memorable. The Bible should be read as literally as any fundamentalist could desire, but the real literal meaning is an imaginative and poetic one. If those who hold the views just listed were to turn their conceptions of language inside out, something quite interesting might happen to whatever commitments are brought to them by words.

The anti-literary prejudices in religious scholarship were, of course, complemented by anti-religious prejudices among literary critics, but as they were essentially the same prejudices in reverse, I need not say much more about them here. Most of them arose from a false notion of the importance of content, of a poet's personal beliefs and the like. What a poet *says* is not what makes him a poet. The situation I describe has changed a good deal in a generation or two. A short time ago, literary critics specifically interested in the Bible were few and defensive: today they are numerous and eminent. The number coming the other way, from Biblical scholarship to an interest in literary criticism, has increased proportionately. However, if I am not the speaker of a prologue, I am not a member of an aging chorus either. *The Great Code* was often regarded as anti-historical because it seemed a priori unlikely on historical grounds that the unity of narrative and imagery it demonstrated could exist in the Bible. As it does exist, so much the worse for history, but not everyone is prepared yet for such a paradigm shift.

A more serious issue, to me, is the number of literary critics who seem to be as unwilling as Biblical critics to admit that myth and metaphor form the primary language of their own subject. Ever since Plato, most literary critics have connected the word "thought" with dialectical and conceptual idioms, and ignored or denied the existence of poetic and imaginative thought. This attitude continued into the twentieth century with I. A. Richards's *Science and Poetry,* with its suggestion that mythical thinking has been superseded by scientific thinking, and that consequently poets must confine themselves to pseudo-statements. The early criticism of T. S. Eliot, though considerably more cautious than this, also exhibited an array of confusions clustering around the word "thought." Since then there has been a slowly growing realization that mythological thinking cannot be superseded, because it forms the framework and context for all thinking. But the old views still persist, if in more sophisticated forms, and there are still far too many literary critics who are both ignorant and contemptuous of the mental processes that produce literature.

The anxiety to develop criticism into a discipline that sounds linguistically mature involves hitching it onto some philosoph-

ical basis, and that in turn means that the very simple and
primitive categories of myth and metaphor at the heart of literature are likely to be misunderstood. I am not speaking of
linguistics or semiotics, where the direction is different to
begin with, but of critical approaches to literature that move
as quickly as possible into non-literary areas.

In the last two decades a bewildering number of new critical theories have developed, and while I have no hostility to
any of them—reservations are not hostility—there is a distinctive theoretical implication in my own position, and it would
be confusing if I did not try to put it in perspective. In its
narrower form, the theory in *Anatomy of Criticism* rested on
the continuity and identity of mythology and literature just
referred to, and although the majority of critics whose opinion
I value have been generous to it, others have tried to embalm
it in a sarcophagus of "myth criticism" unconnected with other
types of criticism. But in that book there was a broader conception closer to what the word *theoria* implies, a conception
originally (1957) directed against the assumption that criticism
must be either parasitic on literature or an extension of another
discipline. The implication for me was that criticism is a coherent but not exhaustible subject. This may seem obvious,
but is far from being so. Coherence is a preliminary intuition
or assumption about criticism: it does not prescribe any pro-
grams or predict any goals, but merely turns the engine on to
enable us to get started. It is what is called a heuristic assumption, adopted for the sake of seeing what comes out of it. What
comes out of it, however, is criticism itself.

When I first began to write it, I realized that criticism was
something different from literature, because I myself was a critic
and not a poet or novelist or dramatist. Yet I felt that I was
no less "creative" than those who were, creativity being an
attribute of a writer's mind and not of the genres he happens
to be working in. The main concern that seemed appropriate
at that time was the defense of criticism as a discipline in its

own right. The situation has reversed itself since then, like one of the trick drawings that illustrate one thing when the foreground is black and the background white, and something quite different when the perspective is white on black. Today criticism looks as though it were taking over the entire verbal area, and it is rather the integrity of literature and other traditional verbal enclaves that needs to be defended. Criticism has the paradoxical task of both defining and opening the boundaries of literature, but there still has to be a continuous dialogue between criticism and what it criticizes.

Every teacher of the humanities employed by a university is expected to be a "productive scholar," and in the present state of criticism not everyone can be that. It follows that there have to be critical methods developed, including my own in its narrower aspect, which enable scholars to produce what are primarily academic exercises, not really increasing the understanding of literature as a whole but demonstrating a certain competence in the subject. There remains however a genuinely "productive" group, who, though operating in a variety of "schools," seem to me to have, for all their surface disagreements, an underlying consensus of attitude, out of which a progress toward some unified comprehension of the subject could emerge, and lead to a construction far more significant than any deconstruction of it could possibly be. This corresponds to the situation in literature itself, where "original" writers form a core within a larger group that follows fashionable conventions and *idées reçues*.

It may seem the height of absurdity to speak of a consensus in criticism, when a glance at abstracts of reviews generally reveals nothing more than an accidental agreement about some temporary vogue or ideological illusion. But a great deal of profound critical insight, even wisdom, can be found in much work devoted to a single author or historical period, which remains isolated, unconnected with different authors or periods. What is usually lacking is a larger perspective that the assumption of coherence for criticism as a whole could give. It is very natural, however, that many humanist academics should feel threatened by the possibility of a coherent criticism, hence the popularity of rather aimless paradoxes that take us from "everything is text" to "nothing is text" and back again.

I have followed my own course in this book without reference to other critical schools, but that will not exclude many parallels to and echoes of them, at least if I am right in my conviction that a consensus does exist in criticism, however much the dialectical divergences among the schools may conceal it. The pluralistic tendency has to work itself out to exhaustion before any effectively unifying movements can replace it. In the meantime it has the disadvantage that while any amount of good work may be done within any one school, each is partly concerned with promoting its own position, which means that such schools form in the aggregate an interlocking body of mutual argument, out of which it is difficult for a real advance in criticism to come.

In this connection, the reader will note a tendency in the present book, which has run through all my writing for the past twenty years or so, to address myself less to a purely academic audience than to undergraduates and a non-specialized public, including, of course, whatever academic critics are willing to take a more detached attitude. I know that this policy has confused even sympathetic academic reviewers, as well as driving others into all the hysterias of pedantry.

There are two reasons for this "public address" format. One is a conviction that radically new directions in the humanities can come only from the cultural needs of this lay public and not from any one version of critical theory, including my own so far as I have one. The other is that books appear from time to time telling us that the educational establishment in our society has betrayed our cultural heritage and allowed young people to grow up barbarously ignorant of its traditions. Such books are often warmly received, with everyone apparently convinced that something should be done. Nothing is done, mainly because the only implicit recommendation for action is to prod the educational bureaucracy. I think this starts at the wrong end, besides introducing assumptions in the philosophy of education that may be mistaken and are in any case unnecessary. Surely only a constant awareness of the widest possible audience for scholarship in the humanities can start the educational breakthrough that everyone seems agreed is needed. So while my critical approach has been said to be deficient in rigor, this does not matter so much to me as long as it is also deficient in rigor mortis.

The view of critical theory as a comprehensive *theoria* may help to explain the role of the Bible in my criticism. The theory of genres in *Anatomy of Criticism* led me up to the sacred book, along with secular analogies or parodies of it, as the most comprehensive form that could reasonably be examined within a literary orbit. It then occurred to me that the perspective might be reversed, starting with the sacred book and working outwards to secular literature. Nobody would attempt to study Islamic culture without starting with the Koran, or Hindu culture without starting with the Vedas and Upanishads: why should not a study of Western culture working outwards from the Bible be equally rewarding? As the Bible is written in poetic language, it should also be possible to approach it as a kind of microcosm or epitome of the unity of literary experience in Western countries. The Bible's authority in matters of religion and the like is not the subject of this book: the subject of this book is the extent to which the canonical unity of the Bible indicates or symbolizes a much wider imaginative unity in secular European literature.

There has recently been a good deal of critical discussion about Poe's story "The Purloined Letter." Much of it deals with the story as a psychological allegory, and with such questions as whether the letter itself is a symbol of a phallus or a clitoris. If we must have such allegorizing, it seems better to have one that does not lose sight of the fact that a letter is a verbal message. A story about a verbal message that various people want to kidnap, can't kidnap because they can't see it, and can't see it precisely because it is staring them in the face, seems to me also an allegory of what I am talking about in this book. For literary critics my "purloined letter" is the Bible, a book normally excluded from discussions of literature, yet the only book, to my mind, that pulls the major problems of criticism together into a single focus. For Biblical scholars the "purloined letter" is the language of myth and metaphor, the essential language in which the Bible is written, and yet a language excluded as far as possible from historical and doctrinal approaches to it. As remarked above, these statements are less true than they were a few years ago, but they are still truer than they should be.

The first half of this book sets out the different idioms of linguistic expression, and tries to approach the question: what is the distinctive social function of literature, and what is the basis of the poet's authority, if he has any? This question may sound now like old-hat Romanticism, the main focus of criticism having shifted from the poet to the reader, the reader being the one who is involved in the Herculean labors of misreading and deconstructing his text. I do not see how the reader can acquire so heroic a role unless something in literature gives it to him, even if this merely throws us back on the question of what gives this something to literature. Whatever the final answer to that, the poet's authority is bound up with the authority of poetic language, which secular poets and most of the Bible have in common.

The second half deals with an image of major importance in literature, the *axis mundi* or vertical dimension of the cosmos. The *axis mundi* seemed to me significant because, first, it has no objective existence, but belongs entirely to the verbal world, and, second, being as frequent and central outside the

Bible as within it, it illustrates my "great code" principle that the organizing structures of the Bible and the corresponding structures of "secular" literature reflect each other. I am familiar enough with such defensive reactions as "unconvincing," but I realize that many readers will find the second part a baffling snakes-and-ladders game, and I have asked myself often enough if I have not attempted an impossibly huge and amorphous subject. There is also the fact that where the possible documentation is so vast, all specific examples may give an impression of thinness or random choice.

Yet I hope, first, that the comments on difficult literary works, however brief and elliptical, may, in the stock phrase, "throw more light" on them, by suggesting a context which is part of their meaning. Second, that this book may help one to understand why the poets whom we consider most serious and worthy of exhaustive study are invariably those who have explicitly used the kind of imagery studied here. And finally, once again, that it will afford glimpses of interconnecting structural principles of literature that are actually connected with literature and the experience of studying it. I am still too close to it to guess how useful this second part will be, but the success of a book that takes no risks is hardly worth achieving.

The critical principle underlying the second part is an inference from the principle of coherence as a critical hypothesis. The poetic imagination constructs a cosmos of its own, a cosmos to be studied not simply as a map but as a world of powerful conflicting forces. This imaginative cosmos is neither the objective environment studied by natural science nor a subjective inner space to be studied by psychology. It is an intermediate world in which the images of higher and lower, the categories of beauty and ugliness, the feelings of love and hatred, the associations of sense experience, can be expressed only by metaphor and yet cannot be either dismissed or reduced to projections of something else. Ordinary consciousness is so possessed by the either-or contrast of subject and object that it finds difficulty in taking in the notion of an order of words that is neither subjective nor objective, though it interpenetrates with both. But its presence gives a very different appearance to many elements of human life, including religion, which depend on metaphor but do not become less "real" or "true" by doing so.

Of course "metaphorical" is as treacherous a conception as "truth" or "reality" could ever be. Some metaphors are illuminating; some are merely indispensable; some are misleading or lead only to illusion; some are socially dangerous. Wallace Stevens speaks of "the metaphor that murders metaphor." But for better or worse it occupies a central area—perhaps *the* central area—of both social and individual experience. It is a primitive form of awareness, established long before the distinction of subject and object became normal, but when we try to outgrow it we find that all we can really do is rehabilitate it.

At this point another recent critical observation comes to hand, from Italo Calvino's posthumous Norton lectures, also a paradox but an exhilarating one: "Literature remains alive only if we set ourselves immeasurable goals, far beyond all hope of achievement." Strictly speaking the writer does not set the goals: these are set by the shaping spirit of literature itself, the source of a writer's ability to write. But in general the same principle should apply to criticism, when the critic sees in the far distance some such axiom as "Criticism can and should make sense of literature," and refuses to settle for anything less.

Much of my critical thinking has turned on the double meaning of Aristotle's term *anagnorisis,* which can mean "discovery" or "recognition," depending on whether the emphasis falls on the newness of the appearance or on its reappearance. Of course every true discovery must in some sense relate to what has always been true, and so all genuine knowledge includes recognition, however interpreted. In any case, at the age of seventy-five discovery can come only from reversing one's direction, going upstream to one's source, like the fisherman in Yeats's "Tower." The negative form of the Greek word for truth, *aletheia,* which means something like "unforgetting," suggests that at a certain point searching for the unknown gives place to trying to remove the impediments to seeing what is there already. I hope that the retracing process, whatever its success, will be profitable for some readers, as it has been for me.

N. F.
Victoria College
Massey College
University of Toronto

I wish you to write a book on the power of the words, and the processes by which the human feelings form affinities with them.

(Coleridge: letter to Godwin, September 1800)

PART ONE

Gibberish
of the Vulgate

CHAPTER ONE

Sequence and Mode

I

May I begin where I have so often begun, with the fact that when we read (or otherwise examine) a verbal structure, our attention is going in two directions at once. One direction is centripetal, trying to make sense of the words we are reading: the other is centrifugal, gathering up from memory the conventional meanings of the words used in the world of language outside the work being read. This relation of signifiers to signifieds is variable, and the variants develop into different kinds of verbal structures, and different emphases in meaning. I am calling these variants modes, a term I have used elsewhere in a different context which I will return to later. Every verbal structure is likely to have its chief center of gravity in one of these modes, though aspects of all the others will be included or implied.

The term traditionally used for varieties of mode within a single work is "polysemous" or having many meanings, a term that can readily be transferred to a critique of the different ways in which words make their impact. In a more restricted sense the theory of polysemous meaning is medieval in origin, and I have drawn heavily on it, especially on Dante's formulation of it, in other writings. The theory is usually bound up with the metaphor of levels, a hierarchical metaphor used for convenience, less likely to be misleading when we remember that it refers to a mental diagram in our minds that we have imposed on the subject, not to something inherent in the subject. The secondary metaphors implied by "level," according to which one level may be either "higher" or "more profound" than another (compare the Latin word *altus,* which means both high and deep), are more likely to lead to irrelevant value-judgments, but sometimes we can hardly dispense with them.

I should like to look at a sequence of such varieties of verbal categories. It is to some degree a sequence of levels, though the levels are (with many qualifications) closer to Hegel than to Dante. That is, they are not so much hierarchical as progressing from the less to the more inclusive. But this is misleading too if it implies that each mode is a self-enclosed entity, which it never can be. Each mode is partial and imperfect, and that is the reason both for the existence of the others and for their co-existence within the same work.

My sequence is not historical—in fact it is practically the reverse of the historical. The mode that it is easiest to begin with was the last historically to become fully mature. This is the descriptive mode, as we may call it, the one in which we are reading to get information about something in the world outside the book. Here we have two structures, the structure of what is being described and the structure of the words describing it. (The first structure is being largely created by the second, but we must not complicate things prematurely.) Words or signifiers are, in theory, being subordinated to what they signify, servomechanisms to the information they convey. The variety of information conveyed by descriptive writing naturally makes for an equal variety of narrative types. Some descriptive narratives, such as textbooks, are expository, preserving some sense of a movement from the better to the lesser known, so that the reader follows a kind of initiatory progress. Others, like most histories, relate their narrative to the sequence of events they describe. This coincidence is possible because both historical events and their narrative counterparts move in temporal order. There are also works of reference, designed not for consecutive reading but for consultation at specific places. Here the narrative falls into a purely arbitrary convention already known to the reader, like the alphabetical narrative of a dictionary. I recall these exceedingly obvious points to emphasize the primary role of narrative or sequence in holding together every mode of verbal expression from the Bible to the telephone directory.

The descriptive style minimizes the aspects of writing that call attention to the relations among the words, to what is peculiarly verbal, or, in vulgar speech, "merely verbal." Ambiguity, pun, multiple meanings within the same word, are avoided: nouns and verbs, at least ideally, have one meaning each, the one suggested by their relevance to the subject the book deals with. Figures of speech, metaphors and the like, are avoided also, except as examples or illustrations. The overriding criterion of descriptive writing is, speaking practically, objective truth. It is important for the reader of a descriptive verbal structure, such as, for example, a newspaper, to know whether he is getting genuine information or merely something the author has made up or heard from others. We call such a verbal structure true, and the details of its content facts, if it seems to be a satisfactory verbal replica of what it describes.

The prestige of the words truth and facts have caused the descriptive mode of writing to be regarded as the most fundamental and essential mode of all, and the one that underlies all the others in hierarchical arrangements. The descriptive is the traditional literal meaning in which words have the function of transmitting the non-verbal. I have many times remarked on the illogicalities of the word literal, and on the absurdity of assuming that in the Bible, for example, the literal (descriptive) meaning must be fundamental, because the Bible could not be true without it. There is no continuous or fully developed descriptive level of meaning in the Bible, and the Bible would be a grotesque anomaly if there were. This difficulty with the word literal was recognized very early, though suppressed by a censorship preoccupied with the anxieties about truth just mentioned. On the whole, continuous descriptive techniques in writing are later than the Bible, because they depend on certain social and technological developments that took a long time to become fully functional.

The writing of history, for example, emerges from chronicle and hearsay and cribbing from other books in proportion as a genuine historiography is formed, with its techniques of research and documentation. Archaeology, which is hardly two centuries old, is essential to its support, particularly in the ancient period. I am not suggesting that history, much less what is now called historicity, is simply a verbal imitation of external events, only that without the descriptive double focus of verbal and actual events we should not have what we now call history. Then again, the study of the external world cannot achieve adequate verbal expression until the techniques of science are developed. The most descriptively minded writer of the ancient world, Aristotle, was greatly hampered, if not crippled, by the absence of such techniques, especially in his biological observations, and so gave his main attention to another mode to be presently described.

There is also a political factor involved. The descriptive writer is a democratic writer, and his truth depends on his putting all his cards on the table, sharing what he knows at every point with his reader. A reader who disagrees with him must simply check his facts or repeat his experiments. It is not a coincidence that the techniques of descriptive writing and the theory of democracy grew up together, beginning perhaps around the time of Locke. The maturity of a democracy, today, is not contained in its voting processes or its choice of leaders, but in the principle of openness in descriptive writing. The authority of open science is recognized in theory in both democratic and totalitarian societies, but both still try to control openness in historical writing by hiding or destroying the relevant documents.

Short-term descriptive statements have probably formed the bulk of human communication from the beginning of time. I am speaking here of continuous forms, which in a pre-technological age are largely confined to memoirs, narratives held together and contained within the memory of the writer. Such narratives are among Derrida's "logocentric" forms, where the writer is really a speaker.

In the descriptive mode, especially in non-historical genres, we follow the Lockean procedure in which perception leads to reflection, perception here including the pre-arranged perception of experiment. It is in the reflection stage that one normally begins writing, and the word contains the metaphor of the mirror, what is reflected in thought being the wordless data of sense perception. But this can hardly mean that we leap across a gap from the wordless to the verbal. Any perception that leads directly to reflection must be a verbalizing impulse from the beginning: the ordering of words does not suddenly appear in the middle of the process. Unthinking people often accuse scholars in every field of finding only what they have previously wanted to find, as though all genuine discoveries resulted from ignorance or pure chance. But perception itself is potentially verbal, starting off with a verbalized hypothesis already in the mind (e.g. "I wonder if"), and it moves directly to its own fulfillment in a verbal goal.

The initiative of descriptive writing, then, the force that starts it all going, is the ordering of words, which on the conscious level involved in such writing is the syntactical or grammatical ordering. But this initiative is in a sense excluded from the descriptive operation: it is centrally there, but has to remain a largely unexamined assumption, if descriptive writing as such is to retain its fullest integrity. The descriptive writer normally wants his non-verbal facts to "speak for themselves," and directs the reader's attention away from the role of his own word-ordering, not merely in connecting his data, but in creating them, in the sense of transmuting something non-verbal into a verbal structure.

However, words can never directly transmit to our minds anything that is not verbal. Words transmit the non-verbal only in their own terms and grammatical conventions. In English, a central convention of this sort is the subject-predicate-object convention. The authority of the non-verbal fact gets considerably cut down in this process: we may try to pretend that the subject-predicate-object relation is inherent in the nature of things, but even if it were the grammatical convention would still be the limit of what we can reach by this road. The difficulties in trying to understand much of contemporary science, for example, through a cumbersome verbal grid of nouns and verbs that insist on turning processes in space-time into things in space and events in time are recognized by everyone now. A naive confidence in the perfect transparency of language as a communicator of the non-verbal has largely disappeared from our culture.

The word-ordering process, then, in descriptive writing may be called the excluded initiative, assumed but not the focus of attention. Once it becomes the focus, we move into another mode of writing, one that we may call the conceptual or dialectic mode. In conceptual writing the element earlier called truth has to be looked for inside, so to speak: in what the words contain rather than in what they reflect from the environment. The movement from descriptive to conceptual runs parallel to the movement of imitation or mimesis in Aristotle when he is illustrating the relation of art to nature. When we say "art imitates nature" we instinctively think of a work of art, say a painting, as a copy of a natural model, landscape or whatever, outside it. To some extent it may be that, but we eventually come to see that the relation of art to nature is better thought of as an internal one, where, in Aristotelian terminology, art is the form and nature the content, nature being something contained by the art and not something reflected in it.

This gives a wider perspective to the criticism of painting, despite all the painters who assert that they paint only what they see, and despite the incompetent critics (a very diminished band now, but once dominant) who think that a painting's merit depends on the similarity of its content to something non-pictorial. But the main emphasis in photography, like other descriptive modes a fairly recent development, is still on the pictorial transmission of an external model.

The conceptual writer, like the descriptive one, is searching for whatever objective truth words can give him, and he is still appealing to the conscious mind and its sense of objectivity. But he is searching for it within the verbal order he is constructing, and this shows itself in an intense tightening up of the narrative movement. It is most important that sentence B should "follow" from sentence A, and rules of logic are developed to ensure that such following is correct throughout. The narrative becomes an argument, and argument is designed to exert a compulsive force on the reader, evoking such responses in both writer and reader as "I am forced to think," "I am compelled to accept," and the like. For many centuries this sense of compulsion in argument was an immense cultural force (GC 11), and there was a widespread assumption that the force of argument was a central determining factor in behavior. A question is thus raised which is implicit in the title of this book: the relation of words to power.

In conceptual writing the emphasis is on the power of words to co-ordinate verbal elements, hence conceptual writing concentrates on the elements most closely related to co-ordination. These are expressed in such terms as time, nature, substance, being, all of which are necessarily abstract, related immediately to the verbal construct itself and withdrawn to some degree from the external world.

Two features of such writing are important for us here. One is that ambiguity may become, not a mere obstacle to meaning, but a positive and constructive force. Such words as time in Bergson or substance in Spinoza have to be used in a great variety of contexts, and while the different uses may be consistent, consistency is not simple identity. The other feature is that, especially when the relation to the concrete seems uncertain, conceptual writing is sometimes called "speculative." Here the metaphor of the mirror (*speculum*) recurs, in a different mode from the "reflection" of descriptive writing. If we ask what the speculation is a mirror of, the traditional answer is being, a conceptual totality that transcends, not only individual beings, but the total aggregate of beings. Heidegger endorses the statement that the first question of philosophy is, "Why are there things rather than nothing?" But things are not what Heidegger means by being, and the question leads to another: "Why is there being beyond all beings?"

It seems clear that, while there is any amount of conceptual writing in the world, the most impressive achievements in this mode are the great metaphysical systems, the structures that seek to present the world to the conscious mind. The word system is a spatial metaphor, and in proportion as temporal metaphors came to replace spatial ones in the nineteenth century, philosophical genres became more fragmented and more emphasis was given to the linear aspects of argument. Along with this went a tendency to try to integrate conceptual and descriptive modes, as in the movement called logical positivism earlier in this century. In this period we were even told that metaphysics was a gigantic verbal illusion based on a misunderstanding of what language can do. One who has read, say, Aristotle's *Metaphysics* to the great enlargement and refreshment of his mind is not likely to take this very seriously, whatever his own philosophical qualifications. In any case logical positivism assumed an antithesis between meaning and nonsense which is no longer with us. But its prejudice against metaphysics was of very long standing.

Anything that sounds anti-intellectual always becomes popular, and we often hear a couplet quoted in the belief that it asserts the superiority of those who get along with common sense, like just ordinary folks, to the great explorers of thought:

> He knew what's what, and that's as high
> As metaphysic wit can fly.

But this is the seventeenth-century Samuel Butler speaking of Hudibras, who is not a person of common sense but a pedantic and pretentious ass. Hudibras has studied philosophy, and knows that a central question of that subject is *quid est quid:* what is whatness, or being? Butler does not say that Hudibras knew the answer to the question, only that he knew that the question existed.

The metaphysical structure in itself, with its speculation reflecting being as a lake does the sky, has a contemplative quality in it, as though the beta rhythms of ordinary awareness were being relaxed into the more meditative alpha ones. The massive calm of Spinoza's *Ethics* is an example. But there are other elements in conceptual writing that qualify this impression. Behind most of it is the traditional dialectic that splits every question in two, accepting the true inference and rejecting the false one. This is potentially an aggressive and militant use of language: there would be everything to be said for it if the true knight always won, but the defeated knight may put on new armor and overcome his rival in his turn. Descriptive writing, in contrast, attempts to escape from argument. Here are the data, the descriptive writer says: they should be established facts if they are right, and nothing at all if they are wrong. But once we make the arranging of the data the center of the activity, we enter a world where argument is central, and there is no end to the possibilities of argument. Arrangement means selecting for emphasis, and selecting for emphasis can never be definitively right or wrong.

The impersonal and objective quality of dialectical writing is an ideal, and a very important one at that, but the impersonal leaves out the personal, and one wonders if the personal can be left out indefinitely. Anyone who says openly, like Orgon in *Tartuffe,* "But I *want* it to be true!" disqualifies himself from being taken seriously in either the descriptive or the conceptual modes. Yet Aristotle's *Metaphysics* begins with the remark that everyone naturally "wants" (*oregontai*) to know. So the objective style of conceptual writing is started off by something more like a subjective desire or energy. This suggests that other factors are involved besides the logically impeccable construct.

Whitehead, for example, remarks: "Every philosophy is tinged with the coloring of some secret imaginative background, which never emerges explicitly into its trains of reasoning." Here again we run into what looks like an excluded initiative. In considering the logic of an argument our attention is directed away from the fact that the argument is what the person constructing the argument wants to be true. One naturally cannot reduce this want to something purely subjective like Orgon's mother-fixated obsession about the piety of Tartuffe. There is an impersonal argument, an appeal to a consensus, and other marks of an intellectual honesty that has its own authority. Still, something is missing. In theory an argument would not depend for its validity on the person who advanced it: it would be the same argument no matter who worked it out. But nobody quite believes this: there is always some glimpse of relation to a personality.

And sometimes we even wonder whether an entire metaphysical system may not be growing out of a personal metaphor. We often run into diagrammatic illustrations, like the divided line in Plato's *Republic,* and other diagrams are implied by the connectives used. Some things are higher and other things lower; on the one hand we have this, on the other hand that; some data are inside us and others outside. Metaphorical connectives of this kind suggest the orientation of a human body in space. Possibly this concealed body may be the center of the whole operation, a personality speaking through the mask of argument. The conceptual writer himself would say: "Well, of course, I wrote it, and I meant what I said." When this initiating personal factor is not simply assumed but moves into the center and becomes a new focus for the verbal operation, dialectic is transmuted into rhetoric, and in place of the conceptual we have the ideological, the verbal structure that appeals to commitment rather than reason. The existential movement earlier in this century brought into prominence a number of conceptual writers—St. Augustine, Pascal, Kierkegaard—who stressed the inseparability of the personal factor in such writing.

II

In the first book of the *Republic,* a general discussion among Socrates and some of his friends and disciples brings up the word justice. One of the group named Thrasymachus undertakes to show that justice is whatever is to the advantage of the stronger. Socrates easily demolishes this argument, and reduces Thrasymachus to silence. But there are a number of ironies in the situation beyond the ironic role of Socrates himself. The disciples of Socrates are not satisfied, and urge him to go on with the discourse, which implies reconsidering what Thrasymachus tried to say in a more inclusive context.

Thrasymachus is a sophist, one of those whom Plato thought of as teaching that good and evil, truth and falsehood, are relative to specific situations. The sophists were concerned with rhetoric, not dialectic, and with training people to speak effectively in law courts and assemblies. The fact that rhetoric is inferior, even contemptibly inferior, to dialectic is proved, for Plato, by the fact that sophists charge fees for their teachings. Thrasymachus warns the company that he is not going to disgorge his precious definition of justice for nothing. And yet Socrates' refutation of Thrasymachus shows him to be a sophist too, if a more generous and agile one. Socrates demonstrates only that the *word* justice is one of the good words, and that its context is with other good words that mean everything admirable and virtuous. Thrasymachus is not talking about this kind of thing at all: he is speaking for the wordless world of power. He is a forerunner of Machiavelli and Hobbes and Marx and the late Nietzsche, who tell us about a world where material or other forces of power are effective and words are not, and where the use of such a word as justice means chiefly that someone who holds power is rationalizing the fact that he is going to go on holding it.

For Socrates, real justice, the justice to be reached by dialectic, not talked about rhetorically, can exist only in a different world from this. But where is such a world, if the word where in fact applies to it? Is it another world, or the world we enter at death, or this world after a revolution? Or is it simply the community of those who know that it is better to endure than to inflict injustice, because they also know that the word justice, however impotent as a word, still does have a meaning, and to acquire meaning is to acquire power, of a sort? The cause of freedom is not quite hopeless as long as someone realizes that the voice of tyranny is misusing words, that is, lying.

Any of these answers may be right, or even all of them: the ten books of the *Republic* seem to find some place for all of them. But if the victim of injustice is not helped by Thrasymachus' vision of "too bad, but that's the way things are," he is no more helped by Socrates' vision of justice as each man doing what by nature he is best fitted to do. By the time we reach Socrates' "noble lie" that ensures the stability of his ideal state, Socrates and Thrasymachus seem to be on much the same level and to be talking about much the same thing. The *Republic* belongs to Utopian literature, and consequently to the moral rather than the intellectual world.

Whatever the role of dialectic or logical consistency in the *Republic,* it emerges as a personal vision from the mind of Socrates. We have moved into a third mode here, based on the identity of the writer with what he writes. I say writer, but in this area the ideal is speaking rather than writing. Rhetorical structures are those that are peculiarly logocentric, where even written authorship points to a speaking personality addressing a listening audience. It is the association of rhetorical writing with speech that has produced the curious idealizing of the orator, the professional speaking rhetorician, which runs through the history of culture from Cicero to the Renaissance humanists, and lingered beyond them. In the *Republic,* again, there is the identification of the writing Plato with the speaking Socrates; and in Christian iconography the four living beings of Revelation 4:7, derived from Ezekiel 1:10, are identified with the four evangelists, Matthew, Mark, Luke and John, who provided the written vehicle for the spoken words of Christ.

Aristotle did not, like Plato, depreciate rhetoric to a secondary art ranking with cookery, but his treatise on rhetoric begins with a most significant word. Rhetoric, he says, is the *antistrophos,* the answering chorus, of dialectic. He goes on to explain that the essential element in rhetoric is the genuine logic and objective pursuit of truth that dialectic gives to it. Appeals to subjective and emotional factors in the audience are suspect: rhetoric is allowed to proceed by discontinuous logical jumps (enthymemes), but should nonetheless preserve the impersonal continuity of logic. Aristotle thus seems to hold what Plato also holds in theory, even if he often does something else in practice: that there is a disinterested pursuit of truth which is morally superior to rhetoric, and should control it wherever possible. This argument has the difficulty that the rhetorical represents a more inclusive form of communication than the dialectical one. Rhetoric expresses and appeals to a more comprehensive enlisting of the personality than simple argument: it is not an imitation of dialectic, but an incorporation of it into another mode.

A few centuries after Aristotle there comes the rise of Christian thought, and Christianity, at least then, did not believe that a disinterested dialectic was either possible or desirable. St. Augustine is quite clear that the pursuit of truth for its own sake is not merely an illusion but a sin of pride. In the medieval theory of polysemous meaning, or at least in Dante's exposition of it, there is nothing that directly corresponds to our conceptual mode, but there are two levels of what I am calling the rhetorical one. The first is "allegorical" (better called analogical or typological); answering the question *quid credas,* what you should believe; the other moral or tropological, answering the question *quid agas,* what you should do. We can call these the theory and practice respectively of Christian ideology. They are of course inseparable: on the level of belief alone, it is not possible to distinguish what we believe from what we believe we believe (GC 229); our actions alone show what we really believe.

On this basis perhaps we can unscramble our terms ideological and rhetorical. The most elaborate developments of our third mode are the great frameworks of accepted (and by the great majority unexamined) assumptions that we call ideologies. These are normally structures of social authority, so far as verbal structures can articulate and rationalize authority. The *strategy* of ideology may begin with premises beyond argument, but it normally proceeds with some respect for logic and intellectual honesty, even permitting a limited amount of dialogue with those outside the ideology. In this way it preserves the kernel of Aristotle's principle of controlling rhetoric by dialectic. However, when an established social authority insists that certain ideological postulates are essential, and is ready to move in on any dissidents who publicly proclaim a different attitude, the subordinating of dialectic to something else is clear enough.

The *tactics* of ideology are incorporated in works of rhetoric, or oratory, where the aim is to persuade and create a response of *conviction*. In oratory an identification of speaker, speech and audience is what is aimed at. That is, the "I," who is the writer or speaker, is identifying himself with the "we" he is addressing within the common framework of assumptions represented by the speech. Such an identification would be impossible if the audience's attention were diverted to the objective, or sent off for any length of time in any centrifugal direction: the whole emphasis has to be on the inter-ordering of words. We noticed that in medieval theory the moral level of persuading to action is also called the tropological or figurative. This points to the fact that in oratory there must be a strong emphasis on figurative or purely verbal language, metaphor, allegory, simile, antithesis, and above all repetition.

Another and more primitive verbal device also begins to emerge in oratory: a rhythm based not on the syntactical sequences of prose, which express the rhythms of waking consciousness, but on a steady repetitive and recurrent beat like that of verse. Figurative language is literary as well, and a training in rhetorical devices would be equally useful to orator and to poet. From Classical times until past the Renaissance, the rhetorical and the literary were recognized to be next door to one another, two varieties of figured language.

If we look at a fairly genuine and positive rhetorical situation, such as those represented by Lincoln's Gettysburg address or the 1940 speeches of Churchill, we can see how an ideology maintains itself in a historical crisis. The appeal to reason is not primary, though not denounced either. The principle invoked is that we belong to something before we are anything, that our loyalties and sense of solidarity are prior to intelligence. This sense of solidarity is not simply emotional, any more than it is simply intellectual: it might better be called existential. There is an appropriate use of figured speech, most obviously repetition ("of the people, by the people, for the people"; "we shall fight on the beaches; we shall fight in the hills").

When the rhetorical occasion narrows down from the historical to the immediate, as at rallies and pep talks, we begin to see features in rhetoric that account for the suspicion, even contempt, with which it was regarded so often by Plato and Aristotle. Let us take a rhetorical situation at its worst. In intensive rhetoric with a short-term aim, there is a deliberate attempt to put the watchdog of consciousness to sleep, and the steady battering of consciousness becomes hypnotic, as the metaphor of "swaying" an audience suggests. A repetition of cliché phrases is designed to bring about a form of dissociation. The dead end of all this is the semi-autonomous monster called the mob, of which the speaker is now the shrieking head. For a mob the kind of independent judgment appealed to by dialectic is an act of open defiance, and is normally treated as such.

We spoke of the endlessness of argument in the conceptual area, but rhetoric has an *ad hominem* or personal weapon available to stop argument. One may be told "You just say that because you're an atheist, a Communist, a Jew, a Christian, or because you had a castrating mother," etc., etc. Such verbal weapons are illegitimate in the conceptual mode, where an impersonal basis is assumed. But they play an important role in ideology—not always a sinister or violent role, as one may also be led to examine one's position to see what limitations are built into it.

Another issue opens out here. We have been speaking so far of the actively ideological, but there is also a passive side to ideology, where every verbal structure, simply by being conditioned by its social and historical environment, reflects that conditioning. Metaphysical systems, down to Leibnitz at least, show a tendency to present themselves spatially, as it were, as structures devoted to unchanging truth, and so rising above time. However, they do not rise above time, and as time goes on this becomes increasingly obvious. The longer a thinker has been dead, the more likely his work is to be studied as an ideological document.

So ideology seems to be the delta which all verbal structures finally reach. But there are other things to be considered that qualify this, the most insistent being the constant tendency for any ideology to collapse into tyranny or mob rule. An ideology is most beneficial when it has least power, when its assumptions can be most freely challenged by others, when the terrible claws of ideological authority, inquisitions and secret police and the like, are not simply pared but removed altogether.

Hence the importance of the independence of the descriptive and conceptual modes and the maintaining of their standards of verbal authority. A new scientific or historical discovery may undermine an ideology at any time; philosophers, even when in bad times they may seem, like Descartes in a different way, to have some difficulty in proving their own existence, may play a crucial part in uttering the voice of reason and logic whenever society degenerates into hysteria. The voice of reason is often weak and ineffectual, however, because of the difference between the reasonable and the rational. Rational dialectic, being inherently deductive, tends to assume a Euclidean world where courses of action must fit an argument, however unpractical. The reasonable is aware that every rational argument is a half truth, and that the other half should be included within a more tolerant and flexible compromise.

Fact and concept can never be divided from ideology, but they can usually be distinguished. Reactions to this situation are curiously extreme in our day. One extreme speaks of an "information explosion" as a feature of our time, without apparently noticing how much of this information comes in prepackaged ideological containers. The other extreme asserts that because no one is free from commitments or assumptions, and a hundred-percent detachment is impossible, the difference between degrees of it is not significant, and that efforts at being intellectually honest when dealing with people of different commitments are ultimately futile. But the fact that no ideal goal can ever be reached in human life does not diminish the importance of turning in the direction of that goal.

We cannot end here, because ideologies, like other human organisms, are mortal: they come to birth, decay and die, or are metamorphosed into other forms. Decline and metamorphosis, we said, are often obviously results of activity in other verbal modes. The rise of science and secular philosophy meant that a Christian ideology founded on a geocentric universe, a very recent beginning and an imminent end of time, a quasi-spatial heaven or hell awaiting us at death, and an organization devoted to stamping out all manifestations of unapproved thought, has had to regroup its forces and reorder its tactics over the last few centuries, besides being compelled to meet the challenge of other ideologies. It seems to follow that there is some verbal mode more inclusive even than ideology. To look into this we have to start with the question: what creates an ideology in the first place? Why does social authority rationalize its power in words, instead of simply asserting that it has it, which according to Thrasymachus is all it needs to do? Is there not here again some excluded initiative that is really a shaping force, something that could be the center of a fourth mode?

III

The ideological unity of speaker, speech and listener is a human and social one, and the non-human environment seldom enters it directly. Ideologies grow in proportion to man's realization that he is the dominant animal in nature, and that the bull, the eagle, the lion, do not represent anything numinous, any powers that man cannot incorporate into his own cosmos. This realization was doubtless preceded by a more primitive sense of human alienation and helplessness in nature, a sense that became largely outgrown as society got stronger. What feelings of impotence still survived were in part transferred to the gods, and events as late as, say, the Lisbon earthquake of 1755 were still apt to evoke some formula of the "God is punishing them for their sins" type. But the normal historical process moves in the direction of eliminating such formulas and regarding earthquakes and similar phenomena as simply "natural" processes that no God or gods either cause or interfere with.

The ideological world as such, then, tends to become a world of the human and the non-human, with nothing that is personal in it outside the human. The same is true of the previous verbal modes. The scientist is better off if he avoids the sense of the numinous, or the non-human personal. If he is a biologist studying evolution, it is better for him to exclude the sense of the teleological, of a non-human personal design; if he is an astronomer studying the big bang, or whatever alternative he prefers, it is better for him to avoid such words as creation. When I say better I mean less liable to be dragged into what for him would be regressive conceptions that could only confuse his science. It is true that in physics, for example, the principle is established that the observer alters what he observes by the process of observing it. But the word observer is still confined to a consciousness relating itself to the impersonal, and whatever is outside consciousness, such as emotion, belongs to a subjective world that is not functional in physics even yet.

However, the essential feeling of the alienation of human beings in a simply non-human environment is still there. There are still the impenetrable mysteries of birth and death; the mystery of what has been called "thrownness," the feeling that the fact of existence is an arbitrary fact; the sense of awe and wonder in contemplating the stars or the sea or the stillness of a forest that is never quite satisfied with the depersonalizing tendencies of descriptive, conceptual or ideological thought, however flexible. Hence the need for a more inclusive mode of verbal communication of a type that since the Romantic period has usually been called imaginative. Such a mode takes us into a more open-ended world, breaking apart the solidified dogmas that ideologies seem to hanker for.

An imaginative response is one in which the distinction between the emotional and the intellectual has disappeared, and in which ordinary consciousness is only one of many possible psychic elements, the fantastic and the dreamlike having conventionally an equal status. The criterion of the imaginative is the conceivable, not the real, and it expresses the hypothetical or assumed, not the actual. It is clear that such a criterion takes us into the verbal area we call literature.

The narratives of literature descend historically from myths, or rather from the aggregate of myths we call a mythology. A myth is a story (*mythos*), usually about the acts of gods. Because it is a story, it is potentially literary, and is of the same shape as other types of story, such as folktale and legend, which are less preoccupied with the recognized divine beings. As the category we call literature develops, these story-types merge, and the traditional myths modulate into the fictions of novels and romances and epics, besides being embodied more episodically in lyric poetry. All this has to be gone into more fully in the next two chapters in spite of having appeared in my earlier work in different contexts.

Myths take us back to a time when the distinction between subject and object was much less continuous and rigid than it is now, and gods are the central characters of myth because they are usually personalities identified with aspects of nature. They are therefore built-in metaphors, another literary element we have still to examine. Gods repeople, so to speak, non-human nature: sun-gods and sea-gods and storm-gods bring nature back to a personal habitation, and provide it with what has been called, in a different context, an "I-Thou" relationship in place of the environment of ordinary consciousness where everything is an "it." But as the category of literature emerges, the existence of these gods ceases to become important even when it is assumed. After the temples of Jupiter and Venus were demolished and prayers and rituals no longer associated with them, they continued to live with undiminished energy in literature. The poet does not need to assert the reality, or ontological existence, of anything he is talking about. This may seem to deprive him of all social usefulness and influence, and in many respects it does.

The initiative excluded from but assumed by ideology is myth. There is an infinite number of individual myths, but only a finite number—in fact a very small number—of *species* of myths. These latter express the human bewilderment about why we are here and where we are going, and include the myths of creation, of fall, of exodus and migration, of the destruction of the human race in the past (deluge myths) or the future (apocalyptic myths), of redemption in some phase of life during or after this one, however "after" is interpreted. Such myths outline, as broadly as words can do, humanity's vision of its nature and destiny, its place in the universe, its sense both of inclusion in and exclusion from an infinitely bigger order. So while nothing ontological is asserted by literature as such, the imaginative or poetic mode of ordering words has to be the basis of any sense of the reality of non-human personality, whether angels, demons, gods, or God.

An ideology starts by providing its own version of whatever in its traditional mythology it considers relevant, and uses this version to form and enforce a social contract. An ideology is thus an applied mythology, and its adaptations of myths are the ones that, when we are inside an ideological structure, we must believe, or say we believe. Belief, in its usual sense, does not go beyond a declaration of adherence to an ideology (GC

229). An ideology normally conveys something of this kind: "Your social order is not always the way you would have it, but it is the best you can hope for at present, as well as the one the gods have decreed for you. Obey and work." Persecution and intolerance result from an ideology's determination, as expressed through its priesthood, or whatever corresponds to a priesthood, backed up by its ascendant class in general, to make its mythological canon the only possible one to commit oneself to, all others being denounced as heretical, morbid, unreal or evil. This means that there is a strong resistance within an ideology to placing its excluded initiative, the myth it lives by, into focus and examining it in a broader perspective.

As literature asserts nothing but simply holds up symbols and illustrations, it calls for a suspension of judgment, as well as varieties of reaction, that, left to itself, could be more corrosive of ideologies than any rational skepticism. I have mentioned the authority of the voice of reason in a hysterical society, but reason depends on consciousness, and consciousness is a defensive and filtering mechanism, excluding other forms of psychic activity, such as fantasy or dream, which are functional in literature. It is also in the interests of every social contract to reduce these non-rational psychic activities to unreality. That gives the poet a psychic "let's pretend" playground that need not be taken seriously unless he re-enters an ideological mode and devotes himself to expounding it in his own language.

Of course many poets do this, and would feel utterly insecure and lacking in social function if they did not. In the thirties and forties of this century it looked for a time as though literature were about to become a closed shop of ideological believers adhering to some religious or political position, usually an authoritarian one. What else can a poet do, if he can only play around in a vague mythical world or hint darkly at great mysteries that no one will ever comprehend, including himself? Shelley wrote a poem of mythical free play called *The Witch of Atlas,* but even his wife thought he was being irresponsible. So essentially did he, though he defended his right to a holiday.

We saw how rhetoric grew up under the shadow of a suspicion that most of it was simply bad dialectic, reinforcing a legitimate appeal to reason by an illegitimate appeal to emotions or vested interests. We also saw that there was much truth in this, that there are debased forms of rhetoric, and that dialectic has some power, though a very limited one, of fighting against them. Similarly, in an age dominated by clashing ideologies, there is a good deal of suspicion of myth as the inspiration of bad ideology. We distinguish two forms of rhetoric which, if not always debased, are certainly suspect: propaganda and advertising. They are suspect because their approach is ironic: an advertiser attaches very little real commitment to what he says, nor does he expect a committed response from his public. Such a contact, assuming some degree of social control, is relatively harmless: only the forms of rhetorical propaganda that are backed by threats and penalties designed to eliminate the ironic response are actively debased.

When an ideology is enforced or promoted to the extent of hysteria and fanaticism, the mythological basis of it comes out very clearly, but in a pathological form. Examples are the "Nordic" racist myth of Nazism, the myth of a spontaneously creative and ideologically obedient peasantry in gang-of-four China, and the "fundamentalist" or sectarian myths in various religions, often forming around a charismatic leader, that cut off their supporters from the rest of the world. But nonetheless the mythology, good or bad, creates the ideology, good or bad. Hence it is misleading to use the word mythology to mean only (a) bad or trivial ideology, (b) other peoples' ideologies, appropriately denigrated, or (c) sick mythology. In the background here is the vulgar prejudice against literature that has made the terms for literary structure, myth, fable and fiction, into synonyms for something not true. There are even people who believe that all myth is verbal pathology: this was a nineteenth-century aberration, but has survived into the twentieth century.

There is a feature in myth, however, that makes this mistreatment of it plausible. When mythology modulates into ideology and helps to form a social contract, it presents data asserted to be historical, actual events in the past, but presents them so selectively that we can hardly take them to be really historical. The creation and deluge myths in Genesis, for example, say explicitly "This is what happened," and implicitly "This can hardly have happened in precisely this way."

The reason for presenting the past, real or legendary, in such a form is already given in the word presenting. Early societies at least may not have any very clear idea of their own actual history, but they do know that their lives will end in death, that they have seen many disasters and setbacks in those lives, with the prospect of further ones, and that their world is full of cruelty and injustice. Myth exerts a counterbalancing force to such history as they know, with its suggestion that the events they encounter are repeating their ancestral myths or working out their decreed meanings. Such myths are not merely "tales of the fathers," in Thomas Mann's phrase, but confrontations with a present significance, drawing out the reserves of courage and energy needed either to maintain routine or to meet a crisis.

Throughout this book we shall be invoking Coleridge's formula, that we must often distinguish where we cannot divide, in order to preserve both the unity of the whole, and the distinctiveness of the parts, of what we are dealing with. If I am asked where criticism itself belongs in this survey, I should say that criticism is the theory of words and of verbal meaning, and is therefore distinguishable, however intimately involved, from the different forms of verbal practice just considered. Criticism includes linguistic and semantic areas which are not touched on here, as I am concerned with a specific issue affecting only one kind of literary criticism. Many critics today are still unwilling or unable to get past the ideological stage in dealing with literature, because they are less interested in literature than in the relation of literature to some primary ideological interest, religious, historical, radical, feminist or whatever. In such approaches literature is subordinated to something else which by definition is more important and urgent. The historical reasons for the popularity of these approaches will be the main theme of the next chapter. I think there should be some critics, however, interested in dealing with literature in terms of its own mythical and metaphorical language, for whom nothing is prior in significance to literature itself. This is not to deny the ideological relations of literature, or belittle their importance, but to ascertain more clearly what it is that is being related.

More broadly, criticism is language that expresses the awareness of language. So far as this means ordinary conscious awareness, the approach of criticism to literature includes a certain amount of a reduction of poetry to expository prose—in itself a somewhat pedantic and ungrateful task. The aim of such reduction, however, is not to translate poetic language into an inferior and inadequate language, but to establish the relations of poetry with its wider verbal contexts. Different kinds of critical activity begin to open up at that point.

In rhetoric, style and content, the oratorical tricks and the persuasive message, are separable, and this assumption of separability is often carried into literature by critics who are thinking in rhetorical terms. Critics often tell us of writers who write elegantly but have nothing to say (i.e. nothing that that particular critic wants to hear), or of writers who may often write badly but, etc. Literature, we have reiterated, does not say things: literary works communicate in mythical wholes, and if a distinction of style and content seems to be essential, it means that the writer has not escaped from the rhetorical orbit.

The awareness of language may begin with ordinary consciousness, but it soon becomes clear that language is a means of intensifying consciousness. This is true of all four of the modes we have been surveying. The reinforcing of science or philosophy or history or politics with criticism begins by creating canons of authenticity: it is criticism that separates science from superstition, history from rumor and legend, philosophy and politics from propaganda, and the like. In literature the canons of the authentic are much more elusive and flexible, and are apt to change at any time. But the role of criticism is the same there as elsewhere, even if criticism is not built into the structure of literature as it is into the structure of science or philosophy. Such criticism marks out the direction of advance in consciousness, and closes off the deviations and blind alleys that lead us back to where we started. In literature the creative structure is normally produced by an individual; criticism represents the forming of a social consensus around it.

In our day the intensifying of consciousness, in the form of techniques of meditation and the like, has become a heavy industry. I have been somewhat puzzled by the extent to which this activity overlooks or evades the fact that all intensified language sooner or later turns metaphorical, and that literature is not only the obvious but the inescapable guide to higher journeys of consciousness. Once again a purloined letter is staring us quizzically in the face. When Dante wanted to experience states of being beyond life in thirteenth-century Italy the poet Virgil appeared as his guide. Virgil represents literature in its Arnoldian function as a "criticism of life," the vision of existence, detached but not withdrawn from it, that is at its most inclusive in the imaginative mode. Beyond Virgil there is Beatrice, who represents among other things a criticism or higher awareness of the limits of the Virgilian vision. It looks as though criticism is both the controlling and directing force within each verbal mode and the power that enables us to travel between the modes in both directions, until we reach the limit of what words can do for us. But what looks like a limit from a distance often turns out to be an open gate to something else when we reach it.

We have next to compare in more detail the two forms of rhetorical language, the literary and the ideological, the imaginative and the persuasive, and see whether we can learn from this something about the place and social function of literature in the verbal cosmos.

CHAPTER TWO

Concern and Myth

I

Our starting point here is the word myth, in its common and popular sense of a story (*mythos*), usually about gods, and usually referred back to a remote past. I am still emphasizing (I will not use the word "privileging") the narrative aspect of literature. The typical myths just mentioned arise in the earlier stages of social development, before the verbal controls of logic and evidence are firmly established. Literary criticism is mainly confined to the era of written documents, so that oral and pre-mythical cultures have to be passed over here.

To recapitulate briefly what was said in *The Great Code* and in the previous chapter: in structure myths resemble other forms of story that we distinguish as folktales or legends. Folktales however tend to be socially nomadic, traveling through the world interchanging their themes and motifs; legends are typically stories associated with some particular place or culture-hero. Myths have a different and distinctive social function. That function is mainly to tell the society they grow up in the important things for that society to know about their gods, their traditional history, the origins of their customs and class structure. Myths are also regularly used in connection with rituals, whether as forming a commentary on the ritual or as being dramatized by it.

Myths have thus two contexts. In their structure they resemble other types of story, and so are potentially literary. But in early societies they also develop a social function that we have been calling ideological. They play a leading role in defining a society, in giving it a shared possession of knowledge, or what is assumed to be knowledge, peculiar to it. Its proclamation is not so much "This is true" as "This is what you must know." Such a mythology is close to what is meant by the Biblical term *torah,* essential instruction, including the laws, which no one can be excused from learning. So a mythology creates in the midst of its society the verbal equivalent of a *temenos* or sacred ground, a limited and sacrosanct area.

When their ideological function disappears, myths, being left only with their literary structure, become purely literary, as Classical mythology did after the rise of Christianity. The myths of the Bible, on the other hand, retained a special sacrosanct status down to about the eighteenth century, and in a more decadent state to our own time. But as society develops it becomes more pluralistic: different questions are asked with words, and more is demanded of the verbal culture, creating the other types of language and of narrative that we have been examining.

Thus the mythological Greek verbal culture, which gave us Homer, Hesiod, the Homeric hymns and the tragic poets, found itself challenged by the early philosophers who began to ask such questions as: what is the world made of? Is there a primary substance from which the others are derived? What really are the stars? Are there such things as atoms? These are questions that move in the direction of science, and the askers of them soon discovered that mythology had no serious or relevant answers to them. The reason is that mythology is not a proto-science: it expresses human beliefs and fears and anxieties and passions and aggressions, in its context of a tradition or revelation assumed to come from an authoritative though ultimately mysterious source. Of course many myths have proto-scientific implications, such as the myths connected with the forming of a calendar, reconciling the solar and lunar year and the like, just as many myths are oblique accounts of historical figures or events. But mythology is not primarily interested in the speculative, much less the factual: it is a structure of practical human concern—the word concern will meet us again before long.

Such new interests, once introduced, are not easily dismissed, because of the linguistic possibilities they have opened up. The Pythagorean school, for all its occult trappings, left the suggestion that perhaps the primary language for the study of the physical world was not verbal at all, but mathematical. The time of this idea, so to speak, did not come until the century of Galileo and Descartes, when it moved into the foreground of thought. But science could not get very far with an undeveloped technology, and the pre-Socratics have left us mainly brilliant intuitions in speculative cosmology. What is important for us just now is that some of these early speculations collided with the anxieties of society, which was, like all societies, dominated by a myth-begotten ideology. One philosopher, Anaxagoras, a teacher of Pericles, was, we are told, brought to trial in Athens for impiety and atheism—he is said to have suggested that the sun might be a glowing rock, perhaps as large as half of Greece. At that time and place not much could be definitely established about the sun, so the only issue here—though a very important issue—was the right of individuals to make their own speculations, a right that few societies have been willing to concede.

The much more highly publicized trial of Socrates on the same charge symbolized a major and permanent revolution in verbal culture. Socrates' interests were less in the natural world than in the ethical one, and thus were a much more direct challenge to the social monopoly of concern. However wrong the condemning of Socrates may have been, the revolution was lucky to have him for a martyr, and, of course, to have Plato as a witness of that martyrdom, at its very beginning. The revolution turned on the superseding of *mythos* by *logos*. *Logos* means here an ideological rhetoric assumed to be controlled by dialectic, and, at least at first, in Plato and Aristotle, identified with dialectic. Obviously a book on the Christian Bible is going to have to use *logos* in other contexts, and due notice will be given when the context changes. Whatever the limitations of language in reaching reality, it was felt, the prose arrangement of words that advances by propositions and makes definite and particular statements gets us further than language bound up with story-telling and with the poetic self-containment that can be neither refuted nor established, and which at best only pretends to make particular statements. *Logos* thinking comes through an individual mind, but its ultimate source is a social consensus: Plato employs a dialogue form partly to symbolize this.

With many qualifications, we may still take the expulsion of poets from Plato's *Republic,* and the contemptuous reference to the mythological way of thinking in Aristotle's *Metaphysics,* to represent a subordination of poetic and metaphorical to dialectical language which has dominated Western culture ever since, however often the direction of the dialectic has changed. From Plato and Aristotle to the Hellenistic philosophies, from them to Christian theology and scholasticism, and from there to the secular ideologies of our own time, democratic or Marxist or whatever, the ascendancy of dialectician over poet has been relatively constant.

Myth thus, as explained earlier, loses its ideological function except for what is taken over and adapted by *logos*. Myths that are no longer believed, no longer connected with cult or ritual, become purely literary; myths that retain a special status in society are translated into *logos* language, and are taught and learned in that form. This is what happened to the Bible in the

Christian centuries; before reading the Bible one had to learn how to read it from a structure of *logos*-formulated doctrine. The procedure was much the same in Reformed churches, however different the theory. An open Bible was one of the central issues of the Reformation, but a Calvinist, for example, read not the Bible but the Bible through Calvin's interpretation of the Bible.

Accepted myths soon cease to function as myths: they are asserted to be historical facts or descriptive accounts of what "really happened." I have noted (GC 18) the passage in *Faust* where Faust deliberately alters "In the beginning was the Word" to "In the beginning was the Act." I should have added that Faust was simply following the established Christian practice up to his time. In the beginning God did something, and words are descriptive servomechanisms telling us what he did. This imports into Western religion what post-structural critics call the "transcendental signified," the view that what is true or real is something outside the words that the words are pointing to. It seems obvious to me (more of this later) that the opening of John's Gospel is expressly trying to block off that attitude, and to identify *logos* and *mythos*. But the attitude itself is deeply rooted in the human mind. In the twentieth century Trotsky denounced certain Marxist deviants of his time for believing, like idealists, in the primacy of the word, whereas for him all genuine Marxists knew that in the beginning was the act.

It is vociferously said at intervals that myth, fable and fiction, the words for literary narrative, are all euphemisms for lies, and this view in earlier centuries included the extreme Christian doctrine that Classical and other mythologies were the devil's parodies of the true one. Biblical myths, in this view, were not lies, and therefore not myths: the warning against "silly myths" (*mythous bebelous*) comes as early as the Pastoral Epistles in the New Testament. Perhaps, if the dates make it possible, the attack here is on the outpouring of mythopoeia in the Gnostic writings: if so, the line is being firmly drawn to exclude all mythology outside the canon, whatever the canon was at that time. Such an attitude locks us into a binary true-or-false system in which the flexibility of myth is lost, though in Western cultural history a more liberal consensus struggled out of it. We have met, and will continue to meet, however, many survivals and mutations of the traditional prejudices against myth.

Plato's myths, constructed by a dialectician of supreme genius who is still very close to a historically functioning mythology, are the clearest examples we have of how mythology is supposed to work when *logos* is in charge. The myths take over in Plato when the dialectic has gone as far as it can, and we are ready for what is called in the *Timaeus* a probable tale (or, in a livelier phrase, "likely story"). The probable tale illustrates what has been said, or speculates on possibilities still unborn in the dialectic, or, as in the *Phaedo,* indicates the kind of thing that must be valid in areas beyond the reach of direct argument. Aristotle also finds a place for the poetic utterance as able to express universal if not particular truths, and hence to contain its own kind of hypothetical truth.

This means in effect that literature is being very closely allied to rhetoric, and like rhetoric should be regarded as an *antistrophos* of dialectic. This view has maintained a good deal of ascendancy ever since: in fact there are not even yet nearly enough critics who can distinguish poetic language from a special-purpose rhetoric. A readily accessible expression of a cultural attitude descending from Aristotle is Sir Philip Sidney's sixteenth-century *Apologie for Poetrie,* which is clear that the poet "never affirmeth," meaning that all statements in literature are hypothetical or pseudo-statements. But poetry, Sidney says, as compared with (moral) philosophy, turns the abstract precept into the concrete example, while as compared with history, it turns the imperfect human example into the idealized or role-model example of the hero. Therefore poetry has

a powerfully supportive social place among all the elements of
courtesy or civilization, even in military circles, where it is the
"companion of camps."

The stock assumptions that Sidney is partly accepting and
partly qualifying are roughly: the poetic is primitive, and
therefore we should be aware, in reading it, of what aspects of
it are to be outgrown; the poetic is playful, and therefore should
be taken in a different spirit from discursive verbal structures;
the poetic is imaginative, and is therefore not a competitor in
the verbal race to truth and reality. The poet's ideal is to delight and instruct: the sources of delight are within his art, but
for instruction he needs guidance from another verbal discipline. Stories proceed by illustration and example, which are
easier to take in than argument, because they appeal to a more
childlike level of the mind. This gives the poetic an emotional
resonance, even at times a sense of mysterious unexplored
possibilities, that catches a much wider audience than pure
argument. It provides color where argument provides only black
and white. Its essential social function, then, is to supply a
rhetorical analogue or counterpart to whatever ascendant ideology may be contemporary with it. The implication is that
legitimate and useful literary structures are myths of the Platonic type.

The poets adjust to this situation in various ways, two of
which are of particular importance. One is the use of allegory.
In allegory the relation between the story and its meaning is
visible throughout, and meaning in this context is connected
with translation into *logos* language, as when a discursive moral
is said to be the meaning of a fable of Aesop. Here the role of
poetry as a rhetorical analogue to an ascendant ideology is very
clear.

Later on, the literary writer begins to displace his mythical
structures in the direction of the plausible or credible, and from
this procedure comes the rise of realistic and naturalistic fiction. Here, as in allegory in a different way, the function of

literature as an illustration of ideology is inescapable. We find less extreme adjustments in verse—the poetic, in the narrower sense of verse, being the most recalcitrant part of literature to adapt to discursive writing. But even there we have notable forms of what is called in Biblical study "demythologizing." An example is Wordsworth's break with the traditional mythologies of Ovidian metamorphosis and the like, and his use of a more descriptive idiom allied to those of non-literary prose. The kind of Victorian reader who, in Douglas Bush's phrase, believed that he was reading poetry when he was really looking for "great thoughts," was also taking a demythologizing view.

II

We have glanced at the way in which ideological language supports the anxieties of social authority, and of how other types of verbal authority nonetheless establish themselves, for example in science. In the collisions of Galileo and Bruno with the religious functionaries of their time, we recognize that a scientist has a commitment to his science as well as to his society, and that in certain crises he has an obligation to remain loyal to his science, even if silenced or martyred. This may be a simple moral issue of holding on to facts and evidence in the face of reactionary illusions, but it may be something subtler than that. In Galileo's day the evidence for a heliocentric solar system was not yet conclusive: the geocentric theory seemed still reasonable, and Galileo was really making what is called a leap of faith. This term is used in religious writing, but not every leap of faith is a religious one. As for Bruno, his leaps are so vast and various that even specialists on him find him hard to keep up with. But then Isaac Newton presents an almost equally disconcerting picture when the whole of his output and range of interests is considered.

The authority of science, in other words, expands into a

wider and more compelling authority of social and intellectual freedom. This will always be relevant as long as the scientist remains a human being whose work has a personal context as well as a scientific one, involved with ideology even when he challenges certain accepted forms of it. In our day the confrontation of scientist and social reaction may go into reverse. A highly technological society may conscript some scientists into working for its interests, whereupon others will realize that the basis of their commitment to science is a conviction that science exists for the benefit of humanity, not for the promotion of tyranny and terror.

The authority of science is generally recognized today, though grudgingly, and often accompanied by the persecution or social isolation of dissident scientists who do not conform to approved social anxieties. But the authority of the poet is hardly recognized at all, and may be explicitly denied, as it has been, for example, in the "socialist realism" manifestoes of the Stalinist era in the Soviet Union, in the so-called "cultural revolution" in China, or in the waves of middle-class hysteria, often called morality, that periodically sweep over the United States and Canada.

Ideology is supported, or assumes that it is supported, by dialectic, and dialectic, we said, traditionally proceeds by demonstrating that one affirmation is true and that consequently its opposite must be false. Christianity affirms the existence of a personal God, and says (or has said) of anyone who affirms the opposite that he is to be anathema, or cursed. But increasingly, since Hegel at least, we have come to see how every affirmation is a partial statement containing its own opposite, which remains attached to that affirmation. If we say "There is a God," we have suggested the possibility of saying "There is no God," and so in a sense have already said it. The most effective ideologies today are those that have developed enough flexibility and tolerance to take account of this fact.

But as a rule those in power, and perhaps a large part of

society also, regard flexibility and tolerance as dangerous social forces. The twentieth century has seen many poets and novelists exiled, silenced, isolated, imprisoned, murdered, or driven to suicide by ideology-obsessed governments. They have become marked out as martyrs or victims mainly by insisting on the integrity of their poetic vision. So the question, not only of the reality of a poetic vision, but of the distinctive authority that proclaims it, can hardly be dismissed as unimportant. This is especially true when the situation has extended beyond literature into a world-wide ideological deadlock, with fools and psychopaths in every part of the world urging war or systematic terrorism as a realistic way of smashing someone else's ideology.

And although a writer may be devoted to maintaining the integrity of his vision to the point of risking his livelihood or even his life for it, he may still be very uncertain in his own mind about what guarantees that integrity. Against him is the weight of the assumption that poetic and mythological forms of thought are primitive, and that without proper ideological guidance his work will become socially useless if not worse. As early as Petrarch's *Secretum,* a rueful dialogue between the poet himself and St. Augustine, we are made aware of how peripheral a poet may feel in his society as compared with so central a figure as a Doctor of the Church.

We also have Chaucer's "Retractation," where the poet repudiates whatever of his works may "sownen into synne." We may feel that there is a strong smell of "sign here" about this document, and that we should not care to cultivate the acquaintance of anyone who thought that reading Chaucer would lead to sin. But nonetheless a long progression of conversions, repentances and repudiations of earlier work both precede and follow this retractation in the history of literature. It is not hard to think of great writers in every culture—Tasso, Gogol, Yukio Mishima are random examples—who have been driven to nervous breakdown or sterility or worse over doubts and insecurities related to the social function of their work. Of course any one of these could be examined as a psychological problem different from the others, but the number associated with literature and the other arts would still be significant.

In the thirteenth-century French poem *Aucassin et Nicolete* the hero Aucassin is warned that his devotion to love and the arts will lead him to hell. He replies that that is precisely where he wants to go, as it seems clear that everything of any human value is headed in the same direction. For all the gossamer-light humor, many of Aucassin's contemporaries would have uttered the same warning in grim earnest, and when we think again of Chaucer's "Retractation," we realize that it would not be easy to maintain so defiant an attitude indefinitely, in such a society, especially on one's death-bed. Nevertheless an attitude of defiance as well as of self-doubt or submissiveness runs all through literature, at least from medieval poets to our own day. This often takes the form of adopting a lifestyle that seems to say: if society considers us anti-social, we will *be* anti-social, or enough so at least to shock its complacency.

Diderot's *Neveu de Rameau* in the eighteenth century heralds a world in which practically every decade has thrown up some variety of anti-establishment attitude associated with the arts. These include the Bohemians of the late nineteenth century and the Dadaists of the time of the First World War. Contemporary with the latter, many great writers, along with minor ones, flirted with various types of fascism, evidently because that was the most obviously anti-social ideology within reach. In English literature they include Yeats, Ezra Pound, Wyndham Lewis and D. H. Lawrence (whose *Plumed Serpent* is surely proto-Nazi in its implications). What seem in retrospect to be milder if no less perverse ideologies affected many others in the same period, and a tendency to simplistic obscurantism, whether located on the left or the right, extends both earlier, in the work of some very prominent nineteenth-century nov-

elists, and later, in the sub-cultural and counter-cultural movements of the last quarter-century.

The list of writers who have sought the support of an
alliance with religion in the last century needs no commentary,
beyond the observation that the connection is usually volun-
tary on the part of the poet, sought out and chosen, in a way
that it would not have been in periods when religious commitments formed part of the cultural ambience. Hence its context is one of minority protest rather than dominant ideology.
We note also two emerging elements of the picture: first, the
rebellious lifestyle extends to the other arts, notably painting,
as well as literature; and second, the counter-cultural aspect is
as a rule expressly antagonistic rather than simply detached.

In ordinary speech we distinguish work and play (GC 125):
work is energy expended for a further end in view; play is
energy expended for its own sake. Discursive language is
working with words, which means that the words should normally be laid out in a straight line leading to the center of what
is being said. But we speak of playing the piano or tennis, and
of dramas, even tragedies, as plays. Doing such playing well
takes a lot of work, of course, but the end of the work is, or
is closely allied to, the self-contained energy of play. It seems
clear that the popular conception of discursive prose as more
responsible and serious than poetic language is an aspect of the
work ethic, an aspect of ideology strong enough for poets
themselves to feel its pressure. Nonetheless literature constitutes the intensely difficult and exacting operation of word-
play, and even granting that there is something of Hermann
Hesse's *Glass Bead Game* about the arts, the element of play in
them should not be misunderstood as withdrawing from the
serious business of society. The distinction of work and play
is symbolized by Valéry in the contrast of walking and danc-
ing: one has a goal in the distance, the other does not. But
when a highly skilled person is performing his skill, it is hardly
possible to distinguish the two: the dancer *is* the dance, as Yeats

implies. What then is expressed by this work-play? This brings us again to the word concern, a word I have dropped already once or twice, and hope is self-explanatory, as I am not using it in any special sense.

I should distinguish primary and secondary concern, even though there is no real boundary line between them. Secondary concerns arise from the social contract, and include patriotic and other attachments of loyalty, religious beliefs, and class-conditioned attitudes and behavior. They develop from the ideological aspect of myth, and consequently tend to be directly expressed in ideological prose language. In the mythical stage they often accompany a ritual. Such a ritual may be designed, for example, to impress on a boy that he is to be admitted to the society of men in a ritual for men only; that he belongs to this tribe or group and not that one, a fact which will probably determine the nature of his marriage; that these and not those are his special totems or tutelary deities.

Primary concerns may be considered in four main areas: food and drink, along with related bodily needs; sex; property (i.e. money, possessions, shelter, clothing, and everything that constitutes property in the sense of what is "proper" to one's life); liberty of movement. The general object of primary concern is expressed in the Biblical phrase "life more abundantly." In origin, primary concerns are not individual or social in reference so much as generic, anterior to the conflicting claims of the singular and the plural. But as society develops they become the claims of the individual body as distinct from those of the body politic. A famine is a social problem, but only the individual starves. So a sustained attempt to express primary concerns can develop only in societies where the sense of individuality has also developed. The axioms of primary concern are the simplest and baldest platitudes it is possible to formulate: that life is better than death, happiness better than misery, health better than sickness, freedom better than bondage, for all people without significant exception.

What we have been calling ideologies are closely linked to secondary concerns, and in large measure consist of rationalizations of them. And the longer we look at myths, or storytelling patterns, the more clearly their links with primary concern stand out. Human life being what it is, it is not so much the satisfaction of these concerns that are featured mythically as the anxiety about not getting them satisfied. Thus the vast number of "dying god" myths assembled by Frazer, whatever the variety of anthropological contexts they may fit into, seem to have a common origin in anxiety about the food supply, which becomes linked to sexual anxieties through a quasi-magical association of fertility and virility. In literature, a reader of romance might be pardoned for sometimes thinking that romance has no subject except sexual frustration, even when the frustration is resolved on the last page or so.

Any work of fiction written during the last two centuries will reflect the secondary and ideological concerns of its time, but it will relate those concerns to the primary ones of making a living, making love, and struggling to stay free and alive. The ideological issues might be more professionally handled in descriptive or conceptual language, but no sensible person denies that the perspective of fiction is irreplaceable. And however ironic or anxiety-ridden the fiction may be, the positive impulse behind it, the impulse to express a concern for more abundant life, is still a *gaya scienza,* a form of play or self-contained energy.

All through history secondary concerns have taken precedence over primary ones. We want to live, but we go to war; we want freedom, but permit, in varying degrees of complacency, an immense amount of exploitation, of ourselves as well as of others; we want happiness, but allow most of our lives to go to waste. The twentieth century, with its nuclear weaponry and its pollution that threatens the supply of air to breathe and water to drink, may be the first time in history when it is really obvious that primary concerns must become primary,

or else. Some of the writers in our day who have been victim-
ized by a hostile ideology have issued statements defending the
value and relevance of their work, and such statements often
refer to their commitment to truth. By truth they usually mean,
not so much the fidelity to the facts of society that make up
much of their descriptive content, as their devotion to human
primary concerns.

The remarks about ideologies in the previous chapter assume that ideological principles are metonymic: that is, they
are *put for* the ideals envisaged by primary concern. We can't
have a perfect society, the argument runs, but what we have
now is the best available. Thus the primary goals tend to become indefinitely postponed. Marx owes his status as a prophetic thinker to the incisiveness with which he analyzed the
ideology of capitalism in relation to the primary needs and
anxieties of an alienated working class. But the tactical adaptations of Marxism, when it comes to power, turn it into another defensive ideology, in contrast to the original Marxist
ideal of a world without classes or states. Similarly, the dy-
namic of democracy rests on its primary concern for what the
American Constitution calls life, liberty, and the pursuit of
happiness. But democratic ideology is mainly the camouflage
of an oligarchy or of various pressure groups within the society. We notice that for poets involved with revolutionary situations, such as Dante, Milton or Victor Hugo, the eloquence
of the poetry, which is related to primary ideals, often forms
part of a startling innocence about the actual social forces around
the poet, which are expressing themselves ideologically.

This rooting of poetic myth in primary concern accounts
for the fact that mythical themes, as distinct from individual
myths or stories, are limited in number. Naturally we cannot
separate body from mind in concern: curiosity and imitation,
the impulses to know and to make that start off the sciences
and the arts, are also primary, and freedom of movement extends to freedom of thought and imagination. But two direc-

tions of development are distinguishable here. One is toward
the acceptance of the secondary concern: thus the concern for
life may extend to a concern for posterity, for immortality, or
for the survival of one's work or good name, as in the speech
of Sarpedon in the *Iliad*. Such extensions turn increasingly to
logos idioms for expression. The other direction is toward the
metaphorical, as the concern for food and drink develops into
the Eucharist symbolism of the New Testament. The difference is that the metaphorical or "spiritual" direction is thought
of as fulfilling the physical need in another dimension of existence: it may require sublimation, but it does not cut off or
abandon its physical roots.

A further comment may be needed to indicate that literature's relation to primary concern is not withdrawn from the
human situation. The first half of the twentieth century was a
time of polarized conflicts, where one ideology was pitted
against another, as communist and fascist revolutions broke
out against capitalism and movements of national independence eroded imperialism. During the Cold War the Soviet
Union was notorious for chronic food shortages, sexual prudery, reduction of property to the barest essentials of clothing
and shelter, and rigid restrictions on freedom of movement.
The United States offered a consumerism with prodigious
quantities of food and drink, indiscriminate sexual activity, an-
archic piling up of accumulations of property, and a restless
nomadism. One subordinated primary concerns to an allegedly materialist ideology, the other satisfied them to excess on
a purely physical level. The second half of the century has seen
a growing distrust of all ideologies and a growing sense of the
importance of primary concern in both bodily and mental contexts. We now see protests in favor of peace, dignity and freedom rather than an alternative ideological system. Such protests
are called counter-revolutionary or what-not by those who hold
power and are determined to keep holding it, power being for
them something that, in Mao Tse-tung's phrase, comes out of

the barrel of a gun. If the human race cannot come up with a better conception of power than that it is clearly not long for this world. The title of the present book (from Luke 4:32) suggests the verbal aspect of a power that has nothing to do with guns, and is therefore consistent, as the other is not, with human survival.

III

In the previous chapter our survey of verbal modes went backward in time, from the later to the earlier. We also tried to emphasize that all four modes are present somewhere and somehow in every verbal structure, whatever the center of gravity may be. One of my favorite examples (because one of my favorite books) is Gibbon's *Decline and Fall of the Roman Empire*. This is first of all a piece of descriptive writing, an account of the Roman Empire from the Antonine age to the fall of Constantinople over a thousand years later. It soon dates as the definitive authority on that subject, but it continues to be read because of its great conceptual power, its vision of the ancient world gradually taking on the outlines of the modern one. Whether the details of this vision are right or wrong is not relevant just here: they are expressed in a coherent and eloquent narrative, and such things are always right, so far as they go. Eventually the book enters the rhetorical area (GC 92) and becomes a typical example of one aspect of eighteenth-century ideology. Not that it was ever out of this area, of course: I am speaking of the order in which its readers normally discover its qualities.

But how did it all start? Here is an indolent eighteenth-century dilettante minding his own business, sitting on the Capitoline Hill and meditating on the vicissitudes of history and fate, as any tourist might do. What was the force that suddenly picked him up and flung him into a chaos of sources and documents, to scribble his way frantically out of them for practically the rest of his life? The only clue, I think, is in the

"Decline and Fall" of the title. The vague meditations suddenly consolidated into one of the great shaping myths of the human psyche: the myth touched him lightly, said "Follow me," and that was that, for the next twenty-five years.

In the previous chapter I traced a sequence of verbal modes in a direction opposite to the historical one, starting with the kind of descriptive writing made possible by modern technical developments and working back to the mythology from which literature descends. At the beginning of my earlier *Anatomy of Criticism* I traced a series of modes *within literature,* in the reverse order, starting with the mythical and descending through romantic, mimetic, and finally the contemporary ironic modes. In myths the characters are usually gods; in romance they are heroes; then we come down to the tragic figures in Shakespeare, and then to the less heroic, but equally universal, characters closer to our own time: Leopold Bloom, Emma Bovary, Prince Myshkin. The practical criticism resulting from the theory of literary modes often takes the form of examining a highly sophisticated structure, such as a story of Joseph Conrad, to see what mythical and romantic patterns are also present in it.

The conception of modes developed out of one of the first features of literature that attracted me as a critic. This was the strength and consistency of literary conventions, the way in which, for example, the same plot and character types in comedy persist with astonishingly little change from Aristophanes to our own day. Such persistence suggested the crucial importance of a literary history of a different kind from the ordinary chronological survey that treats literary history as only a particular department of history in general. I think of a poet, in relation to his society, as being at the center of a cross like a plus sign. The horizontal bar forms the social and ideological conditioning that made him intelligible to his contemporaries, and in fact to himself. The vertical bar is the mythological line of descent from previous poets back to Homer (the usual symbolic starting point) which carries on into our own time.

It is because of this vertical line of literary descent that we are able to understand poets remote from us in time and culture, and can even admire them for many reasons that they themselves, to say nothing of their original audiences, would have found unintelligible. No doubt there is an "anxiety of influence" within the literary tradition itself, especially since the rise of the conception of copyright. But we have suggested that most of a writer's really obsessive anxieties come from his ambiguous relation to the ideology around him. There are also many ways of getting around a specifically literary influence: a first-rate writer may choose to be influenced by a second-rate one who has no real ascendancy over him, or he may simply avoid reading someone whose influence may become a threat—Joyce, for example, claimed that he had never read Rabelais. The real literary descent is not through personalities, but through conventions and genres.

Of course a writer's contemporary ideology is a historical phenomenon too: in our diagram, the horizontal bar would move steadily down the vertical or temporal line as well. This historical dimension of ideology constitutes the "historicity" which surrounds the writer as a womb does an embryo, and which many critics think makes up the entire area of criticism. But the ideology surrounding every great writer in a past at all remote from us is, so to speak, a great deal deader than he is, and it seems clear that one cannot understand the communicating power of such a writer without a study of the place in the history of literature itself that he inherits and transmits, and the conventions and genres that he found it natural to use. As well as participating in history as a whole, literature has its own peculiar history, and the center of that history is not biographies of authors or dates of publications, but the modifying of conventions and genres to meet varying social conditions. Meeting these conditions, of course, may mean opposing them as well as adapting to them.

A writer's context within literature thus cannot always be established, even with the most learned and self-conscious writers, by normal historical methods. Such methods can deal with sources and influences when they can be shown to exist, but the central literary tradition, like the river Alpheus, goes underground for long periods and resurfaces unpredictably. The tragedies of Shakespeare remind us of the great tragic writers of Athens, but between them there is only the somewhat distorting connection of Seneca. Dante knew that Homer was at the headwaters of his own literary tradition, but he did not know Homer at first hand.

The real literary tradition has to be established in large part from a comparative generic study, which may sound speculative or even eccentric because of the absence of normal documentary evidence. Poets often cannot, and oftener still will not when they can, read in the way that would be easiest for historical critics, and critics have to make the best of the fact. Not that they all want to: the prejudices inherited from the ascendancy of *logos*-language are still so strong that any suggestion that literature, like science, might have a structure of its own, and be something more than simply a reflection of social influences or an inorganic aggregate of imaginative efforts, stirs up the same anxieties that the "art for art's sake" paradoxes of a century ago did.

The fact that mythology is the narrative source of literature gradually emerged during the Romantic period, though encrusted with a great deal of irrelevant jargon. In the latter part of the eighteenth century, in English and German literature particularly, the "primitive" affinities of poetry suddenly became popular, although such distinctions as the historically, the socially, and the psychologically primitive were still not very clear. Homer was primitive because he was historically early; ballads and folksongs were primitive because they sprang from untutored people; Rousseau was primitive because he uncovered the emotional basis of the primitive in the individual. It was noted that few societies are entirely without poetry, whereas prose develops much later, and in fairly advanced civ-

ilizations. Also, the poetic is more concrete and simple than
the rational, and its affinity with the primitive is recapitulated
in the education of childhood, where the imagination seems
the obvious and most receptive aspect of the child's mind to
address.

Rousseau's society of nature and reason buried under luxury and exploitation has a good deal to do with the ascendancy
of *logos* over *mythos* that we have been dealing with, and the
implications of Rousseau's argument are that this ascendancy
is not necessarily desirable or unchangeable. With others, on
the contrary, it becomes a dogma that the simple precedes and
is outmoded by the complex, which would imply that the poetic is also something that is or should be outmoded. This
very common, though usually unexamined, attitude was put
into satiric form by Peacock (GC 23) in his essay *Four Ages of
Poetry,* and Peacock's essay was answered by Shelley in his
Defence of Poetry. Shelley's argument simply reverses the traditional relation of *mythos* and *logos,* putting *mythos* firmly on
top. But such a reversal was accepted by few.

With the more systematic study of unconscious elements
in the mind that culminated in the work of Freud, the notion
that primitive meant historically outmoded was put to rest once
and for all. Freud showed that some of the major myths, including those of Oedipus and Narcissus, were re-enacted in
everyone at childhood, as part of the process of individualizing
oneself. It is also this continuous re-enactment of myth that
makes the most ancient or exotic literature accessible to us as
a recognizable literary experience. The same process of explor-
ing the psyche revealed that consciousness is only one of many
elements that go to make up the imaginative, the mental complex that both produces and responds to literature.

A recent book proposes that consciousness, so far from
being the distinctively human trait, actually comes fairly late
into the historical scene, in Greek culture between the *Iliad* and
the *Odyssey,* in Hebrew between the eighth-century prophets

and the post-exilic writers. Before that, we are told, man worked with a "bicameral" mind, half of which was part of and participated in the world around him. When he felt separated from this world, the other half-brain began hallucinating visions and voices of gods, ancestors, or rulers, telling him what to do next. In consciousness the sense of the subjective became habitual, and the visions and voices were internalized. The history of literature is ingeniously fitted into this thesis, but the negative term "hallucination," and the suggestion that those who inherit such a mentality today are schizophrenics, show that we are still within the attitude of distrusting anything in the mind beyond consciousness, an attitude that has wrought a great deal of damage to the poet's status at nearly every period of literature.

It seems clear that discursive prose and dialectic are typical languages of consciousness, and the poets have always insisted that for producing poetry consciousness is not enough. Consciousness implies a control of the will, and although the controlled will has performed countless miracles in human civilization, the forms of creativity that include literature expand beyond it. From the point of view of the creative mind, consciousness is a partial and premature unification of mental powers, and what is needed for creation is a new bicameral mind in which something else supplements consciousness, though this bicamerality, so far as I know, would be more metaphorical than related to actual brain-structure. From Classical times we have the conception of the inspiring Muse; later comes the God of Love who started Dante on his "new life." The term imagination was usually thought of by the Romantics as a higher form of reason, or a more inclusive consciousness. The present century has produced the surrealists and other explorers of subconscious or dreaming states of mind which are assumed to be closely allied with creative power.

Most writers complain of a difficulty in uniting their minds for full creative work by an act of will. Shelley speaks, for example, of the futility of anyone's saying to himself: "I will compose poetry." Doubtless on the very top levels—Dante, Shakespeare, Goethe—this difficulty is at a minimum. But many of those who find it easy to write by an act of conscious will are those who are primarily concerned to say what is most readily acceptable in their cultural surroundings—in other words they are hack writers. Poets who can at will produce verse on approved moral, religious or patriotic themes seldom make a deep impression on the history of literature. There may be many exceptions and there is no boundary line, but we never seem to be clear of some gap between poetic and ideological language.

Consciousness frequently assumes that it has a monopoly on sanity and common sense, and it is true that a creative personality may often be accompanied by an ordinary one that is allied to neurotic states, even approaching schizophrenia. But there is no rule about this, and in fact most major writers seem to withdraw from the kind of subjectivity that the conscious discursive writer possesses and come out on the other side. Many poets even speak of the disappearance of subjective personality, of their lack of "identity," in Keats's phrase. William Blake was generally assumed to be mad in his day and for several decades afterwards. A story in Gilchrist's biography tells how once he was walking from a pub to his house carrying some beer, and encountered a member of the Royal Academy who had met him the night before and was about to speak to him. But, seeing him carrying the beer himself instead of employing a servant or pot-boy, the R. A. thrust his hands back into his pockets and hurried on without speaking. He was only doing what his social conditioning told him to do, but in obeying its voice *he* was the hallucinating neurotic, not the visionary poet-painter.

If it is true that creative verbal power is associated with something in the mind supplementary to ordinary consciousness, we have inched a little closer to the writer's social context.

Such a mind would often be baffled by the arbitrary conventions of behavior that consciousness more easily masters: one
often finds a naivete in the writer that may sometimes inca-
pacitate him from almost anything except writing. But he might
have in compensation an insight into social phenomena that
would give him, not merely an intense vision of the present,
but an unusual ability to see a conditional future, the consequence of tendencies in the present. This in turn may give the
sense of a distinctive kind of knowledge hidden from most of
society. The element of the *prophetic* in literature is often spoken of very vaguely, but is tangible enough to be worth looking into. In any case the word comes closer than anything we
have stumbled over so far to indicate the quality of the poet's
authority, and to indicate also the link between secular and
sacred literature that is one of our main themes.

If we look at the prophetic writers of the Old Testament,
beginning with Amos, the affiliation of primitive and prophetic emerges at once. Amos has the refusal to compromise
with polite conventions, a social reputation in northern Israel
for being a fool and a madman, and an ability to derive the
substance of what he says from unusual mental states, often
allied to trance. Such prophets also foretell a future which is
an inevitable result of certain foolish policies, like the policy of
the king of Judah toward Babylon that led, as Jeremiah told
him it would, to the destruction of Jerusalem. The principle
involved here is that honest social criticism, like honest science, extends the range of predictability in society.

In modern times the writers that we instinctively call prophetic—Blake, Dostoevsky, Rimbaud—show similar features. Such writers are as deeply pondered by readers as the
Greek and Hebrew oracles were: like them, they shock and
disturb; like them, they may be full of contradictions and ambiguities, yet they retain a curiously haunting authority. As
early as Elizabethan times there were critics who suggested
that the distinction between sacred and secular inspiration might

be less rigid than generally assumed. George Puttenham, writing in the 1580s, pointed to the etymology of poet as "maker," which implied for him an analogy between the poet's creative power and the creative power of God in making the world. He quotes Ovid's phrase in the *Fasti,* "est deus in nobis," which could mean either God or *a* god. In the sixteenth century it would certainly have been safer to settle for a Muse or a God of Love or something sanctioned by convention and not taken seriously as doctrine, but the analogy is still there, though latent until the time of Coleridge. It has been frequently observed that the arts are prophetic also in the sense of indicating symbolically the social trends that become obvious several generations later.

The term prophetic in itself might apply to some writers (Luther, Condorcet, Marx) whom we normally would place outside literature. This troublesome apparatus of inside and outside will not go away even when so many aspects of it vanish under examination. It appears to be the connection with the psychologically primitive that characterizes the prophetic writer who is generally thought of as inside literature or at least (as with Rousseau, Kierkegaard, or Nietzsche) impossible to ignore as a literary figure.

The prophetic affinities of the poet sometimes cause the notion of poetry as historically outmoded to go into reverse, and turn into a conception of poetry as becoming more profound and suggestive the further back we go into the past. We find this implied in legends of early times, when the poet, though as primitive as his contemporaries, was assumed to be uniquely erudite, like the Irish ollaves, the Druid bards (whether historical or legendary), or pre-Homeric figures like Musaeus or Orpheus or Hermes Trismegistus. Such poets were assumed to have been the teachers of their societies, those who remembered in verse form (because verse is the easiest arrangement for memorization) the mythological information that their society most needed to know. In Elizabethan times this conception led to the conclusion that the ancient myths really contained an inexhaustible wisdom. Chapman says of Homer that not only all learning, government and wisdom can be deduced from Homer, but all wit, elegance, disposition and judgment. This conception is as old as Plato's *Ion,* and perhaps includes Ion's fallacious inference that he has absorbed all this by osmosis from Homer through reciting him so often.

I am far from denying this intuition about poetry, but there are very obvious fallacies involved. It is true that myths have been retold and reinterpreted in countless ways by later writers, and will be to the end of human culture as we know it. Also that the great interpretations by the poets themselves become in their turn an inexhaustible source of study, so that one could fill a library with critical commentary on a single Shakespeare play. It does not follow that these repetitions of myths go back to a still more profound myth in the remote past. In reading the Grail romances, for example, we may feel tempted to believe that there must have been a definitive treatment of the Grail story earlier than Chrétien de Troyes which had all the elements unified and reconciled that have come down to us in such tantalizing fragments. Apart from there being no evidence for any such source, it is simpler to assume that the real sense of profundity is derived from the opposite process —that is, the accumulation and constant recreation of Grail stories through the centuries to our own day.

What a poet knows, in any age, is mainly the common stock of knowledge, not a special knowledge of a type that separates the expert from the layman. (This principle would apply only to the content of poetry, not to its craft or technique.) In any case what a myth means is what it has been made to mean over the centuries, and some of its profoundest recreations are very recent. There can hardly be any original mythology that, like Adam in Calvinist theology, contains all its descendants in a single body.

The word prophetic has a popular sense of foretelling the

future, but it seems clear that the poet's perspective on time is very seldom focussed on the future, or, when he is using historical material, on the past as such. The word demythologizing, already used, describes the efforts of some Biblical scholars to remove the more obviously primitive elements in the text of the Bible. If we reverse the procedure, and study the mythological tradition itself as it develops through literature, we can see that myth tends (to use an equally ugly word) to dehistoricize whatever is historical in its structure. Critics interested in mythology, including the present writer, are often described as anti-historical, an epithet that transfers to them what is actually a characteristic of their subject-matter. As many writers on mythology, notably Mircea Eliade, have demonstrated at length, mythology tends to see history as a sequence, not of unique events, but of repetitions of model or pattern situations.

Symmetry in a poet's treatment of a historical situation, such as Shakespeare's making Prince Hal and Hotspur the same age in *Henry IV* when Hotspur was actually twenty years older, is not poetic license indulged in by the poet for arbitrary reasons, but an illustration of the fact that within literature the shaping of events takes precedence over the history. The mythical structures developed by literature are not anti-historical, but counter-historical: they transpose a historical theme into the present tense, and hence modify or alter features that emphasize the pastness of the past.

This feature of literature is connected with the permanence and stability of convention. A good deal of popularity in literature is connected with the curious braking force that literary convention exerts on history. For example, there are thousands of stories based on the Cinderella archetype, one of the folktale themes that get absorbed with mythology into literature as literature grows into a recognizable category of its own. It appears, combined with other mythical features, in Classical myth (the Cupid and Psyche story in Apuleius) and Biblical myth (the Book of Ruth). We pick up *Jane Eyre,* and

read how a girl of high intelligence but no great advantages of
beauty or wealth fights her way out of a hostile family and a
hideous school environment to become a woman who can win
the friendship, and finally the love, of a man in a superior
social position. The story outline is familiar, but the mad wife,
the blinded hero in the burned house, the extraordinary coin-
cidences in the plot, are features of the primitive that give the
story something of a fairy-tale quality, and with it the sense of
being more deeply rooted in the literary tradition, than most
of its analogues.

The poet often adopts a historical theme, but he is also
troubled by the untidiness of history, its mixture of brave words
and foul deeds. One way of meeting this is to develop two
levels of meaning, distinguished by Gerard Manley Hopkins
as the underthought and the overthought. The overthought is
the surface meaning of the poem as presented: it covers most
of what the poet's contemporary readers took in and probably,
as a rule, most of what the poet himself thought he was producing. This is mainly the syntactic or conscious meaning of
the poem. The underthought consists of the progression of
imagery and metaphor that supplies an emotional counterpoint
to the surface meaning, which it often supplements, but also
often contradicts.

Shakespeare's *Henry V* affords a good example, as it is
technically, like its predecessor, a historical play. It has for its
overthought a patriotic theme about a heroic English king who
invaded and conquered France, and that overthought is still
there. But if we listen carefully to the emotional impact of
everything said in the play, we soon realize that many other
things are happening. We hear the counterpoint of two very
different themes in the opening scene, when the gushing Arch-
bishop of Canterbury recalls the great days of Edward III:

> To fill King Edward's fame with prisoner kings,
> And make her [England's] chronicle as rich with praise

> As is the ooze and bottom of the sea
> With sunken wrack and sumless treasuries. (I, ii, 162–5)

The somber image, which comes through in spite of the speaker's shallow conscious insights (perhaps in spite of Shakespeare's conscious insights too, for all we know) suggests, when taken with similar images in the same scene, the injustice and horror of the war, the misery to be inflicted on both France and England by a spoiled child of fortune, and, above all, of the ultimate futility of the whole enterprise.

So we cannot say that, because it is a historical play, *Henry V* is "following" history, with a few alterations allowed only to poets. If we look at the total myth, or whole story, of the play, we get a history along with another dimension of meaning. As he goes on, Shakespeare tends to leave English history for the more remote and legendary periods of Lear, Hamlet and Macbeth, where the titanic figures of tragedy can emerge as they could not have emerged from the battlefields of Agincourt or Tewkesbury. In time these periods are more remote from us; in myth they are far more immediate and present.

For the same reason literature constantly uses its own history. No sovereign of Britain can compare for an instant in power and splendor with King Arthur, precisely because his historical existence is so negligible. Tennyson closes his account of Arthur's last battle with the lines:

> The darkness of that battle in the west,
> Where all of high and holy dies away.

It would be difficult to write with this kind of retrospective resonance about an actual battle, where nothing high or holy is likely to appear even in defeat. When historical material is absorbed into poetry, it is normally combined with a perspective "above" history (pastoral myth) or "below" it (ironic myth or demonic parody) or both.

The critical principle involved here is really one of the relation of the poetic to the ideological or rhetorical, as what the audience gets as history in *Henry V* is essentially what it is prepared to accept as history. In other words, the overthought is the ideological content. The relation of overthought to underthought, in this sense, may cover the whole spectrum from total agreement to total disagreement. In the 1850–1950 period, partly as a result of the influence of Poe on French *symbolisme,* there was an influential movement toward opposing the two, regarding the overthought as a rhetorical scaffolding and wanting to keep only a purely metaphorical texture as authentically poetic. There is an echo of this antagonism in T. S. Eliot's remark that what is often thought of as the meaning of a poem may have only the status of a piece of meat thrown to a watchdog by a burglar—something to keep the audience's anxieties quiet while the real poem acts on them. This view that the poetic should purify itself, as far as possible, of the rhetorical recurs in Verlaine, who urged poets to take rhetoric and wring its neck—itself a fairly rhetorical comment. However, a cult of separating poetry and rhetoric could never have been much more than a temporary change of emphasis: what is interesting is the awareness that two distinguishable verbal modes are involved.

An example or two may illustrate another aspect of the relation of myth to ideology, or, as Blake calls them, vision and allegory. In *The Pilgrim's Progress* we see Christian staggering off to the Celestial City under a burden of sins that falls off at a certain point. This is what we called earlier a rhetorical analogue to the Christian ideology of the forgiveness of sins through the atonement of Christ. As long as the ideology remained central in British Protestant middle-class homes, *The Pilgrim's Progress* was cherished in practically every such home as a kind of appendix to the Bible. After the ideology waned, *The Pilgrim's Progress* fell out of fashion: perhaps it was too closely attached to the ideology to survive the change.

But the story can still be read as a story, though a modern reader might see the sins as mostly expendable anxieties and irrational guilt feelings, and Christian's getting rid of them as a manifestation of human sanity rather than divine grace. Once again, two centers of reference emerge, one contemporary with Bunyan and the other with us. The principle involved is that there is a flexibility in the story that its ideological reference does not permit. To paraphrase an axiom of D. H. Lawrence, we should trust no writer's beliefs or attitudes, but concentrate on his myth, which is infinitely wiser than he is, and is the only element that can survive when the ideology attached to it fades.

Continuing with the image of the burden, critics caught up in a new ideological trend may feel oppressed by the burden of the past, and wonder why we should feel obliged to keep maintaining a cultural tradition that practically ignores the interests of the trend. The next step is to set up a value system that gives priority to whatever seems to illustrate the trend and devalues the rest, or else to devalue the whole cultural tradition of the past in favor of a more satisfying culture to be set up in the future. The Marxist criticism of a generation ago carried these tendencies to such an extreme that knowledgeable Marxist critics now speak of "vulgar Marxism." But there are also a vulgar Christian, a vulgar humanist, a vulgar feminist, and many other forms of what may be called topiary criticism, an art of clipping literature in order to distort it into a different shape. Here it is the ideological trend that becomes the real burden, and the cultural tradition that delivers us from it.

At present "historicity" is a critical buzzword from a trend of this kind, and it is widely believed, or said, that any dehistoricizing tendency of any kind, whether mythical or not, will corrupt the critical process into some kind of static idealism. To me myth is not simply an effect of a historical process, but a social vision that looks toward a transcending of history, which explains how it is able to hold two periods of history together, the author's and ours, in direct communication. It is very difficult, perhaps impossible, to suggest a social vision of this kind, even within an ideology, without invoking some kind of pastoral myth, past or future. The Communist Manifesto does this: if we use, it says, the historical process to deliver humanity from the class struggles of history, we shall also restore some of the pre-bourgeois personal relationships to human life. Such mythical features in social vision do not denigrate history, but help to clarify its function.

Another example brings us closer to the central theme of this book. The crucifixion of Jesus was a historical event, or at least I see no reason for its not being one. There are many historical difficulties about it, however, about its timing and placing, its bias toward the Roman authorities and against the Jewish priestly establishment, its marvels of eclipses and opening tombs and the torn veil of the temple, the essential truths of which are clearly symbolic, whatever their relation to actuality.

The point is not that the myth falsifies history, but that history, the continuous record of what ascendant ideologies do, falsifies primary concern. The historical event assimilates the crucifixion of Jesus to that of all the others who suffered that hideous and obscene death. The myth of *the* Crucifixion confronts us with the reminder that we are as much involved in the death of Christ as his contemporaries, the sense of urgency about getting rid of anyone who disturbs our social conditioning being as intense as ever. When the high priest Caiaphas said: "It is expedient that one man die for the people" (John 11:50), he said something we all agree with—in fact Christian doctrine itself agrees with it, and makes Caiaphas one of the first people in the Christian era to be justified by faith. Hence it is only the myth in the present tense, not the event in the past, that has the power to give all the other poor wretches who have been victims of brutal injustice a place in the center of human vision.

The Gospels themselves are not especially sensitive to the

fact that all brutality is unjust: they are too preoccupied with the innocence of Christ (Luke 23:41). But this element begins to carry us further than myth itself. The Gospel writers are convinced that it was God whom man tried to kill, and that consequently a hatred and fear of God is a central aspect of human nature. Whatever we do with this, it bears on the inevitable question: if in all probability the Crucifixion was a historical event, doesn't its historical nature provide the basis for its real power? Would it make any impact at all without its root in history?

It seems to me that the distinctive non-mythical reality of such an event is less historical than personal. This is not a quibble: the historical as such is assimilated to history, and the mythical event as such repeats, the pure myth being represented by the Good Friday that turns up every year. The recurring historical event, the repeated church ritual, is part of history's dream of revelation. The personal happens once and for all (Hebrews 9:26), and so enters into myth and history from another level. This principle of going beyond myth as well as history will be one of our central themes from here on.

CHAPTER THREE

Identity and Metaphor

I

Literature is an art of words, and the student of it may be interested primarily either in the art or in the words. If his interest is in the words, drawing him in the direction of linguistics and semiotics, the ordinary boundary terms that we commonly use within verbal structures begin to dissolve. We find it increasingly difficult to separate, by definition, literature from criticism, criticism from philosophy or history, or philosophy and history from any other type of verbal communication. All we have are the shifting relations of signifiers to signifieds that we surveyed in the first chapter. If we emphasize the art of literature rather than the fact that it uses words, we have to start with a common-sense practical distinction that indicates an area of words different from other areas, even though there is no theoretical wall to separate them. In this distinction Keats, let us say, is a poet and not a philosopher, and Kant is a philosopher and not a poet. We recall the painter Magritte's highly representational picture of a pipe which he called "This Is Not a Pipe." A picture is a picture, and cannot be identified with or defined by its representational content. Similarly, a work of literature cannot be identified with what it says: whatever is "said" in literature belongs to ideology and rhetoric, not to the poetic as such.

Within literature, the centripetal relation among words takes precedence over whatever extra-verbal information filters through. In reading *Madame Bovary* or *Anna Karenina* or *The Newcomes* we learn a good deal about nineteenth-century society in France or Russia or England, but what is primary is the shaped and molded story. These are realistic novels that have borrowed some of their techniques from descriptive writing. The characteristics of literature come out in a more concentrated way in verse, which normally is highly figured, making a functional use of all the standard verbal devices already glanced at: metaphor, simile, metonymy and the rest, along with rhyme, alliteration, antithesis or parallelism, and repetition.

Valéry remarks that while the musical composer can work with a set of sounds distinct from the sounds heard in ordinary experience, the poet has no such privilege: he must use the same words that everyone else does. This is true, but it needs qualification. Words have an arbitrary, or more accurately a conventional, relation to the things they signify; also, words are characterized by their difference from other words. Hence all resemblances in sound or overlappings of meaning in any given language are accidental, or coincidental, or whatever word of that type we prefer. But poetry exploits these accidents and makes them functional: poetry, in short, involves sound as an extra sense.

Thus the element of *resonance* among the signifiers moves into the foreground. Words are arbitrary in relation to a referent—horse, cheval and pferd all mean the same animal—and a rhyme useful in one language, like mountain and fountain in English, may be unavailable in another. The effect of exploiting the sound resemblances within a language is to *minimize* the sense of arbitrariness. Originally this procedure may often have been close to magic: in magic a causal connection between a word and a thing, a name and a spirit, is often assumed, and in magic the poetic effort to get the right words in the right order may help to affect something in the external world. Poetry drops the mechanical, or cause-and-effect, assumption of magic, but retains the sense of a mystery in words unexplained by theories based solely on differentiation.

Some poets adopt the device known as imitative harmony (onomatopoeia), where, in Pope's phrase, the sound should be an echo to the sense. Thus in Wyatt's

> The rocks do not so cruelly
> Repulse the waves continually

we can hear the wash and roll back of the waves. Or, from the same poet:

> Cracketh in sonder; and in the ayre doth roar
> The shiverd pieces

we hear the sound of a gun bursting. Several English poets, including Spenser, make a continuous practice of imitative harmony. Perhaps there is always something of a trick about it, and yet it may be that a device found so constantly in Homer and Virgil is something very central to poetry. Its significance seems to lie in building up a self-contained aural unit, withdrawing from, though in a measure reproducing, the natural environment.

Another feature common enough in the experience of poetry, if very difficult to account for in theory, is a metaphorically "magical" line or passage that sticks in the memory, often coming loose from its original context. An example is the celebrated line from Nashe's elegy, "Brightness falls from the air," familiar to many who know nothing of its context. Another is Marvell's "To a green thought in a green shade." In Keats's "Ode to a Nightingale" the culminating lines, as most readers would consider them, tell us how the nightingale's song has

> Charmed magic casements, opening on the foam
> Of perilous seas, in faery lands forlorn.

The critical study of poetry depends on a kind of holism, an assumption that the poem in front of us is a unity, in which every detail is accounted for by its relation to that unity. The assumption of wholeness, like the assumption of coherence in criticism, is heuristic, adopted for the sake of seeing what results from it. Theoretical objections to it are easy enough to bring up, but without it there can be no sense of direction in critical understanding. At the same time the wholeness is not the goal of the critical process, but merely a factor in it. So while there is nothing in the Keats passage that violates the unity of the poem, nevertheless it seems to burst through that unity to suggest different orders of existence, like the parallel worlds popularized in science fiction. The inference is that there may be something potentially unlimited or infinite in the response to poetry, something that turns on a light in the psyche, so that instead of the darkness of the unknown we see something of the shadows of other kinds of emerging being. We are concerned here only with the principle that a response to a specific passage in a poem may extend indefinitely beyond the poem.

The emphasis on figures of speech in poetry is also found, as noted earlier, in oratory, which is a next-door neighbor to poetry. But, like other neighbors, poetry and oratory have very different lifestyles. The orator faces his audience, speaks directly to it, speaks for it in fact, and is often taken over by it. He retains more of the sense of magical compulsion in words, because he aims at a kinetic effect on his audience. And his magic has the cause-effect, stimulus-response, mechanical quality we mentioned above. This is because he wants a uniform response, and there is always something of the mechanical about uniformity.

The poet, it is true, often imitates the rhetorician: he often does not realize that *qua* poet he has nothing to "say," and may be impatient with the indirectness and lack of instant contact with his public that poetry never quite shakes off. But in rhetoric there is a speaking presence; in poetry the poet absents himself, turns away from his reader, and creates the poem to serve as an intermediary presence. The poet may not even be there: I give an example from a Newfoundland folksong:

> She's like the swallow that flies so high,
> She's like the river that never runs dry,
> She's like the sunshine on the lee shore,
> I love my love and love is no more.

A reader, however great his distrust of interpretation, could write out a series of, let us say, eight sentences, each a paraphrase of what the last line could mean. A ninth sentence would also be possible: "It doesn't mean anything really: it's just a mistake in oral transmission from an original that said something like 'I love my love when love is no more.' " This statement, if true, would be relevant to certain aspects of criticism: as far as experiencing the line as a line of poetry is concerned, it has no relevance whatever. Similarly, all objections to criticism based on the assumption that the poet is speaking, such as "Did the poet really mean, or intend, or have in his mind, all that?" are merely small-minded nagging.

The poem, like the rhetorical speech, is a focus of a community, but instead of demanding a uniformity of response it fosters variety. In the course of time the variety achieves some kind of consensus, but the flexibility remains. The poet uses many conventions to express his indirect relation to his readers. He may invoke a Muse or a god to write his poem for him; he may address a mistress or, in drama, have other characters do the speaking.

There is also the rather curious convention, which lasted for centuries, that the poet is not using words at all, primarily, but is singing, producing not so much words bearing meanings as sounds transcending verbal meanings. Sometimes the metaphor of song is transferred to a musical instrument, whether lute or lyre or harp or flute. In the epilogue to Milton's *Lycidas* we read:

> Thus sang the uncouth swain to the oaks and rills,
> When the still morn went out with sandals grey:
> He touched the tender stops of various quills,
> With eager thought warbling his Doric lay . . .

which is very lovely if we do not think too closely about the picture evoked. The poet says that throughout the poem he has been simultaneously singing and playing a wind instrument, and a rather crude one at that: an "oat," or primitive recorder. The impossibility of this feat is of no importance: what matters is the preserving of the convention. In any case poetry, more particularly lyrical poetry, as the very word lyrical indicates, has a close and constant connection with the organizing of sound that it shares with music, whether physical or metaphorical music.

According to Derrida, who is thinking primarily of metaphysics, words are essentially written: as long as the convention of a personal speaker remains within the writing, the words are still unborn inside him. A possible, if perhaps unexpected, inference is that poetry, by convention oral but not a discourse, takes us, at least sometimes, into a kind of unborn world. In any case literature does not become a cultural category until writing comes to emancipate the poem or story from the physical body of the reciter. And, of course, there is certainly a large amount of literature which is addressed first of all to the eye: there are shape poems, concrete poems, or typographical designs like those of e. e. cummings, as well as the bulk of prose.

The most primitive form of visual poetry is the epitaph, which manifests Derrida's principle of *différance* very clearly. The epitaph typically says: stop and look at me; I'm dead and you're alive (difference), but you'll soon be dead too (deferral). The fact that the speaker is dead represents another device of indirect communication, the figure of speech technically called *prosopopoeia,* where an inanimate object addresses us to remind us that nothing is really dead in poetry, but that nothing speaks either except through indirection or parody. Such figures are often found in riddle poems, where we are expected to guess or name what is speaking. This goes the opposite way from the magical line, resolving the spell of the poem by taking us back to a world of ordinary subjects and objects again. Of course the sense of visual meaning would be stronger in non-alphabetical languages like Chinese, where the written language does not directly reproduce the spoken one.

The act of reading, or its equivalent, consists of two operations that succeed one another in time. We first follow the narrative, from the first page or line to the last: once this pursuit of narrative through time is complete, we make a second act of response, a kind of *Gestalt* of simultaneous understanding, where we try to take in the entire significance of what we have read or listened to. The first response is conventionally one of the listening ear, even if we are reading a written text. The association of the second response with visual metaphors is almost inevitable.

Someone about to tell a joke may say, regrettably, "Have you heard this?" But after hearing it, we then "see" the joke. The same two-stage response is present in religious ritual also, always a close relative of mythical utterance. The elevation of the host follows the reading of the collect in the Mass; the initiates of Eleusis, we are told, listened to an account of the myth of Demeter, and were then shown a reaped ear of corn as the climax of their initiation. After that they were known as *epoptae,* or "seers." Zen Buddhism has a story that after the Buddha had preached a sermon he held up a golden flower, the only member of the audience who got the point being, naturally, the founder of Zen. Works of fiction often bear such titles as *The Golden Bowl, The Rainbow,* or *To the Lighthouse,* where a visual symbol in the book that represents a focus of its total meaning is employed by a form of synecdoche to describe the entire book. The task of the novelist, says Conrad, is "above all to make you *see.*" A metaphorical seeing of this sort might better be described as vision, which keeps the metaphor but transcends the distinction between the physically visible and the visualized.

The visual analogy, in any case, accounts for the word "structure" as a critical term, where an entire work of literature is characterized in a spatial metaphor derived from architecture. Of course the degree to which structure is seen by any respondent depends on the complexity of what is being presented. Once we see a joke we do not want to hear it again; or, if we read a detective story only to see who the murderer is, we do not normally want to reread the story until we have forgotten his identity. But with the *Divine Comedy* or *King Lear,* the seeing of the total structure is something that there could never be any question of completing.

In my earlier books I spoke of this simultaneous vision of a narrative as "thematic stasis," and identified it with Aristotle's term *dianoia,* "meaning" or "thought." The *dianoia* in this sense *is* the narrative looked at as a kind of still photograph: it should not be regarded as thought in the sense of a translation into discursive language, like the moral of a fable. Henry James's *What Maisie Knew* tells the story of a little girl afflicted with stupid and quarrelling parents who divorce, remarry, and give place to a new pair, stepfather and stepmother: these converge on Maisie with threats of a renewed parenthood, which Maisie avoids by going off with her governess. The "what" of *What Maisie Knew* can only be conveyed by a simultaneous vision in the mind of the whole story, not by any discursive account of the "meaning" of her experiences.

At this point we are not primarily concerned with narrative movement but with imagery, the units the writer works with in putting his structure together, which we then try to see as an image-cluster, or visualized unity. Of all images in literature, the most important are the characters, the personalities that do most to mediate between the author and his public. The stories of literature descend historically from the myths that are mainly stories about gods, and gods are personalities associated with nature, like sun-gods and sea-gods and sky-gods, or have emblematic images attached to them, like Juno's peacocks or Neptune's trident. Thus gods are ready-made metaphors (GC 7), a metaphor being a statement of identity of the type "A is B," where personality and natural object are said to be the same thing, although they remain two different things. At the headwaters of literary experience, therefore, we find myth and metaphor, as two aspects of one identity.

Two critical principles derive from this. One is that literature is always and everywhere polytheistic, however far its characters may have modulated from what we ordinarily think of as gods. The other is that literature always assumes, in its metaphors, a relation between human consciousness and its natural environment that passes beyond—in fact, outrages and violates—the ordinary common sense based on a permanent separation of subject and object.

In its normal "A is B" form, the metaphor is one of many figures of speech. All rhetorical figures have some feature that calls attention to their departure from what is normally taken to be the common-sense (descriptive) use of language. In simile, for example ("My love's like a red, red rose"), the word "like," for some readers at any rate, would convey a reassuring sense of "not really." The hyperbole calls attention to its exaggeration of the external facts, the synecdoche to its understating of them, the oxymoron to its paradox, the metonymy to the signified it replaces. But the metaphor conveys an explicit statement, based on the word "is," along with an implicit one that contradicts it. Just as myth says both "This happened" and "This can hardly have happened in precisely this way," so metaphor with the "is" predicate says explicitly "A is B" (e.g. "Joseph is a fruitful bough," Genesis 49:22), and conveys implicitly the sense "A is quite obviously not B, and nobody but a fool would imagine that Joseph really was," etc. Just as myth is counter-historical, asserting and denying its historical validity at the same time, metaphor is counter-logical. So what is the point of a figure of speech that at least includes the opposite of anything that a reader or listener would think of as the truth?

Metaphor, where so often something related to human personality and something related to the natural environment tend to merge, is, as we should expect, at its least self-conscious in early societies, where the distinction of subject and object is not always clear or consistent. It has been said that there are no metaphors in Homer, but in another sense everything in Homer is metaphor. Whatever moods or powers he ascribes to parts of the body, *phrenes, thymos, hepar* and the like, they seem to be metaphorically linked to corresponding moods and powers in nature, or what appear to be such. Gods also stabilize an identity of subject and object on a basis of belief or social acceptance. The statement "Neptune is the sea" is stabilized when there are temples to Neptune or prayers addressed to him before starting on a sea voyage.

The development of *logos*-language tends to make the split between subject and object more of a primary datum of experience, and with it more and more gods become literary figures, where we have a sense of verbal playfulness or ironic distancing, with no assertions about existence that need trouble us. By the time we get to Ovid's *Metamorphoses,* where we are clearly within the category of literature, this process is well under way. In fact, Ovid's metamorphoses, where personal beings turn into natural objects, as Daphne becomes a laurel tree or Philomela a nightingale, are in a sense stories about the breakdown of metaphor, Classical analogies of alienation myths like the fall of Adam and Eve. It seems clear that it is a function of poetry to keep the metaphorical habit of thought alive. But why should it be kept alive, and why do poets continue to speak with such enthusiasm, as Jules Laforgue does, of "those lightning flashes of identity between subject and object—the attribute of genius"?

Because of its basis in metaphor, the language of poetry is a concrete language, where objects of sense experience are in the foreground. Poetic language differs from conceptual or dialectical language, because of the abstract vocabulary of the latter, for which poetry has only a limited tolerance. Abstraction arises from the difficulty, the practical impossibility in fact, of keeping a logical word-order consistently related to the particularity and discreteness of the world of things. It may be true that every abstract word descends historically from a concrete ancestor: "Is not your very attention a stretching-to?" asks Carlyle. It does not follow that we can translate a sentence made up of abstract terms back to their concrete roots. There are amusing examples in Anatole France's *Jardin d'Épicure* of what happens if we do this: thus "animals have no soul" reduces to "Breath-things have no breath." Clearly, this will not do as a critical technique: we must simply let *logos* terms go their own way, and recognize that, as Milton says, the language of poetry is more "simple, sensuous and passionate" than that of philosophy.

What we "see" when we try to comprehend the totality of a literary structure is a large number of juxtaposed images. This is how the literary mode comes to terms with the miscellaneous plurality of the world of things and still manages to retain a concrete basis for its diction. There is thus always something of a mosaic about a work of literature, a pattern where the units are contiguous—in another Miltonic phrase— rather than continuous. In a logical argument we follow a course of words until we reach the end; in literature, the following in the narrative is less urgent, and what we see at the end is a unity of varied particulars.

Criticism as such begins with what we see, with the stationary "verbal icon" that forms a picture of what we have been reading. The experience of following the narrative preceding this critical vision has to be treated as pre-critical, a collecting of data for understanding. There are no words for the direct experience of literature, only unformed and unexamined feelings that have no focus until an entity forms out of the process signalized by coming to the end. This two-stage response is a special case of the difference between experience and knowledge. Experience is of the particular and the unique, and takes place in time; knowledge is of the universal and the assimilated, and contains an element withdrawn from time.

This conception of a two-stage response may strike many readers as both crude and false to their own experience. What are we to make of a preliminary pre-critical pursuit of narrative where we are inside the literary work, absorbed in it, as we sometimes say, followed by an outside simultaneous view of it? True, the frequent statement that we cannot get outside a structure to examine it is only another misleading metaphor, and in any case has no relevance to our present point, where the reader is outside only in the very simple sense in which the viewer of a picture is outside the picture.

What has to be emphasized is that while it may be theoretically useful to distinguish two stages, in practice they have to be assimilated as quickly as possible. Roland Barthes remarks that all serious reading is rereading: this does not necessarily mean second reading, but reading in the perspective of the total structure, a perspective that turns a wandering through a maze of words into a directed quest. There are many ways of attaining such a perspective even on a first reading. One is through intuitions derived from previous experience in reading; another is through the assistance of criticism, which may be simply commentary on the work or a providing of a context for it through a study of the conventions, genres, and contemporary social background related to it. The first reading of a Shakespeare play is an operation many of us can barely even remember: it is followed by many re-experiences of the narrative, both in the text and on the stage, all of which move in the direction of assimilating the experience and the knowledge of the play until they become aspects of the same thing.

We may note in passing that "rereading," or unifying knowledge and experience, depends on the existence of printed texts, or something corresponding to them that stays around to be re-examined and that does not change however often it is consulted. A rush of experiences with limited possibilities of development into genuine knowledge is the major educational difficulty with electronic media in our society. Oral societies develop astonishing powers of memory, but even these are inadequate for so prolific a network of communications as ours. Further technology may make this problem obsolete, but the panics inspired by it are still with us.

The literary work, then, does not stop with being an object of study, something confronting us: sooner or later we have to study as well our own experience in reading it, the results of the merging of the work with ourselves. We are not observers but participants, and have to guard against not only the illusion of detached objectivity but its opposite, the counsel of despair that suggests that all reading is narcissism, seeing every text only as a mirror reflecting our own psyches. A book focusing (or soon about to focus) on the Bible in particular cannot avoid such issues. So we have to go on to consider an extension of the use of metaphor that not merely identifies one thing with another in words, but something of ourselves with both: something of what we may tentatively call existential metaphor. Needless to say, this takes us a long way past the personal identification with some admirable or heroic character in a story and similar immaturities: they are examples of the narcissism just mentioned.

We are dealing with writers as well as with readers, and the writer also realizes how much more there is to metaphor than simply the juxtaposing of images. As we shall see again in a moment, he often feels that the metaphor of the pregnant mother bringing a separate life into existence is closer to his experience than the metaphor of "creation" in the sense of making up what he writes by himself. The latter suggests too facile a victory, with no angel to struggle with: in fact it suggests the total unreality of anything imaginative beyond the subjective that so many of those who are indifferent or hostile to imaginative writing assume. We have spoken of magic as an accidental effect of the poetic that nevertheless seems to open up a dimension beyond the craftsmanship of the creative process. In actual magic there is an *invoking* of an objective presence, or what seems to be one. Ascendant ideologies are nervous about unauthorized presences, hence the popularity of such themes as the bargain with the devil in Marlowe's *Faustus* and elsewhere. But many a novelist, for example, has found that a character he has created has, perhaps because it coincides with some suppressed personality in his own psyche, taken on a life of its own, as though something had walked into the book by itself. In certain moments of creation there may even be a feeling of actual communication with a personal but not subjective presence. A writer who has once had such feelings or experiences can hardly pretend to himself that he has not had them, whatever the clamoring of ideologies and doctrines around him may say.

II

The question has often been raised about the moral benefits of studying literature. Clearly the relation we have outlined, in which the reader is a subject looking at an object set against him, is not one that will necessarily improve the personal character of the reader, unless he very much wants it to. This fact is particularly clear in painting, because of the accident that so many paintings can be bought and possessed instead of becoming the focus of a community. The narrator of Browning's poem "My Last Duchess," who had his wife murdered because she smiled at other people, but cherished her picture which smiled only at him, was what is known as a cultivated man, but the cultivation had not done much for his moral sense.

In literature there is the factor of the difference, almost the opposition, between the kinetic appeal of rhetoric and the imaginative appeal of poetry. As we saw, rhetoric belongs to a moral, *quid agas* or "What should we do?" mode. Thus rhetoric does attempt to be a moral stimulus—usually a bad one, unfortunately, the stimulus to hatred being by far the easiest available—but literature does not act in this way, except through some historical accident, or unless (as in inspirational verse or propaganda novels) the works of literature involved are really disguised forms of rhetoric. And yet I think almost any serious writer, if asked what kind of contact he wanted to make with his public, would say that his aim had something to do with making his reader a different person from what he was before.

Two forms of identity are involved in studying a work of literature. There is identity *as,* which is a basis of ordinary knowledge, and is a matter of fitting individuals into classes. We know this creature to be a cat, we identify it as a cat, because we recognize it to be an individual of the class cat. But, it will be objected, we are overlooking the uniqueness of the cat: there are millions of cats, every one quite discernibly different in appearance and temperament from this one. This

is a kind of mental confusion which seldom affects the status
of cats, where it is easier to understand the traditional distinction between *esse* and *essentia,* but is constantly obscuring the
theory of criticism. We never know the unique as such:
uniqueness belongs to experience by itself. The contemplation
of the literary structure as a representation, an individual of
the class poem, unites experience and knowledge.

There is also identity *with,* which has several dimensions.
A metaphor of the "A is B" type expresses an identity *with*
that is not found in ordinary experience. We do, however,
experience a form of identity-with in time, as when I feel that
I am identical with all the personalities I have been or had since
birth. Identity in this context means unity with variety, as is
also the identity in which one's hands and feet and head are
identified by being parts of the same thing. Then again, the
book I have just read is in a sense identified with me, having
entered the continuum of my own life. Let us explore this
conception of personally involving metaphor a little further.

I have never found any formula better to begin with on
this topic than "the lunatic, the lover, and the poet" of Duke
Theseus in *A Midsummer Night's Dream.* According to him,
these three groups are compact of imagination, by which he
means essentially seeing things that are not there. In our present context this means that they are the obvious groups of
people who take metaphor, or identity-with, seriously. Let us
start with the lover. There is a common stock of metaphors
connected with two bodies becoming one flesh in sexual union,
and the lover as poet revolves around these metaphors, though
in a somewhat elliptical way. The one-flesh metaphor is Biblical (Genesis 2:24), and of course the starting point of every
human life is the identity of one flesh resulting from the meeting of two bodies, which makes the concern involved fairly
immediate.

In Shakespeare's day it was generally assumed that the poet
was a lover, and that if he was not he was probably a rather

poor creature, and almost certainly a dull poet. That is, one of the chief sources for his inspiration was what I have just called an existential metaphor, the union with his mistress in which the experience of being one flesh, identical with someone else, supplied the generative power for his poetry. This union was nearly always "of imagination all compact": that is, it didn't happen. The great majority of Elizabethan poetic mistresses were as unavailable as Elizabeth: they were coy, proud, disdainful, "sworn to live chaste," like Romeo's Rosaline, married to someone else like Sidney's Stella, capricious or promiscuous. (The convention itself of course was centuries older.) Thus love poetry, and perhaps all poetry, is the child of the frustration of identity, a presence taking the place of or substituting for an enforced absence. Here, of course, the lover is the poet, not the reader, but the reader is usually assumed to be reading as a lover, and to share something of the experience going on.

When the union in one flesh does take place, there is still frustration, this time inherent in the brevity and the many accidents of the act, and above all in the inability to forget that two people never really become one person. The standard example in English literature is Donne's "The Extasie," where some turns of phrase ("And yet the body is his book") indicate a connection in Donne's mind between the sex act and the writing of poetry. The connection is much stronger in "The Canonization," where the two lovers

> die and rise the same, and prove
> Mysterious by this love.

Here "die" also has a connotation of sexual union, and we proceed again to literary metaphors, poetry being the result of imitating the model lovers who are "canonized," or made saints of the God of Love. "We'll build in sonnets pretty rooms," the poem says, a pun on "stanza" being concealed behind the last word. In Shakespeare's "Phoenix and the Turtle," what Donne calls "the phoenix riddle" reappears, with female phoenix and male turtle as partners in a union which is again both death and sexual consummation. There is no book or sonnet mentioned here, but Reason, horrified by the metaphorical union of two in one, pronounces a "threnody" reducing the act to simple death.

The love poet employs the assumed or hypothetical identity of the metaphor, which asks us at least to consider the possibility that A and B are the same person even when we know, whatever knowing may mean in this connection, that they aren't. The lover goes further than the reader into actual experience: he has felt what kind of truth is involved in saying that two lovers united sexually are one person, however soon they have to settle for the reality of being two bodies again. The lover is thus the guarantor, so to speak, of the reality of what the poet is talking about, poet and reader, as we said, being both assumed to know enough about love to feel that something more than a literary exercise is going on.

The medieval poets seem to have introduced the God of Love or Eros to Western poetry as a symbol of their cultural status that would just get by established authority. They also appear to have acted largely on their own initiative, drawing on Virgil and Ovid, and obviously they felt the psychological force of the assumption that creativity has a good deal to do with the erotic drive, whether achieved, frustrated or sublimated. In this post-Freudian era we are less likely to be startled or put off by the suggestion that Eros creates the identity behind the imaginative identities of metaphor in poetry, counterpoint in music, composition in painting, proportion in sculpture and architecture. These last two arts even take us in the direction of the erotic appeal in mathematics, which Yeats speaks of in "The Statues," where he begins a poem on the erotic nature of Greek statuary with the words "Pythagoras planned it," Pythagoras being pre-eminently the philosopher of mathematics.

Behind the lover the administrative mind of Theseus sees nothing but lunatics. But, as noted earlier, there are infinite varieties of madness, some of them traditional attributes of poetry, or activities closely related to poetry. There are the Asian shamans, the sibyls and prophets of the ancient Western world, the cults of divine possession like those of Dionysus that have given us the word "enthusiasm"; there are the mystics and the visionaries. There are also identifications with the natural environment, with society or a social group, or with a predecessor in the literary tradition. In all this there is one factor of the greatest importance. In every such form of identification there is a renunciation of egocentric or subjective identity.

There are certain contexts in which one can no longer speak of oneself as a subject. One cannot, for example, say "I am a wise and good man," without suggesting that one is nothing of the kind, because such predicates as wisdom and goodness will not fit into any sentence starting with "I am." Even Jesus had reservations about being called good (Matthew 19:17). Creation appears to be another of these contexts. We have previously suggested that ordinary waking consciousness is not creative; the reason seems to be that it is ego-centered. Keats speaks of the poet's "negative capability"; Blake calls himself the "secretary" of his poems; Eliot uses his well-known figure of the catalyzer, indicating, like all the poets who have invoked Muses and similar figures, that he is not the maker of the poem but simply the place where it comes to being; Mallarmé speaks of his vision as developing "through what used to be me."

Montaigne, a writer unlikely to be accused of obsession, says: "I have no more made my book than my book has made me; a book consubstantial with its author, concerned only with me, a vital part of my life; not having an outside and alien concern like all other books." The concluding phrase we perhaps may view with some detachment: every author regards his book as different from all other books. But the use of the term "consubstantial," the term Luther uses for the relation of the elements of the Eucharist to the body of Christ, could hardly tell us more clearly that Montaigne, who seems the most personal and accessible of writers, is not talking to us at all, even though he uses the convention of direct speech. He is giving us his book instead of himself, or, more accurately, giving us his book, which is both himself and not himself.

The discoverer of the principle that all verbal structures descend from mythological origins was Vico, and Vico's axiom was *verum factum:* what is true for us is what we have made. But the phrase is less simple than that rendering of it may suggest. What is true for us is a creation in which we have participated, whether we have been in on the making of it or on the responding to it. We are accustomed to think, rather helplessly, of whatever presents itself to us objectively as reality. But if we wake up in the morning in a bedroom, everything we see around us that is real, in contrast to our dreams, is a human creation, and whatever human beings have made human beings can remake. I take it that this is something of what Wallace Stevens means by his "supreme fiction," the reality which is real because it is a created fiction, and recognized to be such.

The type of identification we have been calling existential metaphor may also be called, following Heidegger, "ecstatic." The word ecstatic means, approximately, standing outside oneself: a state in which the real self, whatever reality is and whatever the self is in this context, enters a different order of things from that of the now dispossessed ego. There are many varieties of this ecstatic state in the arts: for example, we expect an actor to be ecstatically identified with his role in a play. It seems clear from all accounts that the ecstatic state, no less than the erotic state, is one that one cannot remain in very long. Many writers who enter it in their great moments develop a ferocious ego for their rest periods.

The imaginative element in the poetic means that all the doors of perception in the psyche, the doors of dream and fantasy as well as of waking consciousness, are thrown open. This is the point at which the metaphor of seeing a poem becomes inadequate, and the word vision, suggesting a greater intensity of the same thing, becomes more appropriate. Vision also suggests the fragmentary and the temporary, not necessarily something seen steadily and whole, to paraphrase Arnold, but more frequently providing only an elusive and vanishing glimpse. Glimpse of what? To try to answer this question is to remove it to a different category of experience. If we knew what it was, it would be an object perceived in time and space. And it is not an object, but something uniting the objective with ourselves.

Our metaphors of hearing followed by seeing are beginning to give out at this point, and need reinforcing by other metaphors. We may characterize the following of a narrative by the metaphor of a horizontal line, and of the thematic contemplation of the complete structure by a vertical one. In looking at a picture we are looking mainly up and down. But if narrative is metaphorically horizontal, irony is built into the very conception of narrative. The fact that there must be a last page and a final "cadence," or falling away from the reader, infuses narrative from the beginning with the sense that the reader is above and the action of the text below. This sense of irony increases in proportion to the degree of irony in the text itself: we have irony in tragedy, for example, when we know more about what is going on than the characters do. In an age when practically all narrative, fictional or otherwise, is ironic in its pervading tone, the reader must be in possession of some norm of vision that oversees what he sees. There are various paradoxes in criticism, designed to show how deeply the reader is involved in the irony of what he reads, suggesting that no such norm really exists. But without it irony could not make its point as irony. There is one consciousness that subjects itself to the text and understands, and another that, so to speak, overstands. It is only the possession of the latter that makes the operation of reading worthwhile: without it a reader is a pedant who understands but does not comprehend.

Wallace Stevens remarks, in one of his less illuminating moments, that the great poems of heaven and hell have been written and that the great poem of earth has still to be written. It is unlikely that it ever will be, because a poem of earth would be an endless narrative, without the vision that looks up and down, and adds at least a suggestion of other perspectives above and below. Eventually time gives out for the longest narratives. Tolstoy's *War and Peace* finally separates into the polarized categories of its title, where the variety of meanings of the word for peace in Russian, *mir,* accentuates a contrast between life with order and meaning in it and life subject to the pure chance and randomness that the most carefully planned military campaign falls into. Victor Hugo's gigantic survey of the centuries of history, *La légende des siècles,* similarly expands into upper and lower worlds, and left him with two additional epics still to write, one on Satan and the other on God. For Hugo Satan is redeemed by being absorbed in "Liberté," but the last poem is in too unfinished a state for us to be sure what God's fate is to be.

The point is that structurally there must be these categories of being-above and being-below, whatever the religious implications. In Proust the sequence of experiences that ends at the point that the writing begins similarly separates into the vertical contrast of *temps perdu* and *temps retrouvé. Finnegans Wake* has a purely cyclical construction, on the principle that a horizontal line on a spherical earth or curved space will eventually end where it began. But even there we have a strong suggestion that the cycle symbolizes something that is more than a cycle.

III

We have now three aspects of metaphorical experience, the imaginative, the erotic and the ecstatic. In each aspect there is an alternation between identity and difference. The imaginative is an experience of the arts, including literature, in which we watch the dance of metaphors in a poem, joining them or retreating from them at pleasure. In the erotic we enter into an act of union followed by a separation, but not a separation into a simple subject-object relationship. According to Plato, using an image that will dominate the rest of this book, the lover climbs a ladder of refining experience: at the top of the ladder there is still a contrast between identity and difference, but this time he knows what it is. On the top level of experience, identity is love and difference is beauty. In the ecstatic state there is a sense of presence, a sense uniting ourselves with something else, even when it soon turns into a sense of absence. Here too are gods, says Heraclitus, lighting a fire; Heidegger, 2500 years later, picks up the water jug on his lecture table and says essentially the same thing.

The ecstatic experience would normally be an individual one: certainly there are social or communal ecstatic states, but they seem to have a strong undertow carrying them from what is above consciousness to something below it. But the individual is not solitary or isolated: the same interchange between identity and difference exists here too. That is, there would be an oscillation between a feeling that he is part of a larger design and a feeling that a larger design is a part of him.

Carrying on with Plato's figure of a ladder, it seems as though with the imagination there is a journey upward into a world where subject and object are at one. This takes place, apparently, in literature, through an interchange of illusion and reality. Illusion, something created by human imagination, is what becomes real; reality, most of which in our experience is a fossilized former human creation from the past, becomes illusory. For me the supreme example of this interchange in literature is Shakespeare's *Tempest*. This is a play about creating a play through Prospero's magic, and in all drama, of course, the reality is the illusion, what we see on the stage. The reality of the action in *The Tempest* is created through the illusions summoned up by Prospero. What we call reality, Prospero tells us, sooner or later disappears like other illusions.

At the end of the action Miranda, reacting to her first sight of a human society, calls it a "brave new world." We say, and Prospero says too, that this is merely one more illusion, a product of her inexperience. So it is, except for the word new. It will become an illusion soon enough—she is, after all, looking at some very shoddy and silly people—but for an instant there has been an epiphany, when how things should be has appeared in the middle of how things are. The fresh or innocent vision is often associated with children—Miranda is still a child in experience, if not in age—and has traditionally been associated in Christianity with the alleged nearness of children to the garden of Eden, the age of innocence before the Fall, when human, animal and vegetable existence were in stable reconciliation.

In all the higher religions there seems to be some difference of approach between those who remain within the ideological framework of its revelation, observing its laws and rituals, and those who attempt a more direct approach through ecstatic metaphor, as we have been calling it. The second group includes the mystics, who appear in both Biblical and non-Biblical traditions. In the Christian tradition there is a strong Platonic influence on those interested in this approach.

These latter include the curious Christian Neoplatonist who gave himself a name out of the New Testament, Dionysius the Areopagite; his Latin translator Erigena; and various medieval and later visionaries—Meister Eckhart, Ruysbroeck, Boehme and others. Their central axiom is normally something like "One becomes what one beholds," that is, consistent and disciplined vision ends in the kind of identification we have been associating with existential metaphor. Such people normally show little interest in literature, though there are literary affinities in some religions, such as the haggadic tradition in Judaism and the Sufi use of parables in Islam, which show clearly enough how relevant literature could be to this type of experience. The *logos* emphasis in Christianity has confused us on this point: we tend to think of Jesus as primarily a teacher of doctrine who, as recorded in the synoptic Gospels, used parables as illustrations and examples. It would be at least as true, and in this context more rewarding, to say that the parables *are* the teachings, and that the doctrinal material is concerned with their applications.

Every image of revelation, whether in the Bible or not, has its demonic parody or contrast. The *descent* of the visionary ladder would take us into a world where subject and object grow steadily further apart, and end by the subject's becoming an object too. The phrase "They became what they beheld" appears in a demonic context in the second part of Blake's *Jerusalem,* where Blake is drawing on the remark in Psalm 135 about idolatry: "They that make them are like unto them." Accepting the objective world simply as a given is a parody-creation. Again, Jules Laforgue, whom we have quoted in the opposite context, tells us that the "Moi," the self-alienated ego, is a Galatea blinding Pygmalion. Galatea is the female statue made by the sculptor Pygmalion whom her creator loved so much that Venus brought her to life, and she blinds by substituting an object for a creation.

I spoke earlier of the series of adaptations that poets have made to come to terms with other types of language. For the last century or so literature has been permeated by an ironic perspective that looks at its subjects, themes, characters and settings with a detachment analogous to that of the descriptive writer. Irony cannot achieve the degree of neutrality that is possible in science, but a pretense of doing so is often a part of its convention. In this situation there has been one development of particular relevance. This is an intensification of the imagery that imitates the descriptive mode, an emphasis on the "thingness" of the objective world, which we find in, for example, Beckett's *Watt* and Robbe-Grillet's *Les gommes,* and in William Carlos Williams's insistence on "not ideas about the thing but the thing itself," also the title of a poem by Wallace Stevens. In various forms of painting, such as the pop art of Andy Warhol, and in the popularity of Zen Buddhism, with its technique of training one to see, not another world but the same world with a new intensity, there are parallel developments. Much earlier, Joyce spoke of "epiphanies," or fragments, often of actual experience, that seem charged with a peculiar luminousness, though not with any additional coded meaning. The principle here seems to be: things are not fully seen until they become hallucinatory. Not actual hallucinations, because those would merely substitute subjective for objective visions, but objective things transfigured by identification with the perceiver. An object impregnated, so to speak, by a perceiver is transformed into a presence.

We may summarize all this by saying that, in proportion as we try to approach literature with a sense of personal involvement or commitment, one pole of it begins to look like the revelation of a paradisal state, a lunatic, loving, poetic world where all primary concerns are fulfilled. It is a world of individuals but not of egos, and a world where nature is no longer alien but seems to be, in the medieval phrase, our "natural place." It is one pole only: the other pole is the imaginative hell explored in tragedy, irony and satire. The hell world may be described as the world of power without words, where the predominant impulse is to tyrannize over others so far as one's ability to do so extends. But it is the paradisal pole that gives us a perspective on the hell-world, or, in our previous figure, provides the norm that makes irony ironic. On the other hand, while there is no human society where we do not find all the horrors of psychotic humanity, we seldom fail to find something in the *culture* of a society that is congenial. The sense of the congenial, of a genuine human communication through words, pictures, textiles, ceramics or whatever, comes from the innocent vision at the heart of all human creation and the response to it. Such a vision is a presence created by an absence, a life that remains alive because the death that was also in it has gone.

Two features of such a world are important for us here. The first is the alternation between two perspectives of existence: one an "oceanic" sense of submergence in a larger unity, the other a sense of individuality which is not that of the ego, that is, is not primarily aggressive or fearful. In the New Testament the conception of Christ in relation to the rest of humanity has this double focus. Paul speaks of all Christians as being one in Christ, where Christ is the whole of which individuals are the parts. But he also speaks of "Christ in me," where Paul is an individual of which Christ is a part, though a part that has the capacity to turn him inside out at any time.

The second feature follows from this. Our environment presents us with a vision of total possible intelligibility, symbolized in the Bible as creation through the Word. The "Word," in the New Testament, has associations of division and discrimination (II Timothy 2:15). Complementing the "Word" is the human-centered impulse to enter into that intelligibility, symbolized by the Spirit, a conception we shall look into in more detail in the next chapter. For the New Testament, the Word clarifies, the Spirit unifies, and the two together create what is the only genuine form of human society, the spiritual kingdom of Jesus, founded on the *caritas* or love which for Paul is not one virtue among others but the only virtue there is.

The two-stage movement from experience to knowledge spoken of earlier in this chapter is the result of living in time, where experience comes first and the consciousness of having had the experience comes later, and sometimes does not come at all. The interval is what T. S. Eliot's "Hollow Men" calls the falling of the shadow, and Eliot's *Quartets* are full of the contrast between the experience with its reflective shadow and an idealized spontaneous experience which carries the awareness of itself with it. This latter, according to the *Quartets,* would give, if we had it, a reality to life in the present moment that we normally lack, as the present moment for us is almost always a vanishing point between future and past. The inadequacy of ordinary experience is one reason for building up analogical structures of knowledge: we have criticism in literature, for example, because our experience of literature is so imperfect, improving only up to a point and then only with incessant practice. The ideal harmony of Word and Spirit in the New Testament is often thought of as restoring the kind of awareness that Adam had before the Fall. In any case it points to some kind of union between the imaginative and the actual that we have not yet identified.

Following a narrative is closely connected with the central literary metaphor of the journey, where we have a person making the journey and the road, path, or direction taken, the simplest word for this being "way." Journey is a word connected with *jour* and *journée,* and metaphorical journeys, deriving as they mostly do from slower methods of getting around, usually have at their core the conception of the day's journey, the amount of space we can cover under the cycle of the sun. By a very easy extension of metaphor we get the day's cycle as a symbol for the whole of life. Thus in Housman's poem "Reveille":

> Up, lad: when the journey's over
> There'll be time enough to sleep

the awakening in the morning is a metaphor of continuing the journey of life, a journey ending in death. The prototype for the image is the Book of Ecclesiastes, which urges us to work while it is day, before the night comes when no man can work. The Biblical vision includes a plug for the work ethic: in Housman the ethic seems to relate to war or adventure rather than merely life itself. In Blake's poem "Ah! Sunflower," the flower that turns its face to the sun through its passage across the sky is the emblem of all those who have repressed or frustrated their desires to the point at which they all consolidate into a desire for the sunset of death:

Seeking after that sweet golden clime
Where the traveller's journey is done.

The word "way" is a good example of the extent to which language is built up on a series of metaphorical analogies. The most common meaning of "way" in English is a method or manner of procedure, but method and manner imply some sequential repetition, and the repetition brings us to the metaphorical kernel of a road or path. One way may be straight and another winding: such a phrase as "That's a funny way to go about it" indicates a winding one. If the situation is one where we get to the same destination whichever course we pursue, we use the word "anyway." If we are speaking of a time when all possible journeys have been completed, we use the word "always." And, of course, if we start out on a quest or anything that initiates a narrative movement, we normally go "away."

In the Bible "way" normally translates the Hebrew *derek* and the Greek *hodos,* and throughout the Bible there is a strong emphasis on the contrast between a straight way that takes us to our destination and a divergent way that misleads or confuses. This metaphorical contrast haunts the whole of Christian literature: we start reading Dante's *Commedia,* and the third line speaks of a lost or erased way: "Che la diritta *via* era smarrita." Other religions have the same metaphor: Buddhism speaks of what is usually called in English an eightfold path. In Chinese Taoism the Tao is usually also rendered "way," by Arthur Waley and others, though I understand that the character representing the word is formed of radicals meaning something like "head-going." The sacred book of Taoism, the *Tao te Ching,*

begins by saying that the Tao that can be talked about is not
the real Tao: in other words we are being warned to beware
of the traps in metaphorical language, or, in a common Ori-
ental phrase, of confusing the moon with the finger pointing
to it. But as we read on we find that the Tao can, after all, be
to some extent characterized: the way is specifically the "way
of the valley," the direction taken by humility, self-efface-
ment, and the kind of relaxation, or non-action, that makes all
action effective.

The figure in the Sermon on the Mount, contrasting the
straight and narrow way to salvation with the broad highway
to destruction, has been the basis of a number of sustained
allegories, the best known being Bunyan's *Pilgrim's Progress*.
To keep the figure of a way going for a whole book, the course
pursued has to be a very laborious one: this is theologically
defensible for Bunyan, even though we can see that the difficulty of the journey is a technical as well as a religious require-
ment. Toward the end of the second book Bunyan says:

> Some also have wished, that the next way to their Father's house
> were here, that they might be troubled no more with either hills or
> mountains to go over; but the way is the way, and there is an end.

One wonders if there is not a suppressed voice also in Bunyan's mind asking why we have to be stuck with this spiteful
and malicious God who puts so incredibly difficult an obstacle
course between ourselves and himself. In the great *danse macabre* with which the second book concludes the dying Valiant-
for-Truth says: "Though with great difficulty I am got hither,
yet now I do not repent me of all the trouble I have been to
arrive where I am," where the suppressed voice is almost au-
dible. When there are dissenting voices like this murmuring in
the subtext, one wonders if the author does not feel some difficulty about his choice of metaphor.

There are naturally many variants of the journey: there is

the choice-of-Hercules or Y journey, where a decision must be taken between two courses. There is the fact that such a decision excludes every other decision, so that every journey is haunted by Robert Frost's sense of a "road not taken." There is the Christian doctrine (not that it is confined to Christianity) that everyone is on the wrong path to begin with, and must find his way back to the real starting point. There is the interrupted journey, a theme ranging from Frost's "Stopping by Woods on a Snowy Evening" to Shakespeare's *Tempest,* where suggestions of death and renewed life creep in. There is the involuntary journey, like that of Mohammed to Jerusalem, which takes place in dream or vision. There is the meandering romantic journey of continual discovery, like that of Tennyson's Ulysses or the medieval knight-errant who will never run out of giants to kill or suppliant heroines in a fix. This last is the wish-fulfillment form of the labyrinthine journey, the trapped movement that either leads nowhere or can be escaped from only by external assistance.

Sometimes there is a journey to a point that symbolizes the end of conscious life, such as the sea, which the soul traditionally crosses at death, or a sacred river, like the Ganges or the Jordan. The Christian emphasis on baptism places this image at the beginning of life, and so makes it possible in theory to avoid the wrong path that is certainly going to be traversed in practice.

The initiations at Eleusis concluded with a journey to the sea, and perhaps the great cry of "The sea!" in Xenophon's *Anabasis* owes some of its resonance to the ritual. The word *anabasis* means "going up." Most journeys in literature are connected with some form of quest shape. The quest, where the hero normally leaves home, performs his quest, and returns, has a cyclical or labyrinthine movement at its base, but in most quests the end of the journey is not a simple return home, even in the *Odyssey,* where it looks so much like one. The horizontal circle acquires the spiral vertical dimension of a directed movement, an end-of-narrative vision. The spiral is among other things a conventionalized labyrinth, and the theme of emerging from a labyrinth, where the winding or mazy course straightens out into a directed one, meets us constantly in literature. Aeneas journeys to the lower world through the cave of the Sibyl, the structure of which is associated by Virgil with Daedalus, the builder of the Cretan labyrinth, and the difficulty and importance of emerging from it is heavily stressed. Yeats in "Byzantium" also speaks of "unwinding the winding path," a phrase sometimes associated with unwrapping a mummy, and linked also to his occult *Hodos Chameliontos,* the way that continually changes its appearance. The Biblical Exodus follows the labyrinthine wandering in the wilderness with the directed conquest of Canaan.

Jesus' metaphors of a way come mainly from the more exoteric parts of his doctrine, addresses to a public still immersed in a time-world, where it seems appropriate to suggest extensions of time, in such conceptions as "the next world" or "the after-life," into unknown forms of existence, and to keep the metaphor of the completed journey for this life. But in the dialogues between Jesus and his disciples in the Gospel of John we seem to be in a more esoteric area.

The discussion in John 14 is, for those who are familiar with it at all, so very familiar that it tends to slide in and out of the mind without leaving much impression, and the paralyzing paradox of what is being said misses us entirely. Jesus tells his disciples that he is going to prepare a place for them, that they know where he is going, and consequently they know the way. They protest that they don't at all know where he is going, and therefore they can't possibly know the way. Jesus' answer "I am the way," explodes, or, perhaps, deconstructs, the whole metaphor of journey, of the effort to go there in order to arrive here. The metaphor of a journey modulates into the metaphor of an erect human body, with a head on top and feet underneath, with which we identify ourselves. Philip asks to be shown the Father, and gets the same type of answer: there is nothing there; everything you need is here. In the synoptics Jesus makes the same point in telling his disciples that the kingdom of heaven, the core of his teaching, is among them or within them. Nothing Jesus says seems to have been more difficult for his followers to grasp than his principle of the hereness of here.

Gertrude Stein remarked of the United States: "There is no there there," meaning, I suppose, that the beckoning call to the horizon, which had expanded the country from one ocean to the other in the nineteenth century, had now settled into a cultural uniformity in which every place was like every other place, and so equally "here." This is a kind of parody of Jesus' conception of his kingdom as here, but it suggests other aspects of it. Several religions (I use this word very loosely), including Taoism and Zen Buddhism, emphasize that there is nowhere to go, attempting to drive us into an intolerable claustrophobia from which there is no escape except by a kind of explosion, or rather implosion, of the ego-self into the spiritual body that is the real form of itself. Similarly with Jesus' "I am the way." Once we form part of a body which is both ourselves and infinitely larger than ourselves, the distinction between movement and rest vanishes: there is no need for a way when the conception "away" is no longer functional.

I am not connecting Jesus' metaphor here with a structure of belief, but with the response of a reader to a verbal structure. Following a narrative is a metaphorical journey, and the journey is metaphorically horizontal, going from here to there. Coming to the end, and trying to understand what we have read, introduces a vertical metaphor of looking up and down. That is why the second half of this book deals with the vertical metaphor of the *axis mundi,* the journey of consciousness to higher and lower worlds. Such journeys go back to primitive shamanism, but even primitive societies seem to be fairly clear about the fact that all such journeys are metaphorical, and that no physical acts of climbing or digging need necessarily be involved. The same is true for us, apart from references to whatever happens at death, where we do not know, any more than Jesus' disciples knew, in what sense such a word as journey may be appropriate. Thus Kent at the end of *King Lear:*

> I have a journey, sir, shortly to go:
> My master calls me: I must not say no. (V, iii, 323–4)

Earlier in *King Lear* we have the confrontation of Lear and Edgar disguised as Tom o' Bedlam. It is not difficult to see the ruined and bedraggled form of a primitive shaman in Tom o' Bedlam, an ecstatic who believes himself impelled by forces beyond ordinary human life. The great song of Tom o' Bedlam is not quoted in *King Lear,* but its last stanza, especially its triumphant final line, sums up this phase of our argument:

> By a knight of ghosts and shadows
> I summoned am to tourney
> Ten leagues beyond the wide world's end,
> Methinks it is no journey.

Literature is a technique of meditation, in the widest and most flexible sense. We journey through a narrative; then we stop and confront what we have read as though it were objective. It is not objective, because it is already a part of ourselves. There is a further stage of response, however, where something like a journeying movement is resumed, a movement that may well take us far beyond the world's end, and yet is still no journey.

CHAPTER FOUR

Spirit and Symbol

I

We have been avoiding the word religion, which so far has turned up mainly in the context of ideology. The many religions of the world belong to an even larger group of ideologies: the majority of them accept a specific mythological background and then translate it into a conceptual doctrine that is to be believed (*quid credas*). Belief then bears fruit in the actions or lifestyle of the believer (*quid agas*). At the center of this belief is a sacred area of ritual acts: in Christianity these include going to church, receiving the sacraments, prayer, etc. Such acts are, in Bishop Butler's phrase, "analogies" of a spiritual life. A temporal life permeated by acts within the sacred area moves on to an eternal life entered at death which forms its "antitype" (GC 79). It is possible to have an ideology that substitutes concepts for divine personalities, such as we have in Marxism. But the absence of personal gods did not prevent Marxism from developing a parallel apparatus of inspired texts, saints, shrines and martyrs, a professional hierarchy corresponding to a priesthood, orthodox and heretical beliefs, and commitment to an accepted ideology.

This book is not about religion as such: it is about the

relation of Biblical myth and metaphor to Western verbal culture, more particularly its literature. I know that there is a widespread desire for a religion that transcends ideological commitment, fixed doctrines of belief, and detailed directives for ordering one's life according to ritual and moral patterns. I think this much less anti-social than any of the fundamentalist reactions also taking place in all Western religions and ideologies, which make a policy of excluding what is usually called dialogue. But at the same time I realize that enlarging the scope of dialogue is easiest for the most indifferent, and can be a very painful process for those who see some of their cherished beliefs and practices inexorably turning into mere anxieties.

Such questions turn largely on language and the modes of language. We have looked at the traditional view (or our version of it) that the three "serious" modes of language relate to the perceptual, the conceptual and the ideological aspects of verbal communication, and we have called these modes the descriptive, the dialectical, and the rhetorical. In this perspective the ideological is as far as we can go, which brings us to the point where every religion is a form of ideology. We noted too the traditional proviso that rhetoric should be dominated by dialectic as far as possible, to prevent it from becoming debased into mob emotion. The phrase "as far as possible" indicates the limitations of the procedure. Each religion uses dialectic, or the appearance of it, to demonstrate that it is the right one—the key to the lock, in Chesterton's phrase. Dialectic is a mode of language expressing the dominance of a conscious will, and the difference between religious and non-religious ideologies is largely that the religious ones ascribe the effective conscious will to God and the non-religious ones to some form of Rousseau's "general will" in human society.

We noted also that a fourth mode of language, the imaginative or poetic, lies on the other side of the rhetorical. Rhetoric is intermediate between dialectic and poetic, and shows as many analogies to the poetic as it does to the dialectical mode. The poetic does not depend on the conscious will to the extent that the other modes do: it depends on a half-voluntary, half-involuntary, integration of the conscious will with other factors in the psyche, factors connected with fantasy, dreaming, let's pretend, and the like. It expresses itself in myth and metaphor, myth being a story which is not the same thing as a history, and metaphor being a verbal relation which is not that of logic. And while it would be an abuse of language to speak of the Bible as a work of literature, there is still the fact that most of it, including nearly all of its prophetic part, is written in the literary language of myth and metaphor.

When any mode is misunderstood or distrusted, its neighbors are likely to move into its territory in a spirit of imperialist aggressiveness. I have elsewhere quoted Newman (GC 85) as saying that the Bible was never intended to teach doctrine, but only to prove it. It is true that the Bible cannot teach doctrine, but trying to prove doctrine by it turns the Bible into something else. Yet nothing else is possible for theologians and Biblical scholars who disregard or underrate the importance of the literary elements in the Bible. Some scholars interested in the historical background and setting of the Bible have learned so much about their subject that they have come to feel that their historical reconstructions *are* the reality of which the Bible itself provides only a mythical or polemical distortion.

To use a famous phrase in literary criticism, this will never do. It is true that rhetoric and poetry are often similar in their techniques of handling words, that much of the Bible is didactic exhortation, and that it is often impossible to distinguish the two styles. Again, the original motivation in the Bible often seems to be closer to the ideological than to the literary, a fact that accounts for the power and the plausibility of its ideological expositions.

Nonetheless the Bible is saturated with myth and metaphor, and few would deny that some of the greatest poetry the world has ever seen is included in it. Such features cannot reasonably be treated as merely ornamental, as in so many "Bible as literature" approaches. The literary element needs to be studied functionally, as an essential part of what the Bible is, and how and why its literary aspect is essential is the point I keep missing in the treatments of the subject I have read. Between every sermon and the text it is based on there lies the shadowy valley of the literary imagination, with all its fictions, illusions, and suspended judgments, and, in the twentieth century at any rate, no one unwilling to pass through this valley is likely to get to the center of the Bible itself. This has always been true, but now it is overwhelmingly obvious that the Bible cannot be treated as simply an illustration of a doctrinal or historical construct. I am not considering here the sectarians who confine themselves to two or three proof-texts, but naturally the same principle applies to them.

In *The Great Code* I adopted the widely used term *kerygma,* or proclamation (GC 29), to describe a verbal aspect of the Bible that has affinities with the two figured languages of rhetoric and poetry, and yet is not quite either. It was with some hesitation that I preferred it to "apocalyptic" or "prophetic." This word kerygma is associated mainly with the theologian Rudolf Bultmann, who contrasts it with myth, and regards the mythical elements in the Bible as something to be removed or transmuted into something else before the kerygma can stand out. As the entire Bible, from the first chapter of Genesis to the twenty-second chapter of Revelation, is written in the language of myth and metaphor, with occasional divergences into other modes, this would be difficult to do. If it were possible, we should be back to our old situation: kerygma would be simply a form of ordinary rhetoric, with the theologian adding a skeleton of his own dialectic (or pseudo-dialectic), the literary element being regarded as left in the Bible by inadvertence or simply to make it more fun to read. I think it is important to keep the word kerygma, but it has to mean not ordinary rhetoric but a mode of language that takes account of the mythical and literary qualities which cannot be separated from the Biblical texture. In short, a mode of language on the *other side* of the poetic.

Of course another fallacy, of assuming that the literary Bible is the real or essential Bible, to which non-literary material, like the begats in Chronicles, has inorganically been added, is theoretically possible. But, first, there is no formal unifying literary element like the dactylic hexameter in the Homeric epics: if there were one there would be little point in looking for a metaliterary mode. Again, a work of literature is normally written or edited by a single person, and the immense overview of history that the Bible attains (*Heilsgeschichte* is the technical term for this) puts such a literary perspective out of account. The conception of "literature" itself is really post-Biblical, even if much of what we now call literature is earlier, and literature is addressed to the imagination, a term with no ancient or Biblical equivalent. To get to whatever the verbal mode of the Bible may be we have to go through the territory of literature; but we also have to go out of it on our way to something else. It sounds as though in the literary mode also our old friend the excluded initiative may be knocking at the door again. But we have several things to consider before we can try opening it.

I am not ignoring or undervaluing the work of *Formgeschichte* and other analytic literary scholars, but I am not speaking of that kind of literary criticism. I said in the previous chapter that holism, the assumption that the work in front of us is a unity, with all its parts fitting together and relevant to that unity, is the practical working assumption that every act of criticism must begin with. It may seem monstrous or freakish to assume such a unity in so miscellaneous a book as the Bible, but that is how the Bible has historically made its impact, so it was worth a try. *The Great Code,* if it succeeded in any degree, conveyed the fact that unity exists, though it is of a kind that opens up further perspectives instead of closing them off.

The Bible is held together by an inner core of mythical and metaphorical structure: mythical in the story it tells of the redemption of man from between the beginning and the end of time; metaphorical in the way that its imagery is juxtaposed to form an "apocalyptic" picture of a cosmos constructed according to the categories of human creative energy (i.e. the animal world appears as pastoral, the mineral world as urban, etc., as in GC 166). This poetic unity is there: how it got there will doubtless always be something of a mystery. It is not a product of history, or authorship, or editing, or of any such conception as "inspiration," a word which may assert something but explains nothing. We can only call it a mystery of canonicity, and let it go for the time being, holding in the meantime to our central principle: the Bible is not a work of literature, but its literal meaning is its mythical and metaphorical meaning.

As for the unity of the Bible, there is an analogy in Homeric criticism (GC 206), where after a great deal of analytical work (and guesswork) critics returned to "Homer," though his neo-Homer is not a specific historical figure but a metaphor for the imaginative unity we now see in the *Iliad* and the *Odyssey*. Similarly, the editors and redactors of the Pentateuch have settled down into a narrative continuity so skilful that we seem well on the way to a metaphorical neo-Moses, as well as a neo-somebody else for the Joshua-Kings narrative, a neo-David for the Psalms, a neo-Isaiah, and so on. There is a legend that the Old Testament was rewritten by Ezra in the fifth century B.C.: nobody believes it, but one can understand how the legend arose. However, the real unity in the Bible is not one of authorship but of something else, whether we call it canonicity or not, to which we still have no real clue.

The final cadence of the Bible, the Book of Revelation,

begins with a general epistle to seven churches in Asia, which, if it stood by itself, might well have been called by Luther what he called James, an epistle of straw. It is full of the anxieties that beset a second-rate mind, starting with the anxiety that unless he ascribes what he says to the mouth of God no one will pay attention to him. Very soon now, John says, when the world blows up, the seven churches will have to hand in their examination papers. Most of them will get low marks: Ephesus will get some credit for hating the Nicolaitan heresy, "which I (i.e. God) also hate," but Thyatira will be penalized for listening to a female evangelist identified only as "Jezebel." If the whole book had been on this level, it might perhaps never have got into the canon.

But, starting with the fourth chapter, there follows an incredible *tour de force* singlehandedly working out the entire *dianoia* or metaphor-cluster of the Bible along with its demonic parody, an achievement ranking with the dizziest technical flights of literature. We shall never know what made the difference, but it may have had something to do with the fading-out of the immediate occasion that marks one point where rhetoric turns into literature. The author may have thought of himself as going on with the same rhetorical job, instructing the all-too-few faithful about what to do when the sun turns into darkness and the moon into blood. But the world did not end as soon as John (or possibly his directing angel) thought it would; anxieties about an imminent future gave way to visions of the expanded present, and the fusspot overseer of Asia Minor churches turned into the magnificent seer of Patmos.

It is highly characteristic of the Bible that episodes in it of such different qualities should apparently be by the same person and belong to the same book. The Bible's literary unity is a by-product of something else—we might call it an unconscious by-product if we knew anything at all about the mental processes involved. The earlier part of the Old Testament, with its references to the Book of Jasher and the like, gives the effect of having distilled and fermented a rich poetic literature to extract a different kind of verbal essence, and on a smaller scale the same process can be seen in the New Testament. Luke has the Magnificat and Nunc Dimittis hymns; the Prologue to John is clearly a separate poem annexed by the writer of the Gospel; several famous passages in Paul, such as the *kenosis* passage in Philippians 2:5-11, perhaps even the great panegyric on love in I Corinthians 13, are sometimes thought to be from earlier hymns.

The editorial work done on this earlier poetic material was not an attempt to reduce it from poetry to a plain prose sense, assuming that there is such a thing. This kind of sense implies a direct appeal to credulity, to the infantilism which is so exasperating a feature of popular religious and other ideologies. What we have is rather an absorption of a poetic and mythical presentation that takes us past myth to something else. In doing so it will elude those who assume that myth means only something that did not happen. The organization of the Biblical story makes both the credulous and the rejecting responses possible, however, and it takes its chances with both.

It is a puzzling feature of the New Testament that the Gospels are not historically its earliest documents. Paul's genuine epistles are earlier, and Hebrews and Revelation at least not obviously later. Evidently there seemed to be no pressing need for a narrative account of Jesus as a historical figure until he actually became historical, a figure in the past who was now gone and had left only the Messianic vision behind him. For Paul, Christ was mainly the concealed hero of the Old Testament story and the post-Easter Christ of the resurrection. The Gospels present Christ in a form that fits this pre-Gospel conception of him: not in a biographical form but as a discontinuous sequence of appearances in which Jesus comments on the Old Testament as a series of past events, laws and images coming permanently alive in the Messianic context, and body, which he supplies.

The latest of the Gospels, John, begins with the tremendous prelude on the Logos that was probably, we said, an earlier hymn incorporated into the Gospel. Up to then, *logos* had had a long and varied history in Greek thought from Heraclitus to Philo, and had implied that the "word," or unit of human consciousness and communication, was something belonging to an order in thought linked to an order in nature. I doubt that the author of the hymn or the evangelist were deeply impressed by this history: they seem to have had something much closer to the Hebrew *dabhar* in their minds. But they cannot have been unaware of it either, or of the importance for later generations of adopting the Greek word.

John then proceeds to tell the story of Jesus in a narrative even further removed from the biographical than that of the synoptics. Very early comes the story of the wedding at Cana. It has been noticed that the behavior of Jesus at this wedding is difficult to account for except on the assumption that he was the bridegroom and consequently he and his mother were responsible for the party. The impression remains even though in the text Jesus is explicitly said to be a guest and the bridegroom mentioned is someone else. John obviously has no interest in presenting the historical Jesus as a married man. The Cana wedding is a parable (or type: there are no true parables in John) of Christ's second coming as the Bridegroom: in other words it is *mythos,* whatever the biographical kernel of the story may be. So the subtext of John conveys not only the statement "Jesus is the Logos," but also "Up to now *mythos* and *logos* have been a contrast; now they are the same thing." It is this *mythos-logos* identity that I am trying to characterize in the present chapter.

II

Let us now approach this question from the opposite end. Philosophers often come to, or feel obliged to come to, a point

at which their meditations on being or substance have to be
related to the traditional God of their culture. The God who
appears when thus invoked may be impressive enough. "By
God," says Spinoza:

I understand a being absolutely infinite, that is, a substance consisting of infinite attributes, each of which expresses eternal and infinite essence.

The point is frequently made that such verbal formulas seem
very remote from a personal God addressed as "Father" in
prayers and petitions. Our present question is rather: how could
a being so described ever have become a character in a story,
which is how God is regularly portrayed in the Bible? In addition to the "mighty acts" for which he is celebrated in the
Psalms, we can hardly overlook the extent to which he is also
an actor in a play. Perhaps he wrote the play and perhaps he
has the power to destroy the theater, like Samson, but in the
meantime he is an actor, and the play he is in casts him in
some very human roles.

Thus we have a God who drowns the world in a fit of
anger and repeoples it with the same kind of people in a fit of
remorse, promising not to do it again; a God who smells the
pleasant savor of a vast slaughter of animals by Noah and is
sufficiently gratified by it to remove the curse he imposed on
the earth at the time of Cain's murder of Abel; a God who
goes through a long bargaining scene with Abraham about the
number of righteous men needed to save Sodom; a God who
inspires Samuel to murder one of Saul's prisoners on the ground
that he should not have been spared but offered as a sacrifice
to himself; a God who demonstrates his superiority to Baal on
Mount Carmel by sending fire on Elijah's altar while his rival
remains asleep. It would perhaps be more in accord both with
our religious sensibilities and with our spiritual experience to

feel that the sleepy Baal was closer to being the true God than a jumpy Jehovah who turns up on cue to do stunts.

One can understand, up to a point, the Gnostic inference that the God of the Old Testament was an evil being; one remembers that most mythologies have a trickster god, and that some episodes in the Old Testament narrative—the fall of man, the hardening of Pharaoh's heart, the treatment of Saul, perhaps of Job—seem to show the trickster element incorporated in its God too. If God inspired this account of himself, he assuredly took no pains to wrap himself up in all the characterological armor, as it is sometimes called, that his human devotees are so careful to supply. It seems to be more important to present God as concerned with the human situation, at whatever cost to the dignity and remoteness that human etiquette usually prefers to associate with its rulers.

The primary fact about the Bible, that it illustrates the crossing of the *pons asinorum* from gods to God, is less simple than it is primary. Swedenborg says that angels cannot even pronounce the word "gods," the atmosphere they live in being too pure to tolerate such a grammatical solecism. The authors and editors of the Bible breathed a thicker air. Of course the Biblical religions are monotheistic, but one of the commonest words for God, Elohim, an intensive plural, sometimes seems to refer to a plurality of beings, and the Authorized Version renders it as "gods" or "angels" when it does so. Whether it is right or not, a monotheistic God can surely solve the logical problem of the one and the many by simply being many when he chooses. Thus in India Krishna could dance with any number of milkmaids, each of whom thought she had the real Krishna, and each of whom was (up to a point) right.

The conception of one God seems to be related to a unity in the mind that is supposed to have a conscious will in charge of all moods and emotions and fantasies, even if in practice it often turns out to be largely dominated by those alleged subordinates. Many visions of God in the Bible are, or more ac-

curately start out as, visions of what human passions and
fantasies dream of what God is or might be. This stage is followed by another, the impulse to approach unity in terms of
uniformity. If God is one, he must be uniformly good, wise,
loving, etc. Unity, or oneness coexisting with variety, is the
opposite of uniformity, where all things are alike and unvarying, and the irascible and whimsical acts of God in the Bible
force us to progress toward a vision of unity where we have
to abandon the easy, or uniform, way out. Such a progress
repeats the story of Job, who would never have got to his final
clarification without a cloud coming between him and his
original vision of God that suggested something irrational in
divine providence.

It takes more time to understand a unity that includes an
infinite variety of elements, many of them in at least logical
contradiction with one another, many of them bursting through
all the consistencies and unvarying reactions that human beings
use in struggling to make infinite acts comprehensible to finite
minds. I am not saying anything here that has not always been
recognized, even in the Bible itself. A thirteenth-century hymn
incorporated into the Jewish liturgy says of the prophets:

In images they told of thee, but not according to thine essence:
they but likened thee in accordance with thy works.

Such "works" would include the states of mind within the
human psyche. If we look back here at Spinoza's definition of
God with its infinity of attributes, we can see that he understood this very well, whatever his linguistic idiom.

But even an infinite number of attributes still does not bring
us to the real meaning of the capitalized terms, such as God,
Word and Spirit, which are at the heart of the Bible. It is not
very easy, to put it mildly, to say what the linguistic nature of
such words is. They are not Platonic forms; they are not really
universals, much less merely unifying terms. "God" in a sense

includes all possible gods, but also transcends the totality of gods; "Word" includes all possible words, as symbolized by the "Alpha and Omega" of Revelation 22:13, but is something other than the totality of words; Milton's Adam in Paradise was convinced that "Millions of spiritual creatures walk the earth" there, but "Spirit" is something else again. We are reminded of the fact that "being" in philosophy also as a rule transcends the totality of beings. What kind of language is appropriate for words that do not represent objects or events, or even the totality of them?

The visionary tradition referred to in the previous chapter, the one running through the pseudo-Dionysius, laid a good deal of stress on the fact that God was a hid divinity, hidden because all language about such a being dissolves in paradox or ambiguity (GC 12). Thus: there is no such thing as God, because God is not a thing. All language in such areas has to carry with it the sense of its own descriptive inadequacy, and nothing but the mythical and metaphorical language that says both "is" and "is not" can do this.

Let us glance at a literary term we have not yet used much: symbol. Originally, a symbol was a token or counter, like the stub of a theater ticket which is not the performance, but will take us to where the performance is. It still retains the sense of something that may be of limited interest or value in itself, but points in the direction of something that can be approached directly only with its help. A symbol may be purely arbitrary ("extrinsic," as Carlyle calls it), but as a rule it has or develops some analogous or other connection with what it points to, so that it can expand in that direction, taking us with it. Practically all techniques of meditation, for example, work with symbols, verbal or pictorial, that expand toward an identity, however defined, with what they symbolize.

The more significant the symbol, the more quickly it is transformed into the next stage of symbolism, the stage of epiphany or manifestation of a divine presence, a real presence appearing as a symbol of itself. With the exception of the great visions in Isaiah 6 and Ezekiel 1, these are usually aural in the Old Testament (GC 116), like the voice from the burning bush or the calls to the prophets. Often the narrator seems uncertain whether to say "God" or "angel," but—a point often evaded by commentators—on that level of existence there may be no difference at all between a manifestation and a messenger. Hence the ambiguity of the angels visiting Abraham in Genesis 18, and such phrases as "the angel of God" in Exodus 14:19 and elsewhere, which for all practical purposes seem to mean simply "God." A more familiar example is that of Jacob wrestling with the angel in Genesis 32, described as a "man" in verse 24, but "God" by verse 30. The name of Israel that Jacob acquired at this time is usually interpreted as meaning "he who wrestles (or struggles) with God."

The emphasis on "word" in the Bible implies that the will to communicate with man is part of the essence of God. To speak means to enter into all the conventions and nuances of language, which means that both speaking and understanding are highly selective processes. This is very obvious in conceptual and rhetorical modes. The poet's speech is also limited, but his abilities are linked to something involuntary in the mind, and he can write in the hope that something less inhibited and with a greater penetrating power may emerge. I spoke earlier of the magical line or passage that seems to break through its immediate context and open up wider ones. The prophetic utterance in the Bible is assumed to be one that is magical in the sense of having the greatest possible penetrating power.

The New Testament is presented as a gospel, a verbal communication coming from a Word made flesh, a presence in whom the distinction between the end and the means of communication has disappeared. Such a message has the gift of tongues, i.e. the ability to make its way through all the barriers of language. The frequently repeated phrase "He that hath ears to hear, let him hear" is not an elitism restricting the message only to those previously chosen to hear it. It is rather an appeal to make one's response depend as little as possible on the conventions of one's conditioning and prejudices.

Our survey of verbal modes put rhetoric between the conceptual and the poetic, a placing that should help us to understand why from the beginning there have been two aspects of rhetoric, a moral and a tropological aspect, one persuasive and the other ornamental. Similarly, we have put the poetic between the rhetorical and the kerygmatic, implying that it partakes of the characteristics of both. The relation of the poetic to the rhetorical preoccupied us in the two previous chapters: we have now to look at the mysterious borderlands between the poetic and the kerygmatic, the latter being still uncharacterized. For the time being we shall use the more familiar "prophetic" along with or instead of it, distinguishing them later. When either would be confusing, we shall substitute "metaliterary."

First of all, we need the guidance of a critic who understands what we have called the ecstatic state of response, and the difference, or contrast, between the ideological rhetoric that persuades and the proclamation that takes one out of oneself. The best of such critics is the first- or second-century writer whom we know only as Longinus. The title of Longinus' treatise, *Peri Hypsous,* is usually translated *On the Sublime,* which refers to an eighteenth-century adaptation of his ideas. The most effective part of *On the Sublime* deals with brief passages— "touchstones," as Matthew Arnold would call them—which stand out from their context. This we may call the oracular or discontinuous prophetic, the passage in the text where we suddenly break through into a different dimension of response. Longinus' examples come from Greek literature, but one—he was probably a Jew or a Christian—is the "Let there be light" verse from Genesis.

An utterance of this sort is one charged with such intensity, urgency or authority that it penetrates the defenses of the human receiving apparatus and creates a new channel of response. It may be experienced in trance, dream, hallucination or drug-induced states, and is often reported as a supernatural or externalized voice or vision. A famous passage in William James's *Varieties of Religious Experience* tells us that the author came out of a trance induced by nitrous oxide with the feeling that

> Our normal waking consciousness, rational consciousness as we call it, is but one special type of consciousness, whilst all about it, parted from it by the filmiest of screens, there lie potential forms of consciousness entirely different.

Of course different does not necessarily mean expanded, and the passage in itself might merely anticipate the science-fiction conception of parallel worlds, previously referred to. But James goes on to say that where there is the experience of difference there is the possibility of expansion. It must be a very rigidly self-censoring person who has never felt any whisper of what is expressed by e. e. cummings as "listen: there's a hell of a good universe next door: let's go."

But, of course, the universe next door might also be simply hell, or at any rate a world of overwhelming terror. According to Vico, communication from an unknown world began with a thunderclap, taken by early men (then giants) to be the voice of God. They dashed terrified into caves, dragging their women behind them, and thereby instituting private property. This symbol is incorporated into Joyce's *Finnegans Wake,* and Joyce adds the symbol of the earwig (*perce-oreille*), as a more intimate penetration associated with dreams and poetry. The chief character in this book is named Earwicker, a name also suggesting "Eire-waker," which in turn suggests the greatest kerygmatic utterance of all, the last trump that wakes the dead.

The mad, obsessed poem "Dies irae, dies illa," incorporated into the Requiem Mass, reminds us that terror is insep-

arable from any apocalyptic or prophetic vision. At present a
fear of the extermination of the human race, or a state in which
only the fortunate are dead, coexists with apocalyptic visions
of an "Aquarian age." But as terror paralyzes verbal as well as
other faculties, we cannot say much about it except that it is
always an aspect of prophecy or kerygma, and we must go
on to the more hopeful and therefore articulate features of the
latter.

Earlier in this century, under the influence of a critical tradition that began with Poe, there was a feeling that the greatest poets were those who most vividly communicate a sense
of oracular, fragmented intensity. Hopkins, Hölderlin, Rimbaud, were preferred over Tennyson, Goethe, or Hugo. I have
no great interest in revisions of value-judgments, but there is
a relevant critical principle involved here. In all verbal modes
there is a reader and a narrative to be read, and the continuity
of narrative inhibits at first the personal appropriation of what
one reads. What we read is, however tiresome we may find
the phrase, "food for thought," or imagination, and like other
food it has to be taken discontinuously, in bites.

If we watch a student underlining sentences in a textbook
(hoping he owns the book) we see the process at work: certain
sentences seem to be keys to the total meaning, and they are
the first parts of the narrative to undergo the transition from
their context in the narrative to their new context in the reader.
What happens in discursive prose happens in a different way
in poetry. Sentimental readers say that it will kill a poem to
analyze it, but reading, like eating, is a predatory activity, except, of course, that what is read exists both *en soi* and *pour
soi,* in itself as well as for itself, and, like Robert Graves's white
goddess, obligingly renews its virginity for the next reader. In
fact, it can, and should, renew it for the next reading by the
same reader.

The metaliterary begins with the process of perceiving some
kind of "that's for me" detail in one's reading. In literature,

this quality may be present in the magical line or phrase, earlier referred to, that suddenly seems to extend one's vision.
Others may find it in the sententious, the great thought or
epigram that may become detached from its context and become a proverbial expression in its own right. Still others will
seize on assonances and inner harmonies, such as Poe's much
admired line, "the viol, the violet, and the vine." In the Bible
this last quality of texture would be particularly significant for
the Hebrew scholar able to respond to the flickering and danc-
ing of pun and assonance in the Hebrew text, a feature with
no real counterpart in the Greek text of the New Testament.
These are simple examples of the way in which we may be
suddenly confronted by a verbal formula that insists on becoming a part of us. As isolated passages become more frequent,
the contact expands from the oracular flash into the possession
of or identification with the narrative, as in Eliot's famous phrase
about listening to music so deeply that we become the music
while it lasts.

In the Bible what we read is frequently presented to us as
something that was originally spoken. This is especially true
of the Gospels, centered as they are on a figure who spoke but
did not write. The followers of Derrida who say that we have
here another "logocentric" use of writing to denigrate writing
have, I think, got this situation the wrong way round. The
Gospels are written mythical narratives, and for casual readers
they remain that. But if anything in them strikes a reader with
full kerygmatic force, there is, using the word advisedly, a
resurrection of the original speaking presence in the reader. The
reader is the logocentric focus, and what he reads is emancipated both from writing and from speech. The duality of speaker
and listener has vanished into a single area of verbal recognition.

Traditional critical theories, from Plato and Aristotle on,
look at literature within a mimetic context. We are told in
both the *Republic* and in the *Poetics* that the poet's work is im-

itative, though very different inferences are drawn from the principle in the two contexts. What the poet imitates is usually assumed to fall within either the phenomena of human society or the order of nature. But the Longinian conception of ecstatic response suggests another dimension of imitation.

We have encountered suggestions of this already, in the Elizabethan critics referred to who traced the poetic tradition back beyond Homer into legendary culture-heroes, and who pointed to the words creation and maker, so often applied to poets, as indicating that the poet's work may not after all belong in a rigidly separated secular or profane category. With the coming of the Romantic movement, this association of the poet's work with the metaphors of divine creation greatly expanded. Coleridge, for example, thought of his entire critical theory as fitting inside a still larger study of the Logos. A historical turning point here is Milton's *Areopagitica*. If we concentrate on the broader issues implied in that pamphlet, we can see that the Reformation issue of the "liberty of prophesying" is being extended from the pulpit, where it was generally assumed to be confined, to the marketplace of publication, and that consequently the prophetic could have secular as well as sacerdotal contexts.

Naturally many critics, speaking for fashionable or ascendant ideologies, are anxious to inform poets that they have no right to prophetic authority. In the early twentieth century T. E. Hulme was one such critic, and he influenced the early attitudes of T. S. Eliot and Ezra Pound, because his anti-Romantic views were tactically useful to them for a time. But Eliot later spoke of wanting to go beyond poetry in the *Quartets,* and Pound expanded—exploded would perhaps be a better word—into even broader dimensions.

The existential movement of the nineteen-forties, also, revolved around a number of figures—Dostoevsky, Kierkegaard, Nietzsche, Kafka, Sartre—who were primarily literary figures, the word existential referring to tendencies in them that were metaliterary, trying to get past the limitations of literature into a different kind of identity with their readers. Kierkegaard divided his works into the "aesthetic" or literary, which he published under pseudonyms, and the "edifying," where he spoke in his own name as an "ethical" writer and teacher. He realized that there was a prophetic dimension on the other side of the aesthetic, but evidently did not realize that it was only in his aesthetic writings that he came anywhere near expressing it. The edifying writings revert to standard dialectical and rhetorical forms, one book on the boundary line between the two, *The Sickness unto Death,* being essentially a work in the seventeenth-century rhetorical genre of casuistry. The implications for the conception of the kerygmatic are, first, that kerygmatic writing normally demands a literary, that is, a mythical and metaphorical, basis; second, that the kerygmatic does not, like ordinary rhetoric, emerge from direct personal address, or what a writer "says."

Ordinary rhetoric does not really proclaim: it gives an emotional tone to arguments and uses poetic figures to color appeals to immediate action, but it seldom comes near the primary concern of "How do I live a more abundant life?" This latter on the other hand is the central theme of all genuine kerygmatic, whether we find it in the Sermon on the Mount, the Deer Park Sermon of Buddha, the Koran, or in a secular book that revolutionizes our consciousness. In poetry anything can be juxtaposed, or implicitly identified with, anything else. Kerygma takes this a step further and says: "You are what you identify with." We are close to the kerygmatic whenever we meet the statement, as we do surprisingly often in contemporary writing, that it seems to be language that uses man rather than man that uses language.

In the first three modes we surveyed at the beginning, there is an emphasis on compulsion: the compulsion to accept ascertained facts in the descriptive mode, the compulsion to accept the logic of an argument in the dialectical mode, the compulsion to accept social and authoritative pressure in the ideological mode. In the poetic mode there is no such compulsion: anything in the imaginative world can be assumed to be true for the duration of the individual work. So the imaginative and its freedom to create must be the basis of whatever goes beyond it. What does go beyond it is the "myth to live by," a myth which is also a model for continuous action, and which is the distinctively kerygmatic feature.

The imaginative in itself cannot provide a "myth to live by," but its freedom is the essential basis of all models that retain any sense of tolerance, and any understanding that there could be different models for other people. There is no individual basis for kerygma, in the sense that anyone could make up an anthology of kerygmatic writing or invent a kerygmatic work of his own. The kerygmatic grows out of social recognition, and the Bible is kerygmatic at least partly because it has been recognized as such for so long. The teachings of Jesus are kerygmatic for Christians, but Jesus himself thought of them as confirmed by the "scriptures," the Old Testament as it came to him.

One may also speak of a secular kerygma: the Communist Manifesto is kerygmatic in Marxist countries, and a more short-lived kerygma was achieved by the axioms of Mao Tse-tung in an earlier period of Chinese Communism. But political kerygma lacks a mythology of traditional stories and archetypal allusions, and the sense of a shared cultural tradition that only such a mythology can give. A kerygma without the full support of a mythology soon becomes a rhetorical vacuum, and a vacuum is something that consciousness, like nature, abhors. On the other hand, even the most penetrating literature, even Dante or Shakespeare, does not attempt to provide the dimension of a model-myth, with its program for reordering the direction of one's life.

In practice, therefore, the Bible is uniquely kerygmatic in the cultural tradition of the West. At this point the term prophetic falls into place as indicating both a metaliterary direction latent within literature and the human medium transmitting the kerygmatic to the idiom of ordinary language. What makes a prophet a genuine prophet, we may feel, is not what he says but what is said to him. But as soon as we use this not-but construction, we are going off the rails. We have to try to get past the verbal barrier implied: if the word inspiration means anything at all, it means the point at which the cleavage between active speech and reception of speech merges into unity. At this point we are in a genuinely kerygmatic realm.

The kerygmatic in the Bible, to confine ourselves to that, is not a form of verbal organization like the other four, even if our phrasing sometimes suggests that it is. It is metaphorically a speaking voice from God transmitted through human agents, of which the final one must be a transcribing secretary. But if we stop with the metaphor of the speaking voice, we are assimilating kerygma to ordinary rhetoric, just as the metaphor of the "sovereign will" of God assimilates him to a barbaric social order. Proclamation in the sense of a herald's utterance is a symbol of a manifestation that eludes the objective metaphors of hearing and seeing.

We now perhaps have some clue to the linguistic nature of the capitalized terms, God, Word, Spirit, Father and the like, that puzzled us earlier. Such terms are, at first, the objective counterparts of subjective psychic elements in the human complex, and as long as they are that they could be called pure projections. But as the subject-object cleavage becomes increasingly unsatisfactory, subject and object merge in an intermediate verbal world, where a Word not our own, though also our own, proclaims and a Spirit not our own, though also our own, responds. We capitalize these terms for the same reason that we capitalize other people's names. To use the terminology of Martin Buber's *I and Thou,* there is an inner movement in the creative life away from a world where everything outside humanity—and sometimes even humanity—is an "It," an object that never releases us from being subjects.

Obviously the ordinary critical value-judgments applied to literature have no relevance to the kerygmatic. For a critic to say on literary grounds that the Bible, the Koran, the Buddhist or Hindu Scriptures are repetitive, chaotic, obscure, obscurantist, illogical, inconsistent, unconvincing or what-not would obviously be a totally futile procedure, whatever might be true of the judgments themselves. In this area the critical faculty can only make the best of what is presented to it.

III

The most explicit directive given in the New Testament for reading the Old is Paul's statement that the text must be "spiritually discerned" (I Corinthians 2:14). What spiritual means in this context we have yet to see, although we have elsewhere suggested (GC 56) that its primary linguistic meaning (as, for instance, in Revelation 11:8) is metaphorical. In the same sense an early Christian father tells us that in addition to the synoptics, John wrote a spiritual or metaphorical gospel.

Descriptive language, apart from history, is concerned mainly with the physical environment; conceptual with the physical and social environment; rhetorical language with the social environment. All three are languages of nature and they express the relation of the physical to its context in time and space. With the poetic or imaginative we move into the spiritual area, where two new factors become apparent. First, the kerygmatic Word of the Bible has traditionally had a secondary relation to nature and a primary relation to spirit, the creative power of humanity. Second, there are spiritual aspects of descriptive, conceptual and rhetorical language which do not exist by themselves but only as elements in a poetic structure. Poetic (and kerygmatic) structures are therefore polysemous in a particularly specific and integrated way.

The spiritual *descriptive* is the narrative or fiction or *mythos* we have been discussing. It describes nothing external, but, by being a structure, it becomes a verbal something. Wallace Ste-

vens has a poem I have often referred to, "Description Without Place," which comes as near as anything I know to
expressing the notion of the spiritually descriptive. The principle is, according to Stevens, that we live secondarily within
our natural environment, but primarily within a creation of
our own inside the natural environment. As this inner creation
does not exist, in the sense of being a place, it has to be located
first of all within the poet's mind and writings, because there
seems nowhere else to put it. But the internalized, in this context, has to be distinguished from the subjective. The subjective is still a chaos of moods and emotions; the internalized is
a creation, and as such it is a part of the totality of human
creative efforts. It thus contains a communicable quality that
expands until, Stevens says, description becomes "revelation,"
with an explicit reference to "the thesis of plentifullest John"
(i.e. the author of Revelation). Spiritual "description" develops a distinct culture or style of creativity inside the "place"
where it occurs. Such a question as "Why does everything in
Spain look Spanish?" is one of those apparently idiotic questions that open up quite unexpected areas of vision.

The spiritually *conceptual* is the "underthought," or progression of metaphors underneath the explicit or ideological
meaning. As the second part of this book will try to suggest
in more detail, every system of conceptual thought has a metaphorical and diagrammatic skeleton beneath it. There is also
a strong polarizing tendency in the mosaic pattern of images
we meet at the end of a narrative suggesting that, to use conventionally religious language, the two real abodes of human
life are heaven and hell, and that the world we actually live in
is an inconsistent and inextricable mixture of the two.

The spiritually *rhetorical* is rhetoric in reverse, so to speak.
Rhetoric uses figurative language to address an audience directly. In poetic language there is no direct address: the writer
turns away from his audience and uses the convention of direct
speech in relation to something else. I have quoted the obser-

vation of John Stuart Mill that the poet is not heard but over-heard. Plato moves closer to the poetic area than practically any other philosopher because of his use of dialogue, where others speak for him, because his main speaker Socrates is an ironist who questions rather than answers, and because the dialogues which are concerned with Platonic forms (courage, friendship, justice) do not depend so much on the argument as on the presentation by the dialogue as a whole of what the ostensible argument is about (i.e. justice is discussed by the intellectually honest, friendship by the friendly, love by lov-ers, etc.).

These three polysemous factors of the poetic make up a total descriptive narrative that I called elsewhere the loss and regaining of identity, a conceptual argument based on a pat-tern of imagery that separates a world of metaphorical unity from its demonic opposite, and a rhetoric based on example and illustration rather than direct assertion. The Bible is a con-densed and unified epitome of this poetic universe, as well as the proclamation of God's message to man. The word mes-sage of course suggests ordinary rhetoric, but a rhetorical di-rect address that by definition comes from an infinite mind to a finite one is a wildly paradoxical notion. The Sermon on the Mount is said to be preached to multitudes, but one cannot imagine it shouted in the open air: its clauses are verbal seeds planted in silence and growing in silence within.

But why is our present direction "spiritual"?

There are two traditional words for the distinctively hu-man element in man as a product of nature, the words spirit and soul, which are distinguished in all languages relevant to the Bible. They cannot be said to be consistently distinguished (GC 20), but soul seems to have a general context of man as creature, as brought into being by a God thought of as exter-nal to man. Soul does not seem to have a capitalized transcen-dental form like Spirit, but remains a plurality, something that each person *has*. Paul's discussion of the soul-spirit relationship in I Corinthians is the *locus classicus* for the Christian Bible (in the next few paragraphs any reference to the Bible not otherwise indicated is to this epistle). Paul speaks of the *soma psychikon,* the "soul-body," as what the AV translates as the "natural" or mortal body, which he apparently equates with the "spirit of man" (2:11). The notion that the soul is immortal by nature is Platonic rather than Biblical (GC 19). The soul-body seems to be thought of as a duality, the soul being "in" the body, so that when the physical body dies the soul would either vanish into non-being or survive without its body in a discarnate state. The beings encountered in Dante are discarnate souls of this kind.

The conception of soul begins with the fact, which has been noted from earliest times, that the human psyche consists of a variety of elements, all of them linguistically structured. Man is a being who can argue with himself, yield to himself and despise or congratulate himself for doing so, play jokes on himself, blank himself out and let some other voice, still himself, take over. In pathological states a number of quite separate personalities may emerge. The word individual, if it has any connection with the undividable, could hardly be less appropriate. The simplest way of normalizing this state of affairs is to put a consciousness in charge which has acquired certain habits of procedure and has learned what is socially effective. Putting it in charge means giving it control of the will. The consciousness may then claim to speak for the whole psyche, and, if it temporarily loses control, may even use metaphors of foreign invasion ("I don't know what got into me").

In Plato's *Republic* the just society is an allegory of the wise man's mind. The latter is an intensification of the normal arrangement: the consciousness is the ruler, the guards are his will, and the rest of the population represent moods and desires and needs that are generalized as bodily. Aristotle's less rigorous conception of the soul as the unity that the variety of perceptions and impulses builds up was the one that Christianity, despite the New Testament, tended to adopt. Through most of the Christian period, the soul was regarded as what is essential to man: the soul is immortal, and saving it is man's primary duty. Thus soul becomes largely identical with the spirit as soon as it has got rid of the body. But because the New Testament's language introduces a distinction that this view of it ignores, the doctrine had to be added that at the end of time the body will rise and re-attach itself to the discarnate soul.

The Greek conception of soul and body corresponds closely to our first three linguistic modes, the body's awareness of its environment being expressed in descriptive language, the soul's in the language of argument and ideology. In the *Republic* the ruling power has to be philosophical, because without a philosopher's command of dialectic the consciousness will simply be rationalizing impulses or decisions made elsewhere in the psyche, which is what most of us, not being wise, do most of the time. Poetic language has a low rating in this view: if we tolerate it at all we should make sure that it confines itself to panegyrics on the soul and the rightness of its views and decisions. Many poets come to terms with this situation, and hence the "dialogue of soul and body" has become a common literary genre. "Body" here is a metaphor, and a very confusing one, for another context of the psyche.

Usually in such poems the soul condemns anything resisting it as merely bodily, in what often seems an arrogant and self-righteous tone. There is one magnificent exception in Marvell, where the body gets the last word:

What but a soul would have the wit
To build me up for sin so fit?
So architects do square and hew
Green trees that in the forest grew.

Yeats remarks that we make rhetoric out of quarrels with others, poetry out of the quarrel with ourselves. So we are not surprised to see the dialogue of soul and body recur in such poems of Yeats as "Dialogue of Self and Soul," the fourth part of "Vacillation," and "Ego Dominus Tuus." The soul comes off rather badly in these debates because Yeats reflects a century in which the doctrine of the immortality of the soul seems very close to the prospect of living indefinitely as a cantankerous and censorious superego. In general, in their social attitude and personal behavior, poets are fairly flexible about their inner parliaments, knowing by experience how a dictatorial consciousness inhibits the creative faculties.

Spirit, on the other hand, is identified in the New Testament both with God and with the kind of understanding response it wants us to develop about God. Paul distinguishes the *soma psychikon,* which is mortal, from the *soma pneumatikon,* the spiritual body (I Corinthians 15:44). This is also a body (Paul means that it *is* a body, not that it *has* one). We possess it in this life also, and it is the element in us that enables us to understand the scripture and other aspects of revelation (2:14). It is a highly individualizing power, and Paul is emphatic about the infinite variety of its gifts and operations (12:4).

We recall our previous discussion of the paradisal vision as the upper pole of the imaginative one. In Pauline terms the *soma pneumatikon* enables us to live continuously on the paradisal level, as the quickening spirit created out of the "living soul" of the first Adam in Genesis (15:45). It goes without saying that the spirit is the immortal aspect of ourselves, and that the soul-body unit has to dissolve before it becomes fully emancipated (15:36). It is the body that Jesus assumed at the resurrection, and is for us the "risen body" in which we share that state. Angels, or whatever forms of existence are assumed to occupy higher levels than our ordinary one, are regularly called spiritual beings. These are the traditional associations, but the word spirit is versatile enough to include secular areas as well. Behind the crowds lining up in Red Square to view the body of Lenin is some such axiom as: "Lenin is dead, but his spirit still lives on." No other word than "spirit" would seem appropriate here.

The soul is usually thought of as the seat of consciousness (Genesis 2:7), and consciousness includes a will to keep on being conscious: no consciousness is separable from such a will. Machines may do many things that resemble consciousness, but as they have no will to do these things, but depend on being plugged in or turned on, we do not think of them as conscious. So the soul-body unit is a persisting hierarchy in which the will of a soul continuously dominates. This persistence gives the unit a single identity, in which, as we noted, we call ourselves the same person at seventy that we were at seven, despite all the obvious changes.

The persistence of identity is thus the persistence of a hierarchy of authority, and all order in the *soma psychikon* is a product of this hierarchy. What is true of the individual expands into society: within a society of such individuals all order depends on assigned authority, and the individual's dignity is greatly enhanced by identifying himself with a more continuous social institution, such as a nation or church. We have noted the Platonic context of the soul-body relationship, and a certain amount of Platonism about such larger institutions seems inevitable: most students or churchgoers or voters sense an ideal form within university or church or state that is not destroyed by the pedantry or stupidity or dishonesty also to be found in their practical operations.

In English the word body has two meanings, the physical individual and an aggregate that may include a number of individuals, as when we speak of a committee or army or nation as a body. In fact the whole of mankind may be called metaphorically a single body, even though we say that such a complex unity is really an aggregate. But the "spiritual body" seems to have some genuine independence of the single permanently anchored identity to which the *soma psychikon* is confined. The

Jesus of history, according to most Christian views, was a soul-body unit like anyone else; the spiritual body of the risen Christ is everywhere and in everyone, and, as noted earlier, it may be a part of us or we may be a part of it. The *soma pneumatikon,* then, suggests a certain fluidity of personality, in which such metaphors as the "one flesh" erotic metaphor, or metaphors of being influenced by another personality or the work of a creative artist, begin to take on more reality.

In *The Great Code* I used the word interpenetration (168) to describe this fluidity of personality in its complete form. The word love means perhaps too many things in English and for many has an over-sentimental sound, but it seems impossible to dissociate the conceptions of spiritual personality and love. The capacity to merge with another person's being without violating it seems to be at the center of love, just as the will to dominate one conscious soul-will externally by another is the center of all tyranny and hatred. John Donne uses a beautiful figure in this connection based on the metaphor of an individual life as a book. The spiritual world, he says, is a library "where all books lie open to one another."

The metaphorical kernel of spirit, in all languages, is air or breath. Breathing is the most primary of all primary concerns, the act marking the transition from the embryo to the baby, and our most continuous activity thereafter. We can go for days without food, or for a lifetime without sex, but ten minutes without breathing and we "expire." The transition from the embryonic to the ordinary world suggests by analogy a second transition from a natural to a spiritual world, which we reach by taking a second breath or inspiration in a higher kind of air. This process is a rebirth or second birth. In its transcendental or capitalized form, spirit in Christian doctrine becomes the Holy Spirit, but the imagery can be independent of this application. In Rilke's *Orpheus Sonnets* there is a magnificent poem about breathing (II, i), which speaks of it as a pure interchange of world-space and one's own being:

Immerfort um das eigne
  Sein rein eingetauschter Weltraum.

Some mythologies make a good deal of the metaphor of the spirit as child (*puer aeternus*), born from the soul and body. In this context soul and body would be psychological parental residues. The implication seems to be that this spiritual child escapes from the conditioning factors of the time-bound influence inherited from parents and transmitted to progeny. Perhaps Jesus had such blocking elements in mind when he spoke of the duty of his disciples to "hate" their parents and others close to them, including themselves (Luke 14:26), and the same myth may be a factor in the reference to Melchizedek, the prototype of Christ, as "without father, mother, or descent" (Hebrews 7:3). Elsewhere there seem to be suggestions that the emancipation of the spirit restores an original androgynous form of humanity: thus the statement in Revelation 14:4 that the redeemed are all male celibates, which we shall have to look at again. A variant of the same myth may lurk in the background of the verse: "Whosoever is born of God doth not commit sin; for his seed remaineth in him" (1 John 3:9; AV: modern translations try to make it mean something else).

As for the "air" aspect of the metaphor, the air we breathe is invisible because if it were visible nothing else would be (GC 124). Hence the spiritual or higher air world is not an invisible order independent of the visible one, but an invisibility that enables another kind of reality to appear, a mystery turned into revelation. This upper air is one in which the relation of divine and human becomes reciprocal, as the spirit is part of the human as well as of the divine being (6:17). The demonic parody of this spiritual air in the Bible is the *hebel,* the vapor or "vanity" of the Book of Ecclesiastes which is the normal characteristic of life without any vision of or desire for renewal.

Valéry, in an essay on Mallarmé where he is following

Mallarmé's thought very closely, says that in Mallarmé language becomes an instrument of spirituality, which he explains as "the direct transmutation of desires and emotions into presences and powers that become 'realities' in themselves." The word spiritual in English may have a rather hollow and booming sound to some: it is often detached from the spiritual body and made to mean an empty shadow of the material, as with churches who offer us spiritual food that we cannot eat and spiritual riches that we cannot spend. Here spirit is being confused with soul, which traditionally fights with and contradicts the body, instead of extending bodily experience into another dimension. The Song of Songs, of which more later, is a spiritual song of love: it expresses erotic feeling on all levels of consciousness, but does not run away from its physical basis or cut off its physical roots. We have to think of such phrases as "a spirited performance" to realize that spirit can refer to ordinary consciousness at its most intense: the *gaya scienza,* or mental life as play, that we glanced at earlier. Similar overtones are in the words *esprit* and *Geist.* (The phrase "in good spirits" is different: it comes from an abandoned medical theory.)

It is not hard to understand that spiritual may be used to mean the highest intensity of consciousness. But Valéry and Mallarmé are saying much more than that, and implying still more. They are in fact suggesting that the initiative excluded hitherto from the imaginative and poetic, the principle that opens the way into the kerygmatic, is the principle of the reality of what is created in the production and response to literature. Such a reality would be neither objective nor subjective, but essentially both at once, and would of course leave the old opposition of idealism and materialism a long way behind. It would also abandon the schizophrenic efforts at faith in the old dialectical sense of a simulated knowledge, according to the schoolboy's definition of faith as "believin' what you know ain't so."

But perhaps not in the New Testament sense. Faith is defined in the New Testament (Hebrews 11:1) as the *hypostasis* of the hoped-for, the *elenchos* of the unseen. *Hypostasis* is a term in Greek philosophy for which the Latin equivalent is *substantia,* and hence the AV, following the Vulgate, renders it "substance." Modern translations usually say "assurance," because Paul uses the word in that sense, but Paul is not the author of Hebrews, and I suspect that "substance" is closer to what is meant here (see also Hebrews 1:3). The believer is being told that he has got something, not that he is sure of getting it eventually. *Elenchos* means proof or evidence. The point is that substance cannot here possibly mean a metaphysical substance, proof a logical proof, or evidence anything that a scientist or historian would call evidence. These words refer normally to conceptual processes, but the context does not suggest a ground arrived at by conceptual arguments, however powerful, much less a literal acceptance which is really pseudo-descriptive in its basis.

Whatever one thinks of the Tertullian paradox ("I believe because it is impossible"), the opposite of it is the reduction of the substance of belief to the credible, which is a dreary desolation of the spirit. The credible is, by definition, what is believed already, and there is no adventure of the mind there. The Wright brothers getting a heavier-than-air machine off the ground when the most distinguished contemporary scientists had proved that such a thing was impossible: that is closer to the kind of thing the author of Hebrews means by faith, as the examples he goes on to give from the Old Testament show. Belief is rather the creative energy that turns the illusory into the real. Such belief is neither rational nor ideological, but belongs on the other side of the imaginative. One could practically paraphrase the Hebrews verse as: "Faith is the reality of hope and of illusion." Both these words need a further comment.

The Bible is framed within a gigantic metaphor of a court trial, ending in a last judgment, with an accuser and defender.

In the Book of Job the accuser is Satan and a defender (*go'el*) is postulated by Job (19:25); in the New Testament, of course, the defender is Christ. The accuser stands particularly for the past and for what one has done. Every moment, as it passes, vanishes from the potential into the forever actual: the mouth of hell is the previous moment, and the passing of each moment makes the next one more predictable, until life ends. The souls in Dante's hell represent the aspect of life in which one is imprisoned forever within the sum of one's past deeds, when what one is and what one has done become, at death, the same thing.

The hope that the New Testament writers relate to faith and love refers to the future and the still potential. One may lose hope for some specific thing, but it may not be psychologically possible to lose altogether the hope that the future may bring something more than the past would lead us to expect. At the end of life this residual hope may spill over into a hope for a "future" life, whatever future would mean in a life that has passed beyond time. All hopes, Emily Dickinson reminds us, are written in the literary or fictional mode:

> Could Hope inspect her basis,
> Her craft were done:
> Has a fictitious charter,
> Or it has none.

So literature, with its sense of "anything is possible" and its convention of suspending disbelief even in the most fantastic assumptions, is a mode of language with a particular relation to hope. The New Testament implies that this hope is an analogy of a more substantial virtue, in Hebrews the faith which is the substance of hope, in Paul the love which is the substance of both, the love that "believeth all things, hopeth all things" (I Corinthians 13:7).

As for illusion, its central importance in imaginative writing needs little emphasis. It would be difficult to take such a scene as the blinding of Gloucester in *King Lear* without the realization that it was not really happening. But the situation is more complicated than that, because what is physically absent is spiritually present. We suggested earlier, in connection with the imagery used in *The Tempest,* that the play is a reality created out of illusion, in the teeth, so to speak, of what we usually call reality, a reality which itself eventually dissolves into illusion, leaving not a rack behind. Such created reality is neither objective nor subjective, though it preserves elements of both.

There are two kinds of illusion: the negative illusion that merely fails to be an objective reality, and the positive illusion which is a potential, a something hoped for that can be actualized by a creative effort. Freud spoke of "the future of an illusion" in connection with religion, meaning that religion was a negative illusion. If the illusion of religion is positive, he was right in a way he did not intend. Nothing except a positive illusion can possibly have a future. Reality is something that obviously changes only on its own terms: as far as we are concerned, its future has already occurred. To realize an illusion is to abolish its future and turn it into a presence.

It has been shrewdly observed that for many poets of our age, verbs that have been traditionally transitive have become intransitive. Rilke, for example, speaks of praising as a central activity of poetry, but he does not praise God or nature or his fellow man or anything else objective: he simply praises. Similarly many poets of the last century, reflecting an increasingly common attitude in society, do not necessarily believe this or that, but believe intransitively, preserving an openness of attitude which closes nothing off dogmatically, but is the opposite of gullibility, the readiness to believe anything transitively. As soon as we stop trying to prove the existence of God and believing our proofs, we are faced with the challenge of manifesting that existence.

There are many approaches to faith, and one would hesitate to condemn any faith unless its practical results were hatred and cruelty. But we can hardly help noticing how often faiths of the type described as orthodox, fundamentalist, or what not, are pernicious in their social influence whenever they get into a position of secular power. The news media constantly confirm the principle that the more explicitly any society is based on religious foundations of this kind, the worse off it is. Societies based on atheistic and anti-religious dogmas preserve the same contrast between orthodoxy and heresy (or deviationism), hence although they start from the opposite end they usually arrive at much the same goal. There are many reasons for this, but the one that concerns this book is that they are based on false linguistic assumptions. Their approach to language has its own area and its own function, but in an age of primary concern the hewers of doctrines and drawers of boundary lines should always be servants, never masters.

Critical theory today converges on what were originally Biblical questions, and the Bible is still the clearest example to use in explaining them. For critical theory there seems to be a point where a change of elements from "words" to "Word" takes place. This Word is not the Bible or the person of Christ for, say, Mallarmé or Lacan, nor does it have to be those things for anyone. But apparently it does have to be there. So the question arises: if we use the Bible as an illustration of so many central critical problems, how far are we committed to its theism?

It seems to me that as soon as we start taking such terms as Word and Spirit seriously, we have already dissolved the clumsy either-or dilemma of a choice between a religious view with "a" God in it, and a secular or humanistic view with only man and nature in it. Some years ago the phrase "God is dead" was transferred from its context in the teachings of Nietzsche's eccentric guru Zarathustra to a movement in Christian theology, where it turned into an extreme version of Paul's conception of kenosis (Philippians 2:7). That is, it proposed that Christ "emptied himself" of the divine nature at his incarnation, or at least of a divine nature separate from the human one. This appears to mean that what is really dead is the antithesis between a human subject and a divine object.

A related remark by Michel Foucault, which seems to me highly relevant whatever implications the author himself would have drawn from it, is: "God is perhaps not so much a region beyond knowledge as something prior to the sentences we speak." This puts into a secular context what the opening of the Gospel of John puts into a sacred one, relating the Word that begins everything to the power behind the beginning which Jesus expresses by the metaphor of Son and Father.

The theism of the Bible raises another critical problem that we may conclude this part of our survey with. If the New Testament, to keep to that for the moment, is written in mythical and metaphorical language, why does it seem so hostile to everything else expressed in that language? The Word in the New Testament, we said, is associated with metaphors of dividing and cutting (II Timothy 2:15), and we are urged to cut away all mythical accretions on a central body of truth which transcends myth. What transcends myth is still myth in the terms of this book, but those who originally responded to the Gospel must have felt that they had got clear of something futile in the mythopoeic imagination and its undirected procedures. So the New Testament illustrates, and revives, one of the most primitive features of myth, one referred to at the beginning of this book. Some stories seem to have a particular function of telling a society what it needs to know, and thereby should be distinguished from other stories without such a function. Perhaps the existence of the Biblical canon, by opposing itself in so many respects to secular literature, did something to mark off and outline the conception of "literature" as we know it now.

We glimpse traces here of a larger context in the history of culture, and one that should further clarify the place of the Bible in that context. We may think of the verbal imagination as forming first an age of gods, a vast spiral ascending from early Sumerian and Egyptian times, where we can first identify it, up to the age of Virgil and Ovid, at a time when a contrasting spiral was beginning to unfold from the New Testament and extend itself gradually over the verbal culture of the next two thousand years. Something of this conception entered the vision of Yeats, and Yeats drew the conclusion that a third age would follow, that this third age needed a prophet to proclaim it, and that he was that prophet. Whatever the merits of this vision, it was the ability to conceive of his (or any) poetic function on such a scale that made Yeats a major poet, and not, as in Auden's poem on Yeats, some vague "gift" for "writing well."

By the time of Virgil and Ovid the age of the gods had become essentially monotheistic, although its monotheism (GC 114) was wholly different from the revolutionary monotheism of the Bible. The Messianic figures of Virgil and Ovid were Caesar and Augustus. But still such poets had begun to realize that the gods were the first-fruits of the human creative imagination. The Christian counter-movement made God the only creator, man a creature, and the creations of man illusions to be kept in a shadowy limbo for fear they should become idols. In the course of centuries the sequence of human creations, from gods to characters in novels and metaphors in poetry, has steadily risen in significance and reality. The dialectic of the Biblical God who is what he is and the human creations that are not what they are is exhausted now, raising the sardonic question of Emily Dickinson about whether the jealous God of the Bible

> will refund us finally
> Our confiscated gods.

Many poets, including Yeats, have hailed a coming return of the gods in various forms, but cycles as such are only cycles.

We have invoked Vico's axiom *verum factum,* that what is true is what we have made true, as an essential axiom of criticism. The structure of the Bible suggests that this axiom has two sides. The Bible begins by showing on its first page that the reality of God manifests itself in creation, and on its last page that the same reality is manifested in a new creation in which man is a participant. He becomes a participant by being redeemed, or separated from the predatory and destructive elements acquired from his origin in nature. In between these visions of creation comes the Incarnation, which presents God and man as indissolubly locked together in a common enterprise. This is Christian, but the answering and supporting "Thou" of Buber, which grows out of the Jewish tradition, is not imaginatively very different. Faith, then, is not developed by clogging the air with questions of the "Does a God really exist?" type and answering them with equal nonsense, but in working, in words and other media, toward a peace that passes understanding, not by contradicting understanding, but by disclosing, behind the human peace that is merely a temporary cessation of a war, the proclaimed or mythological model of a peace infinite in both its source and its goal.

PART TWO

Variations on a Theme

Prefatory Note

In *The Great Code* I spoke of the traditional Christian view of the Old Testament as a set of "types" of which the New Testament provides the "antitypes," the types being the symbols and the antitypes the realities. It should be clear by now that this type-antitype distinction is closely parallel in shape to the mythical-kerygmatic relationship just expounded. But we obviously cannot say that the Old Testament is all type and the New Testament all antitype, or that there are no types except in the Old Testament and no antitypes except in the New. The New Testament, being just as mythical as the Old, is a type of its own spiritual understanding; the mythical elements in both testaments are closely related to mythical analogues all over the world.

What follows is a series of essays on comparative mythology, organized around four primary concerns: the concern to make and create, the concern to love, the concern to sustain oneself and assimilate the environment, with its metaphorical kernel of food, and the concern to escape from slavery and restraint. Each essay relates these concerns to the Bible and to various themes in literature—necessarily chosen somewhat at random, and with a strong bias toward English literature. The two chief aims are, first, to relate the Bible and literature more closely within the cultural history of the Western world, and, second, to provide a more intelligible account of the relation of mythology in general to what is often vaguely described as "the myths we live by." These latter are the kerygmatic points on which myth seems to focus, the antitypes for which comparative mythology provides the types.

The previous chapter brought us into the area of such words as faith and love, words that perhaps mean too many things in the language and tend to sound sentimental. The word sentimental is one of many euphemisms for the infantilism that is, as noted, the besetting sin of an uncritical attachment to an ideology of any kind—in fact, it is the most dangerous form of original sin. I said earlier that the secondary or ideological concerns, such as social loyalties or religious orthodoxies, have usually taken precedence over the primary concerns of "life, liberty and the pursuit of happiness," so that we continue to go to war in spite of our primary concern to live. There are many reasons for this: the one that concerns us here is that secondary concerns, which depend on verbalization, are distinctively human concerns, and reinforce our sense that humanity is the apex of creation. The ability to postpone, subordinate or sublimate our appetites and desires is further evidence of human ascendancy. However, the master-slave relation being what it is, man's superiority to nature has another side. As Swift's bewildered Gulliver gradually discovered in his travels, the human mastery of nature tends to identify the human with the most ferociously predatory aspect of the natural, along with a sadistic nastiness which is peculiar to the human species, and is a product of verbalizing. That is, man does not sink to his lowest level of brutality until he has worked out some rationalization for doing so.

Myth, concentrating as it does on the primary concerns that human beings share with animals and even plants, is more closely linked to man's genuine kinship with nature. The Bible speaks continually of the alienation of man from God and of man's eventual redemption or reconciliation with God. This latter movement, if we are right about primary concern, cannot be achieved without a corresponding redemption and reconciliation of nature, something that moves in the direction of restoring the original paradisal environment. So far as we can see, a complete redemption of this kind is entirely impossible, and is therefore one of the proper studies of faith, as previously defined.

This redemption is part of the Bible's final apocalyptic vision in which there is an ultimate separation of life from death. When death is so separated, it appears in the form of a parody of the apocalyptic, hence the phrase "demonic parody," which is so essential a critical conception both for this book and its predecessor. In early Christian centuries the main extra-Biblical source of mythology was the Classical one, and some die-hard Christians tried to regard all Classical myths as demonic parodies of the true Biblical ones. However the myths moved from the position of demonic parody to that of positive analogy—Gentile "types" added to the Old Testament ones—as it gradually dawned on the poets that "gods" were not really in competition with the God of a monotheistic religion, but had much more in common with human beings themselves.

The principle of what I call in *Anatomy of Criticism* "displacement" is involved here, the process by which mythical and metaphorical structures become altered, in certain cultural situations, by demands for plausibility and resemblance or ordinary experience. The degree of incarnation of literary characters may vary from the discarnate god of pure myth or semi-discarnate romantic hero to the total immersion in the world characteristic of the ironic mode which dominates contemporary literature. When I speak of an "undisplaced" hypothetical form of a fiction I am speaking of the more concentrated structure of myth and metaphor that forms its imaginative skeleton. Undisplaced structures take us back to the gods, that is, beings who have metaphorical connections with both personality and objects in the natural environment. They are "spiritual" entities, being both conscious and bodily.

In the first three chapters of this book we began with the different kinds of verbal narrative, where the act of reading or listening is a movement in time. This movement stops at the end, and there follows what is metaphorically an arrest of time, where our main effort is directed toward a simultaneous understanding of what has been presented. Still metaphorically, we are in front of a flat surface, like an inscription on a rock, where we are not looking ahead to see what comes next but looking up and down over the whole surface.

The metaphor of a flat surface represents the beginning of the critical operation, after which, so to speak, time resumes its movement and the critic is no longer a separated subject but a participant in a social enterprise. The amount of disagreement within the enterprise slows down its development, but is not otherwise significant. An army is not less an army for the number of soldiers who would rather shoot their sergeants than the enemy. The presentation of the flat surface is, as suggested earlier, one of the things that Derrida appears to mean by *écriture,* the emancipation of the metaphorical listener into the metaphorical viewer.

The flat surface of primary understanding turns three-dimensional as soon as the critic enters it, and a variety of directions, contextual, intertextual, subtextual, begins to open up. In the infinity of possible relationships one would naturally prefer one with some kind of answer to the question "So what?," one that suggests a definite direction leading to genuine knowledge. The direction that interests me is a contextual one, relating works of literature, through their conventions and genres, to a co-ordinated view of literature. Such a view brings out its historical descent from mythology, which in turn is the contextual term for myth. The next part of this book plunges into a "garden of forking paths," as Borges might call it, the chaos of echoes and resemblances that we find in comparative mythology, to which I have added literature as an inseparable body of further analogies. Out of all this I hope that some indication of how coherent lifestyles, connected with primary concerns and the kerygmatic mode, will emerge from the infinite possibilities of myth.

CHAPTER FIVE

First Variation: the Mountain

I

The Bible, we are suggesting, demands the active and creative response that the imagination makes to literature and mythology; the faith it calls for must be able to accept divergences from historical fact as one of its conditions. The Bible also concentrates on the existential form of "myths to live by": there is a minimum of *speculative* mythopoeia, or efforts to explain or rationalize things in mythical terms. We can see this at a glance if we turn from the New Testament to the Gnostic writers who are contemporary or slightly later, with their catalogues of demons and angels, their eons and emanations, their Barbelos and Ialdabaoths. There is a similar contrast, if a less dramatic one, between the Old Testament and most of the pseudepigraphic writings.

It is not hard to understand how the clean and crisp outlines of the Gospels impressed themselves on the Western world as representing a truth far above all myths. Nor is it hard to understand the exclusiveness of the Christian attitude, or the feeling that a principle had to be kept to of "no more myths." At that time, of course, the only way to establish such a principle was to deny that the Christian story was in any sense a myth, and we are still struggling with all the confusions in verbal theory that have resulted. The issue later became involved with the brutal intolerance that normally accompanies the transforming of mythologies into ascendant ideologies.

In the prefatory note to Part Two I briefly alluded to the resemblance between Biblical and extra-Biblical (mainly Classical) mythologies. If Biblical myths were true and Classical ones false, then the only way to account for the resemblances was to call the latter demonic parodies of Biblical ones, or, perhaps, fairy tales begotten by confused human memories after the Fall. This notion of demonic parody lurked at the bottom of the Christian view for centuries: even as late as Cowley in the seventeenth century we hear about the oracles of the "fiend Apollo." But a more liberal view of Classical mythology as a kind of supplement or counterpoint to the Christian one soon established itself in spite of this. The Renaissance produced elaborate commentaries on Ovid's *Metamorphoses* and other sources of Classical myth that emphasized every resemblance to be found between Christian and Biblical myths, treating them not as demonic parodies but as positive analogies. Giles Fletcher, Milton's contemporary, says:

> Who doth not see drown'd in Deucalions name
> (When earth his men, and sea had lost his shore)
> Old Noah; and in Nisus' lock, the fame
> Of Sampson yet alive; and long before
> In Phaethon's, mine own fall I deplore:
>   But he that conquer'd hell, to fetch again
>   His virgin widow by a serpent slain,
> Another Orpheus was than dreaming poets feign.

The story of the world-wide deluge in Ovid, which Deucalion and Pyrrha survived, is a positive analogy of the story of Noah in Genesis; the story of "Nisus' injur'd hair," as Pope calls it in *The Rape of the Lock,* has resemblances to the Samson saga;

the story of the fall of Phaethon is an analogue of the fall of Adam, and so Fletcher may deplore Phaethon's fall as an emblem of his own as a son of Adam; the descent of Orpheus to hell to reclaim his bride Eurydice is an analogue of the harrowing of hell by Jesus and his rescue of his bride the Church. The final phrase is an example of the traditional ingratitude of Christian poets who levy such tribute on Classical writers while officially denouncing the truth of their stories. Of course Orpheus did fail in his quest, a fact which underlies a line in the introduction to the third book of *Paradise Lost:* "With other notes than to th'Orphean lyre."

A different and subtler aspect of the same kind of tension appears in the first canto of the *Paradiso,* where Dante uses the Classical images of Marsyas, who was flayed alive for challenging Apollo to a contest in flute-playing (the Olympians were notoriously poor losers, but Apollo had not even the excuse of losing), and of Glaucus, who ate some miraculous grass that turned him into a sea-god. The images are very precise: Marsyas stands for the divesting of the garment of flesh in paradise and Glaucus for the plunge into a new and unknown element. But the touch of grotesquerie in the same images still keeps a hint of negative analogy or demonic parody, their original context in the Christian view.

It was much easier for poets to avoid the dogmatic barriers of Christianity and use Classical myths in a purely literary or imaginative context, and this of course became a regular procedure, though as a rule it needs little commentary beyond looking up the allusions when unfamiliar. More elaborate devices included the introduction of an Eros cult, to be dealt with in the next chapter, which is a close and detailed replica of Christian themes, with the God of Love and Venus corresponding to Christ and the Virgin.

I have elsewhere tried to explain the critical attitude involved in the apparently very obscurantist passage in Milton's *Paradise Regained,* where Jesus is tempted by Satan to become a Greek philosopher but refuses to have anything to do with any culture outside the Old Testament. The main theme of *Paradise Regained* is the spiritual side of the temptation in which Jesus gets his mind totally detached from Satan's illusory world: once he has done that, and defined the nature of his own Messianic mission, he can start on his work of redeeming everything human that is not inseparably attached to the demonic. It is because Jesus excludes Plato and Aristotle from the prophetic tradition that Milton himself can study them, and the same is true of Classical mythology and literature.

For many centuries a punctilious etiquette had to be observed in treating Biblical and Classical themes together. In the twenty-second *Amoretti* sonnet Spenser begins with a reference to the Christian Lent, and immediately takes us into a building where we meet saints, altars, sacrifices and the like. The building is the temple of Venus built in the poet's mind, not a Christian church, and the icon of devotion is his mistress. But the sense of two mythical traditions is quite clear. Elsewhere Spenser writes hymns to love and beauty in the Eros idiom, then explains that these were youthful and immature works, and supplements them with hymns to heavenly love and beauty that incorporate explicitly Christian themes.

Milton himself sends his early *Nativity Ode,* a Christian poem, to his friend Diodati along with a Latin poem outlining the responsibilities of the major poet which it was obvious he was going to be. The life of such a poet is described in entirely pagan terms. He is to live like Pythagoras and like the prophet Tiresias, "before his eyes were darkened," and he is to regard himself as a sacred priest whose whole soul is devoted to Jupiter. Among the false gods abolished by the birth of Christ in the *Nativity Ode* is the pagan "Genius," the spirit of nature; but in other early poems that have a less doctrinally Christian content, such as *Arcades, Lycidas* and *Comus,* a Genius is introduced as a benevolent and imaginatively quite real character.

Later, with the influence of Boileau and similar critics, and with the growth of their view that Christian mythology was too high for poetry and other mythologies too low and puerile, there came a new type of secularization. This affected the period of English poetry that falls between Dryden and Johnson, but had a more long-term influence in prose fiction, which grew increasingly realistic, meaning that the shapes of the stories it told were implicitly rather than explicitly mythological. In the Romantic period poetry and prose diverged even more widely: in prose fiction the mythological affinities of the stories told have been largely neglected or ignored by critics, while in poetry Christian and Classical mythologies, at least, began to achieve imaginative parity with each other.

I have spoken of the popular view that poetry cannot reach the highest levels of meaning by itself, and of allegory as one of the devices by which poets came to terms with this view. In Romantic times a contrast in critical theory between "allegory" and "symbol," in which the latter was generally preferred to the former, marked the beginning of a sense that literature creates and lives within its own cosmos, and advances into or retreats from other verbal modes on its own terms. The development of realistic fiction, on the contrary, was often accompanied by the assumption implied in the word realistic itself, that literature needed to get out and mingle with the non-literary world if it was to avoid becoming over-subjective, self-indulgent, ingrown, snobbish, elitist, and all the other things that are so often assumed to be endemic diseases in literature and criticism. This attitude is still going strong in Edmund Wilson's *Axël's Castle,* but had been earlier opposed with great wit and charm by Oscar Wilde, especially in his essay "The Decay of Lying."

Works of literature follow, like dreams in Freud, the opposed principles of condensation and displacement, though these processes function quite differently in literature from the way that they do in dreams. Displacement in a literary context means the alteration of a mythical structure in the direction of greater plausibility and accommodation to ordinary experience. Thus the final scene of *The Winter's Tale,* where a statue comes to life, is displaced with a more plausible explanation that there is no statue and that Hermione has simply been hidden away for fifteen years, practising standing still at intervals. Condensation means the opposite movement, where the similarities and associations of ordinary experience become metaphorical identities. Anyone seeing a jealous and possessive lover breaking the spirit of the person he thinks he loves may be reminded of a parasite destroying a flower, but Blake's "Sick Rose" gives us the two things in a single metaphor, along with a good deal more that the condensing operation also makes possible. An explicit allusion to Biblical or Classical mythology in an otherwise representational context is a condensing image. It may be a casual or even a deliberately incongruous allusion, but it regularly has the function of reminding us that we are still within a literary orbit.

In the socialist realism movement promoted by Stalin in Russia we met the principle of displacement in its most extreme form, where an ideology tried to make all literature into an allegory of its own obsessions. The most extreme form of condensation is probably represented by *Finnegans Wake,* where we have a huge body of words and verbal sounds echoing one another, with apparently no continuous sequential narrative. The reader is compelled to find all its meaning within its interlocking structure. T. S. Eliot remarked that one *Finnegans Wake* was probably enough, and one ideological tyranny crippling all the first-rate creative power within its reach ought to be more than enough.

Assuming that literature as a whole lies somewhere between these extremes, it ought, to be totally intelligible to criticism, to present the appearance of a cosmos of human phenomena, some of them belonging to that special category of the human that we call the world of the gods. The Bible, sitting in the middle of this cosmos for the Western world, can be used to show that the cosmos of myth and metaphor has an overall structure, and is not simply a chaos of endlessly tantalizing echoes and resemblances. Our next logical step, then, would be to venture into an area that might be called literary cosmology.

Cosmology is a subject usually associated with philosophy. Whitehead's *Process and Reality* is subtitled "an essay on cosmology." But we have quoted Whitehead as saying that philosophical systems usually conceal something much more simple and naive behind them, and Bertrand Russell is even more explicit on this point:

> Every philosopher, in addition to the formal system which he offers to the world, has another, much simpler, of which he may be quite unaware. If he is aware of it, he probably realizes that it won't quite do; he therefore conceals it, and sets forth something more sophisticated, which he believes because it is like his crude system, but which he asks others to accept because he thinks he has made it such as cannot be disproved.

It seems to me to be part of the literary critic's task to look into some of these indecently naked formal systems that won't quite do: the cosmologies, for example, constructed out of the metaphors that lift us up or bring us down, that oppose one hand to the other, look in or out, go forward or back. Occasionally poets themselves work out such naive metaphorical constructs, which are usually, as we might expect, received only with baffled stares even by those who admire their poetry. Examples are Poe's *Eureka* and Yeats's *Vision*.

Valéry's very discerning essay on *Eureka* points out that cosmology, in this metaphorical skeletonic form, is a product of the literary imagination, though in earlier times even naive systems could be more readily projected into the environment as a form of speculation. *Eureka* itself is based on an in-and-out breathing or cyclical metaphor, like the myth of the alter-

nating of control and relaxation in Plato's *Statesman,* or the
Hindu myth of the days and nights of Brahma.

We saw in our third chapter that the end of a *mythos* or
narrative movement brings us to a "thematic stasis" or simultaneous apprehension of what we have been following up to
that point. For literary structures, we said, we generally use
metaphors of vision to describe this simultaneity of response.
Also, as there is no more narrative to keep us moving ahead,
our perspective shifts to an up-and-down vertical pattern. Out
of this emerges the central metaphor of the *axis mundi,* a vertical line running from the top to the bottom of the cosmos.

In the days of the geocentric universe, there was some
scientific status for an *axis mundi,* but there is none now, or
certainly not in any area that I am competent to discuss. For
the purpose of this book, the *axis mundi* is related only to a
verbal universe, though naturally the images used to illustrate
it suggest climbing into the sky or descending into the depths
of the earth or sea. To the imagination, the universe has
always presented the appearance of a middle world, with a
second world above it and a third one below it. We may
say, with many qualifications, that images of ascent are connected with the intensifying of consciousness, and images of
descent with the reinforcing of it by other forms of awareness,
such as fantasy or dream. The most common images of ascent
are ladders, mountains, towers and trees; of descent, caves or
dives into water.

Jacob's dream of the ladder in Genesis 28 is, in its immediate context, merely another of the various Genesis visions in
which a great and numerous posterity is promised to Israel,
but it has symbolic overtones extending infinitely beyond that.
The story tells us that Jacob came to a place called Luz, and
lay down to sleep there, with his head resting on a stone. Evidently the Biblical writer assumed, as we do, that dreaming
takes place in the brain. If we are to believe tradition, the stone
his head rested on still lies under the throne at Westminster. In

his sleep Jacob had a vision of a ladder, as it is called in the AV and other translations, stretching from earth to heaven, with angels ascending and descending on it. When he awoke in the morning he said, according to the same translation, "How dreadful is this place!" He meant, of course, how holy is this place, as the sense of the holy originates in a sense of awe or dread. Jacob called the place of his dream the house of God and the gate of heaven and vowed to build an altar there. He also changed its name from Luz to Bethel, meaning house of God.

The antecedents of such a story would most naturally relate to a pre-Israelite sacred site, featuring either a sacred stone or a group of stones. In this earlier version the stone might have belonged to a megalithic monument of a type still found in that part of the world among other places. Whether or not traditions lingered of a connection between such monuments and movements of the heavenly bodies we do not know: the Biblical narrator describes the taking over of a pre-Biblical cult site for Biblical purposes, but has no further interest in its original context. The process probably anticipates, however, the building of Christian churches on sites of pagan holy places in Northern Europe many centuries later.

The ladder of the dream was a ladder *from* heaven rather than *to* it: it was not a human construction but an image of the divine will to reach man. Further, if angels were going both up and down on it, it was really a staircase, not a ladder (GC 158). Finally, although Jacob calls the place the house of God, he does not build a temple there, merely an altar. The altar is also an image of a connection between earth and heaven, but one that subordinates the human side of the connection. So the story, as it reaches us, is the acceptable version, as the Bible sees it, of an image found in most of the ancient religions of the Near East. Similar images in a heathen or non-Israelite context would represent demonic parodies of the accepted one.

In Mesopotamian cities the temple to the god of the city

would normally be in the center and would be the highest building: it would therefore be, symbolically, the connecting link between the earth we live on and the world of the gods, which is usually assumed to be in the sky, or above the sky. In Mesopotamia such temples usually took the form of what is known as the ziggurat, a building of several stories, with each story recessed from the one below it. The different stories were connected by stairs, usually winding stairs, so that the ascent would be in a spiral. There were winding stairs in Solomon's temple, even though it was only three stories high (I Kings 6:8).

Herodotus tells us of more elaborate temples in Babylon and Persia, where there were seven stories and seven flights of steps, colored differently, perhaps to symbolize the planets, including the sun and moon. At the top was a chamber representing the place where the bride of the god was to await his descent: this aspect of the symbolism we must leave for later. The bridal chamber indicates that there are two groups of metaphors involved, one mainly cosmological and the other sexual, a ladder of wisdom and a ladder of love. The first of these is the one that concerns us at present.

In Egypt the step pyramids had a similar symbolic reference to the heavens, and in the Pyramid Texts the ascent of a stairway was a crucial stage in the Pharaoh's journey after death to the realm of the gods. The judge of the dead in Egypt was the god Osiris, and one of the earliest epithets for him was "the god at the top of the staircase." The phrase indicates that in mounting a ladder it is the last step which is the supremely important one, and we are reminded of this by the Greek word for ladder, *klimax*. In an Egyptian ritual where the raising of a ladder occupied a prominent place, the ladder is identified with the spine of a cosmological body.

In these myths the emphasis seems to be mainly on the human construct: man builds the temple, or tower, in the form of something that points to heaven and suggests a final entry into it. This is the emphasis that is ridiculed in another story in Genesis (11), the story of the Tower of Babel, whose builders thought to reach heaven but had to abandon their project when their speech was broken into different languages. The Genesis story derives the word Babel from *balal,* confusion, but Babel actually means what Jacob called the place of his vision, the gate of God. We notice that the contrast between the central image of connection between heaven and earth and its demonic parody or ironic negation is bound up with the use of language. Just now we are concerned only with the principle that every image of revelation in the Bible carries with it a demonic parody or counterpart. In a play of Strindberg, *The Keys of Heaven,* the final scene contrasts the Tower of Babel with Jacob's ladder, the hero escaping the first and climbing the second.

Neither Babel nor the stairway seen at Bethel are explicitly said to be spiral or winding structures, though that is how they appear in Brueghel's painting of Babel and Blake's of Jacob's dream. In any case we have a cluster of images, ladders, towers, winding or spiral stairs, all with the general symbolic sense of connecting with a higher state of existence from the ordinary one. The earth we live on seems connected with the sky by mountains, and it is clear that such temples or towers are symbolic mountains. There appears to be a world-wide practice of making sacred pilgrimages up mountains, usually on a spiral course: one such spiral ascent has been claimed for Glastonbury Tor in England, and perhaps the later Psalms, especially those headed in the AV as "a song of degrees" belong to the same ritual area (GC 158). Jerusalem in particular is symbolically the highest point in the world: it is as impossible for returning Israelites to go "down" to Jerusalem as it would be for a student in England to go "down" to Oxford or Cambridge.

There are several other types of *axis mundi* imagery: one is the world-tree rooted in the world below with its upper branches in the world above, which appears, somewhat vestigially, in the reference to the tree of life in Eden. This tree is not said to reach heaven, but it obviously is linked to a connection between earth and heaven broken at the Fall. There are also demonic parodies of this world-tree associated with the world empires of Assyria and Babylonia by Ezekiel and Daniel corresponding to the Tower of Babel (GC 149), as well as demonic mountains in Isaiah and elsewhere.

It seems clear that the very widespread images of ladders and stairs and mountains and trees leading to a higher world must owe their existence, at least in part, to the fact that man cannot fly, and finds climbing the easiest metaphor for raising himself, whether physically or symbolically. Some people tell us that the ancient Near East preserved a race memory of visitors from other planets who could blast off in rocket ships: if so, it seems rather a lame conclusion to come down to so homely an image as climbing a tree or ladder, or even a mountain. John Donne also comments on the self-restraint of angels, who confined themselves to walking up and down Jacob's ladder, even though they could fly.

If the seven-story towers in Persia and Babylon were painted in different colors to represent the planets, the building would be even more explicitly a stairway to heaven. This heavenward stair seems to have been an important element in the symbolism of Mithraism, the Persian sun-cult that was a rival of early Christianity. In Mithraism there were seven degrees of ascent after death associated with the planets. This association, we are told, was so deeply rooted that Mithraism, if it had won out over Christianity, would have found it difficult to survive the Copernican revolution in astronomy. But by now it is obvious that this stairway imagery is expanding in the direction of a creation myth.

What is really dramatic and powerful about a creation myth is not any account of how the order of nature came into being, but the account of how the sense of nature as an order dawns on a conscious mind. Again, creation carries little conviction when presented as an event occurring at the beginning of time, as time for the imagination really has no beginning. Creation is rather an intensely vivid image of the objective world as a spread-out picture of intelligibility awaiting discovery and interpretation. Traditional religion claims that creation is a product of the Word of God, the creation itself being a second Word of God, an infinite source of what is intelligible to man and can be responded to by him:

> Set the Word at its origin and put the Maker in his place.

So counsels the *Sepher Yetzirah* (Book of Formations), a pioneering work of Jewish kabbalism that takes the letters of the Hebrew alphabet, along with the numbers they also stood for, to be the formative principles of the cosmos.

There are two creation myths in Genesis, distinguished by the names they use for God. The first extends from Genesis 1:1 to Genesis 2:3. Although it stands first, it is the later of the two accounts; it uses the word Elohim for God, is probably post-exilic, and is known as the Priestly account (P). The second, which begins at Genesis 2:4, is called the Jahwist account (J), as it refers to God as Jahweh Elohim (in the AV one may distinguish the "God" of the first chapter from the "Lord God" of the second). Although both accounts are involved here, we shall be examining the J one more particularly in the next chapter.

The P account, as everyone knows, is fitted into the unit of the week, and is said to consist of six days of creative acts and a seventh day of rest. This myth has already acquired a strongly ideological content: the day of rest is the model for the law of doing no work on the sabbath, and the sun and moon are created "for signs" to mark the ritual days of the year. The somewhat parenthetical remark, "He made the stars also," indicates that there is little if any zodiacal or astrological background to this myth, despite a probable recent sojourn in Babylon. Familiar as it is, there will be still some point in setting out the phases of the myth:

1. Creation of the primordial light.

2. Creation of the firmament or sky, separating waters above from waters below (GC 146).

3. Creation of the trees (strictly, command to the earth to bring forth the first growing things), and separation of land and sea.

4. Creation of the heavenly bodies, sun, moon and stars.

5. Creation of the creatures of water and air.

6. Creation of land animals, including human beings both male and female.

7. Institution of a seventh day of rest.

In this account there is a strong emphasis on hierarchy and on differentiation. Cosmos is separated from chaos; land from sea; the sky or firmament from waters above and below; the kinship of human beings to land animals is clearly recognized, but man is said to be the supreme ruler of the animal and vegetable creation. He is also allowed to eat what he chooses of both plants and animals, but there is a sense of divine regulations still overshadowing him. The four elements are also clearly distinguished, and darkness and the chaos symbolized by the sea are thought of as both outside and incorporated into the creation, so that the forces of darkness and chaos may be represented either as enemies of God or as his creatures (GC 194).

The P account is a vision of the natural environment as what is called *natura naturata,* nature as a structure or system, the nature of physics. The significance of the day of rest is in part that the creation becomes objective to God himself; in human terms, God withdraws from his creation sufficiently to enable man to study it on his own, and also to guarantee, so to speak, that while both man and nature are finite the amount of knowledge and wisdom available to man is inexhaustible. The second withdrawal caused by the fall of man later is something else again.

The sense of a hierarchical universe is reflected in the progression of events. First we have four elements: light, air, water and earth appear, the habitations of all living things. Then we have a sequence of created beings, trees, birds and fish, land animals, then man as the lord of creation. On the seventh day we get a glimpse of God's presence at the top. The vision seems to suggest authority and subordination, where the fulfillment of life consists in occupying one's "natural place."

We have two themes to examine here. One is the hierarchical cosmology derived from it (or at any rate strongly influenced by it: any other mythology in the Near Eastern or Classical cultures would have produced a very similar ideology). The other is the set of images that form the metaphorical kernels of the vision. The two Biblical images we have looked at, Jacob's ladder and the Tower of Babel, are not explicitly linked to creation myths, but the affinities emerge when we look further afield.

A tale current among British Columbia Indian tribes tells us of an original war between the Sky People and the Earth People, the latter being apparently animals. An animal or bird, generally the wren, shoots an arrow into the moon; another shoots a second arrow that hits the notch of its predecessor, and so on until there is a complete ladder of arrows from earth to sky. Then the animals climb up, until the grizzly bear breaks the ladder by his weight. In other versions the ladder remains in good shape. I am concerned here with two points. First, there are both ideal and ironic aspects of the theme, outside as well as inside the Bible, and the ironic ones are usually connected with the folly or presumption of the underdogs. Second, the image of the ladder is clearly being linked to a myth of an original connection between this and a higher world which is broken at some point.

A Classical counterpart of the ironic version is the story of the revolt of the Titans, the sons of earth who piled mountains on top of each other to reach their enemy in the sky. Closer to our own time is the drawing in Blake's sequence of illustrations of human life called *The Gates of Paradise*. It has the caption "I want! I want!", and shows a young man starting to climb a ladder leaned against the moon. A young couple makes a gesture toward him, but he ignores them, no doubt in the spirit of Longfellow's mountain-climbing hero, responding "Excelsior" when invited to sleep with an Alpine maiden. There is an ominous bend in the ladder, however, and we are not surprised to find that the next picture, with the caption "Help! Help!", shows him fallen into the sea, like his prototype Icarus.

We should naturally expect these image-clusters to be prominent in Christian literature, and of course the great exemplar is Dante's *Divine Comedy*. Purgatory is the connecting link between earth and heaven, and has the form of a mountain with seven main spiral turnings. The ascent of Purgatory is followed by a second climb through the planetary spheres in the *Paradiso*. In the seventh of these spheres, that of Saturn, we see Jacob's ladder again, symbolizing the remainder of Dante's journey from the manifest spheres of the redeemed into the heart of the eternal light.

Students of Dante never cease to marvel at the completeness with which Dante has grasped the entire range of the myth, and have even suggested influences through Islamic sources that might have brought him in touch with such conceptions as the Mithraic ascent already mentioned. However, images of arrows appear with great frequency in *Purgatorio* and *Paradiso*, and Dante could hardly have heard of any myths of a ladder of arrows. Where a major poet gets his mythical data will always have some residual mystery about it. In any case, Dante's poem being Christian, Dante's ascent is not directed by his own will, but by the divine grace manifested in Beatrice.

In Milton the emphasis on divine initiative is even stronger. In the third book of *Paradise Lost* we encounter the "paradise of fools" on the smooth surface of the *primum mobile,* or circumference of the universe, where those arrive who have tried to take the kingdom of heaven by force or fraud. A reference to the Tower of Babel precedes this description, and indicates its archetype. There follows a vision of stairs descending from heaven to earth, which, Milton tells us, were "such as whereon Jacob saw" the angels of his vision. These stairs are let down from heaven and drawn up again at the pleasure of God: Satan, on his journey to Eden, arrives at a lower stair, from which he descends to earth by way of the planets.

Dante and Milton are following the religious tradition that starts from Jacob's ladder, where there can be no connection between heaven and earth except through divine will. Mystics also seem to have a curious affinity with ladders and staircases in their writings (John Hilton's *Ladder of Perfection* is a medieval English example), but they always remember that they are not climbing on their own power. Ladders going back to the ladder of love in Plato's *Symposium* have to be passed over for the moment.

About sixty years ago four leading writers, T. S. Eliot, W. B. Yeats, Ezra Pound and James Joyce, converged on the same imagery. In Eliot's early poems there is a curiously urgent emphasis on the highest step of a staircase, where Prufrock and the narrator of "Portrait of a Lady" think of turning back, and where the girl in "La Figlia che Piange," standing "on the highest pavement of the stair," remains to haunt her deserting lover. In *Ash-Wednesday* Eliot joins the Christian tradition of ladders, and follows Dante's *Purgatorio* in placing a turning stair at the center of his poem. In *Four Quartets* there is a great variety of such images, some derived from the Spanish mystic St. John of the Cross, whose *Ascent of Mount Carmel* is one of the best known mystical climbs.

In "Burnt Norton," the first of *Four Quartets,* we have a fully developed vision of the *axis mundi,* its top among the circling stars, crossing the line of ordinary experience at "the still point of the turning world," and going below a world associated both with the London subway and Homer's Hades to a world of death. Packed around the roots of this "bedded axletree" is the great variety of objects in the physical world symbolized by the phrase "garlic and sapphires."

At the time of *Ash-Wednesday,* around 1930, Yeats was publishing books of poetry with such titles as *The Tower* (1928) and *The Winding Stair* (1933), and searching for spirals and gyres in every aspect of experience. All ladders, he remarks, are planted in the "foul rag-and-bone-shop" of the human heart, but, under the influence of *A Vision,* his later poetry comes increasingly to revolve around a double spiral like those suggested by some aphorisms of Heraclitus and by the Chinese yin-yang duality. The image of the tower with a spiraling staircase is at the center of this, and Yeats even went to the length of buying one of the round towers that still survive in Ireland and living in it. The double gyre extends to a vision in which human life from birth to death is supplemented by an after-life which is purgatorial and runs from death to birth again, taking the form of a "dreaming back," a kind of total psycho-analysis. The image of unwrapping an Egyptian mummy is sometimes used in this connection. We notice that the purgatorial theme in Dante also includes the image of moving from death back to birth again, as Dante is traveling toward the place of his original birth as a child of an unfallen Adam.

Joyce built his last and most elaborate work, *Finnegans Wake,* on the Irish ballad of Finnegan, the hod-carrier who fell from the top of a ladder, an event Joyce associates with the fall of man on his first page. In the ballad, Finnegan comes to life at his own wake and demands a share of the whisky, but in Joyce he is persuaded to go back to death by twelve mourners representing the cycle of the Zodiac. Finnegan then modulates into the figure known chiefly by his initials HCE, who remains asleep and dreaming, and whose dream takes the form of a cyclical repetition that is the shape of history as we know it. Joyce makes us aware of another aspect of the imagery of ladders and their relatives: human life is not a straight line but a sequence of cycles in which we get "up" in the morning and "fall" asleep at night.

Ezra Pound begins the first of his *Cantos* by adapting the *Odyssey* story of the summoning of spirits from Hades by Ulysses, the first of whom is Elpenor, who fell asleep at the top of a ladder and broke his neck in falling, like Finnegan. For his main body of imagery, however, Pound went back to Herodotus and his account of the staircases in Ecbatana and Babylon. Even the *Pisan Cantos,* written out of the terrible experience of being confined in a cage after the war, begin with the still unshaken resolution "To build the city of Dioce whose terraces are the colour of stars." In the final fragments that record his sense of failure to do what he had hoped to do in the *Cantos,* one of the shattered hopes he mentions was that of constructing a "paradiso terrestre" like the one at the top of Dante's purgatory. The Babel theme of the confusion of tongues, so pervasive in Joyce, appears in *The Waste Land* also, especially in the final lines, as well as in various parts of the Pound *Cantos.*

What is important, of course, is not that these poets were fascinated by the same group of images, but why they were. Eliot, for example, in "Burnt Norton," identifies his *axis mundi,* at the point where it crosses the horizontal line of ordinary life, with the Incarnation: the word is used explicitly in "The Dry Salvages." Yeats, who, like Pound, preferred to resist Biblical imagery when he could, says in a letter that the confusion of modern times comes from the abandoning of the old hierarchy ascending from man up to "the one." Much the same figure as Eliot's is in the background, though it is Neoplatonic rather than Christian in reference.

II

Let us start again with the ladder and its metaphorical relatives as an image of communication between earth and heaven through angels, along with its demonic parody, the Tower of Babel. The former is based on the primacy of the word, the latter on the primacy of the act. The demonic tower signifies the aspect of history known as imperialism, the human effort to unite human resources by force that organizes larger and larger social units, and eventually exalts some king into a world ruler, a parody representative of God.

The Bible springs from an intensely tribal culture that marked its historical origin by a revolt against the imperial power of Egypt (earlier "Chaldea" for Abraham), and maintained its tribal organization under various dominant powers: Assyria, Babylonia, Persia, Rome. Israel never got anywhere in the imperial direction itself, partly because its tribes could not stop fighting with each other, but it continued to prophesy the imminent collapse of other empires, and associated them with other parodies of the ladder image, including the world-tree (Ezekiel 31) and the world-mountain (Isaiah 14; see GC 149, 163). In its great creative period Greek culture was also tribal, and attributed the fact that it was able to stop the invasion of Xerxes, the greatest military enterprise that had yet appeared in history, to the fact that the gods don't like big empires.

The rising tower, then, soon turns into the falling tower, with its attendant confusion of tongues, hence Babel is really a cyclical symbol, an example of the rising and falling of great kingdoms that forms a kind of counterpoint to Biblical history. The image of the cycle of empires does not really come into focus in the Bible, however, before the book of Daniel, written on the eve of the Maccabean rebellion. After the *Consolation of Philosophy* of Boethius (6th century A.D.), the image of the cycle of empires consolidated into the image of the wheel of fortune, which became the central image of tragedy in medieval and Renaissance times.

The twentieth-century poets just referred to are of course aware of the same imagery. In *Finnegans Wake,* after Finnegan has fallen off his ladder, he falls into the sleep of history, which moves in the cyclical rotation indicated by one of Joyce's chief mentors, Vico. This turning cycle, which includes awakening and rebirth but never a climb up the original ladder again, is a kind of parody of resurrection or restoration to the original state, a parody which encircles the whole book, as the sentence left unfinished on the last page is continued on the first. In Yeats too there is a cyclical movement in history, a sequence of alternating "primary" and "antithetical" periods, one democratic and the other heroic in tendency. In the Tarot pack of cards, the imagery of which appears to be late or post-medieval, both the wheel of fortune and the falling tower are featured, and both are referred to in *The Waste Land,* despite Eliot's professed lack of interest in Tarot symbolism.

The closed cycle, the Tower of Babel built and abandoned innumerable times, is traditionally symbolized by the *ouroboros,* the serpent with its tail in its mouth. The *ouroboros*—and closed circles generally—is sometimes said to be an emblem of eternity, but it presents a somewhat lugubrious picture of whatever that impressive word is supposed to convey. If the *ouroboros* is actually feeding on itself, it is presumably a spiral narrowing into nothingness. I am aware that Kekulé's discovery of the circular structure of the benzene molecule was inspired by a dream of the *ouroboros,* just as I am aware that the DNA molecule has affinities with a double spiral. But I am not sure just what to do with these analogies.

Jacob's vision was of angels ascending and descending: angels are messengers of God, and messages are normally verbal.

The real or metaphorical tower, then, would be what Dylan Thomas calls a "tower of words." In the New Testament the first chapter of John ends (1:51) with a prophecy of Jesus cast in the form of a vision of Jacob's ladder: "You will see the heaven opened, and the angels of God ascending and descending upon the Son of Man." While a messenger of God may be a fellow-creature of man, on no account to be worshipped (Colossians 2:18; Revelation 22:9), the messenger, as we saw, may be symbolically an epiphany or manifestation of God himself. When Jesus speaks of his Father as "him that sent me" (John 4:34, etc.), he is in effect referring to himself as an angel. According to Paul, the descending angels are messengers of revelation (Galatians 3:19), who brought the Scripture to man. With the Incarnation, or descent of the Word in flesh, the symbolic apparatus of ladders and the like becomes entirely verbal. Ladders, temples, mountains, world-trees, are now all images of a verbal revelation in which descent is the only projected metaphor.

The interest of modern poets in ladders and spirals is not nostalgia for outmoded images of creation, but a realization that because such images stand for the intensifying of consciousness through words, they represent the concern of concerns, so to speak, the consciousness of consciousness. The same figures appear outside the poets. In Hegel's *Phenomenology* we are obviously climbing spirally as well as following an argument, and Hegel drops the word "ladder" into his Preface. Wittgenstein's *Tractatus* may give the impression of a horizontal logical sequence, but we are told at the end that we have been climbing a ladder, and are urged to throw it away. In a much earlier time a famous passage in Donne also gives us the spiral ascent form of the image in a context of words:

> on a huge hill
> Cragg'd, and steep, Truth stands, and he that will

Reach her, about must, and about must go;
And what the hill's suddenness resists, win so.

What we tried in the previous chapter to clarify as "spirit" is mainly the ascending movement, the human response to the revealing of intelligibility in the natural and social orders. According to Paul the typical message from man to God is the prayer, which is formulated by the Spirit out of ego-bound requests for special favors (Romans 8:26). It is not difficult to associate this conception of prayer with the articulate imaginative expression of literature, which so often seems to take shape independently of the conscious will.

The movement of descending Word and ascending Spirit is reversed in the first two chapters of Acts, where we see first Jesus ascending into the sky, and then the Spirit descending on the Apostles. The Ascension is a New Testament antitype (GC 79) of the objectifying of the creation on the seventh day, or sabbath vision, the withdrawal of the Word from the world it creates. The descending Spirit brings the gift of tongues, emphasizing the contrast with the demonic parody, the confusion of tongues at Babel, and also forming a community of response. This reversed movement comes in between the Incarnation and the final descent of a new heaven to a new earth (Revelation 21:2–3). The physical images are gone, but the ascending and descending movements are still there, a double movement that fulfills an aphorism of Heraclitus: "Immortals become mortals, mortals become immortals: they live in each other's death and die in each other's life." This aphorism is quoted, as something very like a prophecy, by two early Christian writers.

III

We said earlier that the P creation myth suggested a hierarchy of being, rising from the elements up through plant and animal forms of life to man, the lord of creation, and from man to God. The Latin word for ladder is *scala,* and that word extends the image of the ladder to the scale, or measurement by degrees, which is so fundamental in scientific work and in some of the arts as well, notably music. The scale also forms the basis of one of the most persistent conceptions in the history of thought, one very clearly expressed by Sir Thomas Browne in *Religio Medici* (1643): "There is in this Universe a Stair, or manifest Scale of creatures, rising not disorderly, or in confusion, but with a comely method and proportion." This is the famous "chain of being" version of the *axis mundi* image, a cosmology that sees the whole of creation as a ladder stretching from God to the chaos at the bottom of God's creation. The feature that particularly concerns us here about this chain of being is that it represents the primary ideological adapting of the ladder metaphor to a rationalizing of authority.

The categories of thought that form part of the chain of being are very complex: some of them are set out in a fascinating chapter of Michel Foucault's *Les mots et les choses.* Here we have to stick with the most elementary and well known, of which there seem to be three. First is the cosmological chain, which is polarized by the Aristotelian conceptions of form and matter, and extends from God, who is pure form without material substance, to chaos, which is the nearest we can get to matter without form. The material principles of the cosmos were the four elements, which are the fixed combinations of four "principles," hot, cold, moist and dry. Chaos, according to Milton, is a world in which these principles combine and recombine at random, so that when Satan is traversing chaos he does not know whether his next movement is a step or a flight or a swim. We notice that the conception of an order of nature resting on a basis of controlled randomness is still with us.

Above the elements comes the hierarchy of creatures: angels first, then human beings, then animals, plants and minerals. The proportion of form to matter determines the rank in the hierarchy. Man being exactly in the middle, halfway between matter and spirit, he is a "microcosm," an epitome of the "macrocosm," or total creation.

The second aspect of this version of the *axis mundi* is the parallel construct of the Ptolemaic universe, which gave the chain of being a quasi-scientific status. The universe in this construct extends from the *primum mobile,* the circumference of an order of nature thought of as finite, down through the circle of fixed stars, through the sequence of seven planetary spheres, of which the lowest is the moon, then into the "sublunary" world of the four elements, in the order fire, air, water, earth. Since the Fall these elements have been subject to corruption and decay, but their separation was a major element in the creation out of chaos, and each element still seeks its own sphere. The principle that everything in nature has its natural place and tends to seek that place accounted for many of the phenomena that we now ascribe to gravitation. A solid object held in the air and let go will drop, because it is seeking the sphere of the solid earth.

The physical and philosophical views of the *axis mundi* partly reinforced, but partly collided with, a third view, which was theological and was based on the conception of man as a fallen being. This view contradicts the conception of the natural place to the extent of regarding man as a being who does not occupy the place he was originally assigned in nature, and takes the form of a sequence of four levels that involves the Biblical story more directly in the world picture. I have expounded this sequence many times, but in a book of the shape that this one seems to be expanding into I can hardly avoid repeating it here.

From the early Christian centuries down to at least the end of the eighteenth century, then, it was widely assumed that there were four levels of the cosmos. At the top was heaven in the sense of the place of the presence of God: it was not of course heaven in the natural sense of the sky with its sun and moon and stars, but the sky was metaphorically associated with it. Below heaven was the order of nature, on two levels. One was the level symbolized by the Garden of Eden in the Bible and the Golden Age in Classical myth, which is specifically the proper level of human nature. Below this was the level of physical nature, which, since the Fall, man has been born into but does not really belong to. Below physical nature was the demonic world, the hell of the rebel angels which is below the order of nature, but still exerts considerable power over the third level as a result of the Fall. The Garden of Eden has gone, but the starry heavens, assumed to be made out of an immortal substance purer than the four elements, remain to symbolize it.

A table will be useful at this point:

Heaven, in the sense of the place of the presence of God, usually symbolized by the physical heaven or sky.

The earthly paradise, the natural and original home of man, represented in the Biblical story by the Garden of Eden, which has disappeared as a place but is to a degree recoverable as a state of mind.

The physical environment we are born in, theologically a fallen world of alienation.

The demonic world of death and hell and sin below nature.

Man, born into the third or physical world, is subjected to a moral dialectic from his birth. He must either go downward into sin and death, sin being a demonic state that the animals cannot reach, or upward, back as far as possible, to his original home. Many things are natural to man that are not natural anywhere else, such as using reason and consciousness, being under specific social discipline, and the like. Most important here for the understanding of verbal culture, down to the eighteenth century at least, is the conception of man as belonging to an order of nature that is, since the Fall, peculiar to man himself. As man wears clothes and lives in buildings, art and nature are interdependent on the human level. Edmund Burke, attacking revolutionary doctrines of natural rights, was asserting that "Art is man's nature" at the very end of the eighteenth century. Also, the question "What is really natural for man?" has a completely circular answer, for the answer depends on which level of nature we are talking about. If we are talking about the human level, then, because the garden of Eden has gone, what is humanly natural can only be what is decreed by custom and authority to be natural: there is nothing in external nature to serve as a reliable guide.

In the foreground of these cosmologies are the structures and ideologies of social authority that they do so much to rationalize. Like the cosmologies, the social structures vary in shape, from the feudal and chivalric myths of the Middle Ages to the mystique of the Renaissance prince, and from there to the verbal auras surrounding the enlightened despots of later ages. But as a rule they converge on the figure of a sovereign vested with supreme authority who, whatever theology says, is for all practical purposes a divine incarnation. Donne's "Anniversaries," or extended elegies on the death of Elizabeth Drury, were said by Ben Jonson to be blasphemous, and poems that should have been written only about the Virgin Mary. But they are apparently blasphemous only because Elizabeth Drury was a commoner: I have elsewhere quoted Ben Jonson himself

on King James, very thinly disguised as Oberon the king of
fairies:

> He is a god, o'er kings; yet stoops he then
> Nearest a man when he doth govern men . . .
> 'Tis he that stays the time from turning old
> And keeps the age up in a head of gold;
> That in his own true circle still doth run
> And holds his course, as certain as the sun.
> He makes it ever day and ever spring
> Where he doth shine, and quickens every thing
> Like a new nature; so that true to call
> Him by his title is to say, He's all.

This is from a court masque, and the masque dramatizes
the parallel between social and cosmic structures very vividly.
In masques of the Jonsonian type, we normally start with a
stage set representing something very low on the chain of being,
such as rocks. Then we proceed to the antimasque, the vision
of lower-class disorder, which was usually performed by professional dancers and got most of the applause. Then the vision goes up the social scale to the lords and ladies who take
over the masque proper, and ends with a spotlight on the most
socially prominent character (e.g. Prince Charles in *Pleasure
Reconciled to Virtue*). Donne himself, despite his excursions into
areas of symbolism less approved by Jonson, was well aware
of the same cosmic-social link:

> The earth doth in her inward bowels hold
>   Stuff well dispos'd, and which would fain be gold,
> But never shall, except it chance to lie
>   So upward, that heaven gild it with his eye;
> As, for divine things, faith comes from above,
>   So, for best civil use, all tinctures move
> From higher powers; From God religion springs,
>   Wisdom and honour from the use of Kings.

The underlying figure here is the belief that the planets engender metals out of the mineral world, gold being engendered by the sun.

In the eighteenth century, the chain of being was still in place for many contemporary writers. Berkeley says in *Siris* (1744), for example: "There is no chasm in nature, but a Chain or Scale of beings rising by gentle uninterrupted gradations from the lowest to the highest." But once the Ptolemaic universe was gone, the conception lost most of its scientific status, and began to look more like a purely verbal construct. Voltaire in particular was very doubtful about the "échelle de l'infini," which he saw to be so largely a rationalization of political authority, and under the impact of the later American, French and Industrial revolutions, it began to modulate into other forms. I quote Berkeley partly because of the uneasy emphasis he puts on the gradualness of his version of the great chain, and its total exclusion of any revolutionary breaks.

Metaphorical structures of this sort do not become untrue in a descriptive sense, because truth in that sense does not apply to them. They go out of fashion when they become, or when certain aspects of them become, imaginatively unconvincing as metaphors. They are then replaced by other metaphorical structures. Originally, one of the poet's central functions was to celebrate the hero, that is, his counterpart in the world of action. It is this tradition that survives in the extravagant flattery of King James by Jonson or Louis XIV by Racine, and we recognize that such writing, even if it bores us, had still some cultural validity in the seventeenth century. After listening to the St. Matthew Passion or the Christmas Oratorio, we may be startled to realize that music from these works can also be used for the greater glory of the Elector of Saxony, but we can come to terms with that too. In this century very little panegyric has survived its occasion, although fulsome praise was bestowed by some poets on Hitler, Stalin, Mao and similar figures. A contributing cause of the metaphorical shift was the rise of the Romantic movement, in which the poet himself and his art began to replace the hero as the main subject of poetry. As Hölderlin says of Napoleon: he belongs to his own world, and the poets should leave him there.

The ideologies derived from the P creation myth were always somewhat self-defeating for poets, because they suggested that there was only a very limited place for human creativity in a cosmos where, as Browne says, "Nature is the art of God," where the artist can do nothing but make inferior imitations of what God does infinitely better. Not always better: it is also Browne who shakes his head over the unaccountable absent-mindedness of God in filling the New World with such a variety of animals and yet forgetting to supply "that necessary animal, the horse." But despite this, and despite the puerilities of the arguments from design which demonstrated how ingenious God had been as a craftsman, the prestige of the metaphor of creation as applied exclusively to the work of God helped to keep the arts in a subordinate position. The most obvious example is the subordinating of painting to representation.

For many poets, of course, the old symbols of spiritual authority retain their cogency, however much their metaphorical context may have changed. Such symbols are still there, for example, in the Eliot *Quartets,* in Hopkins, and in Francis Thompson, the last of whom saw Jacob's ladder pitched between heaven and Charing Cross. We notice however that the modern poetic use of the older images is often associated with a strong emphasis on the informing power of tradition, the continuity of social institutions and doctrines, and their incorporation into the conventions and genres of literature. Mediating human institutions, including literature itself, replace the older authority figures.

In Goethe's *Faust* there is a significant discussion between Faust and Wagner at the city gate, just before the entrance of Mephistopheles. Wagner, who temperamentally needs a sense

of authority but is a keen student nonetheless, remarks that
when he unrolls a parchment manuscript it seems to him as
though heaven were descending. He is invoking some minor
Biblical modulation of the ladder, like the flying scroll of
Zechariah. Faust's famous answer, that there are two souls in
his breast, one earth-bound and the other longing to ascend to
a higher community of angels, associates the latter world with
ancestral spirits (*hoher Ahnen*), where again tradition and continuous descent are involved. The same metaphors are there,
but the ideologies they have incidentally inspired are dissolv-
ing and reforming into new ones.

The coming of mythical analogies to evolution in the nineteenth century did not change much in this picture, except that
it usually cut off the top, leaving man, who was assumed to
be the highest product of evolution, with nothing above him
unless he surpassed himself, as he was urged to do in Nietzsche.
Here again myth develops an ideology: certain aspects of what
is called social Darwinism, for instance, tried to rationalize the
authority of European societies over "inferior" ones. Such ideology had a very pervasive influence in popular mythology,
but had much less effect on imaginative literature.

IV

What we have now is a structural model of intensified consciousness, once linked to various physical phenomena and
transformed into a hierarchy rationalizing certain types of authority. There is no reason for the metaphorical structure to
disappear from literature when its application to authority or
the physical world does. There remain, however, two types
of the axial image that we have been considering. We notice
that although angels ascend and descend on Jacob's ladder, there
is no suggestion that what goes up must come down, that
there is any mechanical rotation. With the parody imagery that
starts with the Tower of Babel it is, as we saw, different: there

an inevitable rising and falling movement pervades everything.

Let us look back at the theological form of our universe with its four levels, the heaven of the presence of God, the unfallen or regenerate order of nature, the fallen nature of ordinary life, and the demonic world. Even if there are no paradises, lost or hidden, no angels, no divine presence and no hell, there is still the range of human mentality, which could be immensely more powerful and efficient than it normally is, or fall far below even its average performance now. We can understand this best, perhaps, by thinking of each level of this imaginative cosmos as a way of experiencing the primary categories of consciousness, time and space.

I have often reverted to the unreality of our ordinary experience of time, where none of the three dimensions of time, past, present and future, really seems to exist, and where the word present means only a never-quite disappearing between a no-longer and a not-yet. It is obvious enough why, in the four-level construct mentioned above, the highest level, the presence of God, should be associated with a real and continuous present moment, a moment where, as Eliot says, the past and future are gathered. In the Elizabethan period we have Sir John Davies' poem *Nosce Teipsum,* a wonderful grab-bag of epigrams giving us a great number of the common mythical axioms of the time, where we read:

> But we that measure times by first and last
> The sight of things successively do take,
> When God on all at once His view doth cast,
> And of all times doth but one instant make.

Eliot's *Quartets* are largely concerned with the Incarnation as a descent from the divine world into our time-world, where it creates the possibility of experiencing a real present moment for us, however often we miss the chance of it. Ordinary time can be represented as a horizontal line, the *axis mundi* as a vertical one, and the point where the *axis mundi* crosses time, the moment of incarnation, is, we saw, "the still point of the turning world," and the center of the axis. The still point and the response to it are clearly verbal and spiritual. The conception of a verbal still point recurs in Pound, where it is called the "unwobbling pivot" and is associated with Confucius. Many other examples could be given of a "timeless moment" reached through the verbal imagination, from Blake's "pulsation of an artery" that includes the whole of time to the paradox of the Grecian urn in Keats.

In the unfallen, paradisal, angelic or other modes of experience more intense than the ordinary one, time would exist without the sense of external compulsion that we feel in being continually dragged into the future with our faces toward the past. Such an existence would be a *musical* one, in harmony with nature, in counterpoint with other living beings, and in itself a pulsating inner exuberance. Images of music and the dance have always been inseparable from images of upper worlds. We remember the dance in the *Paradiso,* and the dance in heaven described by Raphael in *Paradise Lost.* Sir John Davies, again, in his magnificent poem *Orchestra,* gives us a vision of the whole cosmos as an interlocking dance. Davies even picks up the symbolism of ritual as the special occasion when a society imitates the same kind of disciplined spontaneity:

> Since when all ceremonies, mysteries,
> All sacred orgies and religious rites,
> All pomps and triumphs and solemnities,
> All funerals, nuptials, and like public sights,
> All parliaments of peace, and warlike fights,
> All learned arts, and every great affair,
> A lively shape of dancing seems to bear.

Orchestra is a most comprehensive vision of man as *homo ludens,* expressing the energy of his life within a cosmos of perpetual

exuberance. The poem is said to be sung to Penelope during
the absence of Odysseus by the chief of her suitors, Alcinous.
I think the reason for this is not some concealed irony but the
opportunity to associate this cosmic dance with a mythical expansion of the web of Penelope:

> So subtle and curious was the measure,
> With such unlooked-for change in every strain,
> As that Penelope, rapt with sweet pleasure,
> Ween'd she beheld the true proportion plain
> Of her own web, weaved and unweaved again.

Schiller, in his *An die Freude,* which was incorporated into
Beethoven's Choral Symphony, also gives us a vision of the
whole chain of being, from the worm in the dust to the angels
standing before God, in possession of an inner energy of life:

> Wollust ward das Wurm gegeben,
> Und der Cherub stets vor Gott.

Not the greatest poetry, perhaps, but good rhetoric about a
great poetic theme, and possibly all the more useful to a musical composer for that reason.

Demonic time, of course, would be pure duration or clock
time, "tomorrow and tomorrow and tomorrow" with no significant alteration. Normally this is the aspect of time in which
it is the universal destroyer, sweeping everything away into
annihilation. Our experience of time contains a cyclical movement besides a linear one, and the upward phases of the cycle,
youth, morning, spring bring a temporary, or time-domi-
nated, sense of the exuberance and gaiety of the world above.
Hence the *carpe diem* theme of the urgency of snatching at happiness while there is still time, that runs through lyrical poetry
from Horace to Herrick. In demonic time all cyclical movement is seen as closed and completed, and we have only rep-

etition of the same thing, or the same kind of thing. The immense gap between our ordinary experience of time, or clock time, and our experience of it at the extremes of existence, indicate how easily we adapt ourselves to a kind of minimal sense of reality. The legend that the whole of life appears before our eyes at the moment of death or near-death conveys something of this. Its most famous literary expression comes in the last canto of Dante's *Paradiso,* where we are told that an instant in the divine presence covers more time than has elapsed since the beginning of all human journeys with the Argonautic voyage:

> Un punto solo m'e maggior letargo,
>   che venticinque secoli alla impresa,
>   che fe' Nettuno ammirar l'ombra d'Argo.

At the other end of experience, we have the intensity of awareness of time while awaiting execution which Dostoevsky experienced and conveys so poignantly through Prince Myshkin in *The Idiot.* This in its turn is contrasted with the second of illumination before an epileptic attack that seemed to him as full of significance as an entire life.

The center of time is now, but every moment of time we can point to is a partly alienating then, in the past or future. Similarly, the center of space is here, but every actual point of space is there. In the four-level cosmos the aspect of space corresponding to the musical experience of time is the natural place, one's allotted position in the chain of being. Schiller's worms and cherubs would not feel joy except in their natural place. In the demonic world, of course, space would be totally alienating; in the divine world it would be a real presence corresponding to the real present of time. In the divine world the words eternal and infinite would mean the reality of now and here; in the demonic world they would have only their vulgar meanings of time and space going on without ever stopping.

Once again a table should be useful:

Cosmic Level	Time	Space
Heaven	Time as total "now" or real present	Space as total "here" or real presence
Unfallen world	Time as exuberance or inner energy (music, dance, play)	Space as home or "natural place"
Fallen world of experience	Time as "then" (linear and cyclical)	Space as "there" (objective environment)
Demonic world	Time as pure duration and power of annihilation	Space as alienation

We have to make one more effort to integrate the four-level cosmos with ladder and wheel symbols. In between the "heaven" or whatever that Jacob's ladder points to, and the worlds revealed in descending journeys to be examined later, there comes the order of nature, where living things struggle upward to their natural place and fall backward into death, in other words a cyclical order. This is the world of metamorphosis, bodies continually changing into new forms, the principle around which Ovid gathered so many of the traditional Classical myths.

Although theologically the two orders of nature, the lost

paradise and the fallen world we now inhabit, form a dialectical contrast, in poetic practice they form an interlocking cycle. The images of the upper order are invariably derived from the earlier phases of the natural cycle: paradises are always associated with sunshine, youth and fertility, and form a *locus amoenus* or pleasant place where it is always spring and autumn at once. Darkness, cold, sterility, old age and the sea have readier connections with the lower order. The essential image, however, especially for the older poets, is that man is an exile and a wanderer in the lower world of nature, and comes to his home in the upper one.

Spenser gives us an account of such an upper world in his description of the Gardens of Adonis, a place of seed or *locus amoenus* apparently above the world rather than below it. Most scholars associate the mountain described in connection with it with the female genitals, the womb of Mother Nature made visible, as it were. A similar image is in Yeats's "Dialogue of Self and Soul," where the self looks downward into a cyclical world of rebirth and sexual symbols (sword, flowers of "heart's purple," mirror).

Chaucer's *House of Fame* provides a brilliant parody of such themes. This poem first summarizes the *Aeneid* story to the point of the descent in the sixth book, then tells us how an eagle seizes Chaucer and carries him upward. Evidently he is to go to some kind of paradisal place (*locus amoenus*), as a reward for writing so much about love. However, Ovid mentions a house of Fama or Rumor which is at the *center* of the order of nature, and that is where Chaucer is taken instead. The eagle is an uncommonly loquacious bird, and we get the impression that he has a white-knuckled passenger who would prefer not to be told the stories of Icarus and Phaethon with so much relish. But the main point of the eagle's harangue is that the principle of motion in nature is for heavy things to fall and light things to rise, and words, being only "ayre ybroken," rise in the order of nature, ascending toward their natural place, or, as the eagle calls it, their "kindly stead." What Chaucer finds in this upper place is a vast confusion of rumors illustrating the total irrationality of fame and reputation. He does not get to the top of the cosmos, but to what Ovid calls the middle of the threefold world (*triplicis confinia mundi*), the hub of the wheel of fortune, so to speak.

This is an ironic parody, by anticipation, of Eliot's still point at the center of the *axis mundi*. And just as Eliot's still point derives from Dante's axis, of which Jacob's ladder forms the highest part, so Chaucer's center of noise, rumor and confusion of tongues suggests Babel. There is a strong element of parody too in what for English literature is perhaps the greatest single vision of the four-level universe and the ideology that accompanies it. This is the curious pendant to Spenser's *Faerie Queene* known as the *Mutabilitie Cantos*. This poem is printed as though it were a fragment in the middle of a lost seventh book of the epic, but it is nothing of the sort: it is a beautifully designed and unified poem complete in itself, though cast in the regular *Faerie Queene* format.

Mutability, a demonic goddess of the lower world of change and decay (our third and fourth levels), claims jurisdiction over the planetary world as well, on the ground that planets revolve, and therefore change. What follows is the lawsuit of the goddess against the god, as Graves calls it, the god being Jove, the ruler of the heavens. Mutability contemptuously dismisses Jove's claim to be such a ruler, and appeals to Nature, who is supreme over both. Nature's decision is:

> I well consider all that ye have said,
> And find that all things steadfastness do hate
> And changed be: yet being rightly weighed
> They are not changed from their first estate;
> But by their change their being do dilate:
> And turning to themselves at length again,
> Do work their own perfection so by fate:

So over them Change doth not rule and reign;
But they reign over Change, and do their states maintain.

The effect of this decision is to confine Mutability to the sub-lunary world, and to confirm the authority of Jove in "his imperial see." But that is not the real point of Nature's decision, which speaks of "all things," including the things of this world as well. The cycles of nature are geared to two movements, one downward into death and annihilation, the other upward into "perfection." The former is the direction of Mutability herself: "For thy decay thou seek'st by thy desire," Nature says to her.

The *Mutabilitie Cantos* form a secular apocalypse, a high metaphysical comedy, some of it written in deliberate doggerel, yet ending with two deeply serious stanzas contrasting the world of becoming, where Mutability reigns, and the world of unchanging being in the presence of God. To this last Spenser applies the pun "Sabbath-Sabbaoth," a good enough pun in the language Spenser is using, however indifferent in Hebrew. The vision of being beyond change is a Sabbath vision, a human glimpse of creation corresponding to the contemplation of it by God himself on its seventh day. It is also a vision of the hosts or multitudes (*tzabaoth*) that the divine creation has made into an order.

Wallace Stevens, in "Sunday Morning," seems almost to have written a rejoinder to Spenser's poem: here a woman stays home from church, meditates on the Resurrection, and comes to the conclusion that a world beyond change is not humanly conceivable: "The imperfect is our paradise," as the poet says elsewhere. Spenser's point, however, is that it is only in Mutability's world that all change moves in the direction of death, and that above her world there is an energy that changes but rules over change and is not subject to death.

There are two themes in Spenser's poem: the main theme contrasts the first and fourth worlds of Spenser's cosmos; a subordinate theme, the farcical Ovidian metamorphosis of Faunus, deals with the cyclical order of nature in between. Faunus the satyr bribes a nymph to let him see Diana naked: the glimpse of Diana's genitals, which is too much for his gravity, corresponds to the symbolism of the womb in the Gardens of Adonis, Venus being readily interchangeable with the triple goddess Cynthia-Diana-Hecate. Mutability is not Hecate, but she is associated with her, and she begins her lawsuit by thrusting herself into the sphere of Cynthia, the moon. This is a violation of decorum in counterpoint to the voyeurism of Faunus, and perhaps reinforces the association between an epiphany of nature and a view of female genitals. Faunus is changed into a stony brook, in the regular metamorphosis tradition, and emphasizing the two aspects of Ovid's metamorphosis stories that made them so fascinating to poets of Spenser's day: the vision of life as fallen from a higher category of consciousness and as bound to a natural cycle of life in which life is always renewed in a different form.

The *Mutabilitie Cantos* are in a secular idiom, where the highest entity is Nature. There is only one Biblical reference to indicate that for Spenser's readers Nature would not really be the supreme being, and that is to the Transfiguration:

Her [Nature's] garment was so bright and wondrous sheene,

That my fraile wit cannot devize to what
It to compare, nor finde like stuffe to that:
As those three sacred saints, though else most wise,
Yet on Mount Thabor quite their wits forgat
When they their glorious Lord in strange disguise
Transfigur'd sawe: his garments so did daze their eyes.

I think there are three main reasons for choosing this particular New Testament image. One is that the word rendered "transfiguration" in the Greek text is *metamorphosis*. Another is that the Transfiguration, unlike the Resurrection, is a mountain-top epiphany. Like Mutability's lawsuit, it takes place on a height that suggests the summit of the order of nature, whatever the actual height of "Arlo Hill" in Ireland may be where Spenser's trial is located.

Third, the Transfiguration represents the identity of the Word as the person of Christ with the Word as the Bible. Jesus appears in the Transfiguration with Moses and Elijah, the law and the prophets, the major components of scripture. The reference, brief as it is, indicates that the Sabbath vision Spenser prays for in the final line of the poem is not simply rest from change but an understanding of the order that governs change, an order to which the term Word both in Spenser's day and ours still gives the only real clue.

Spenser associates his Sabbath vision with a rest which is, he says, contrary to Mutability: it is difficult to express the final "rule over change" except in images suggesting the unmoving. In our day Valéry's *Cimitière marin* expresses a similar vision through the paradoxical images of death (the graveyard), and oceanic obliterating of identity (the sea) and Zeno of Elea's vision of a motionless universe. But the deep repose at the heart of the last stanza of the *Mutabilitie Cantos* is not immobility, but the result of occupying one's natural place in the scheme of things.

In each of our variations there are three elements to be considered: an authentic myth, an ideological adaptation of the myth to a form of social ascendancy, and a demonic parody. Here the demonic parody is the Tower of Babel and the cycle of empires it develops into, and the ideological adaptation the vision of hierarchy, through the chain of being and the like, which rationalizes the authority of kings, dictators and similar leaders. The authentic myth is the vision of order prompted by the P creation myth, an order which passes through our normal awareness of passing time and receding space into a real present and a real presence. Authority in this context is the authority that we gradually learn through science, dialectic and poetry, an authority which emancipates instead of subordinating the person who accepts it. The authentic myth of order accounts for the fact that anyone learning the cosmology of the *Commedia* or *Paradise Lost* is not burdening his mind with obsolete pseudo-scientific rubbish, but studying the structural principles of very great poems. Similar imagery in twentieth-century poets is not inspired by pedantry but by the same vision of order.

We also said at the beginning of the book that the poetic imagination deals with primary human concerns, which we classified in four groups as (1) concerns of bodily integrity (breathing, food and drink); (2) concerns of sexual fulfillment or frustration; (3) concerns of property or extensions of power, such as money and machinery; (4) concerns of liberty of movement. The concern mainly informing the present variation is freedom of movement, which is expressed in the images of exuberance, of music, dance and play that we glanced at earlier. We soon come to see that the ultimate sources of hampered movement are time and space as we normally experience them, and at the top of the ladder of wisdom these elements in time and space disappear.

The idealized image of free movement in the Bible is that of the wandering sheep of the twenty-third Psalm, for whom everywhere is home, and who represent a pastoral existence whose disappearance in the Bible is symbolized by the murder of the shepherd Abel. Cain introduces the contrasting image of human life as an exile, and the exile, who can go everywhere except home, becomes intensified in the post-Biblical Jewish dispersion, symbolized in legend by the story of the Wandering Jew. This type of wandering exile is ascribed by Jesus to his own earthly life (Luke 9:58). More intensified assaults on freedom of movement, such as imprisonment, binding or torture, need no further commentary at this point. This physical symbol extends into the spiritual world, and Paul is emphatic about the freedom of movement brought by the spiritual life (II Corinthians 3:17). This includes freedom of thought and consciousness, as Paul says when he speaks of the Spirit searching the deep things of God (I Corinthians 2:10). The next step takes us back to the image of a circle or sphere, though of a very different kind from the cycles operated by fate or fortune.

In the last two or three lines of the *Paradiso,* after Dante has finished his journey and is in the presence of God, the words "cerchio" and "rota" appear. The contemporary scientific vision of nature, in spite of its millions of galaxies, continues to speak of a universe, or "one-turning" totality which forms an infinite circumference enclosing us on all sides. Here the human being's natural place is the center of an expanding sphere, instead of hanging between an upper and a lower world like the samphire-cutter in *King Lear.* The corresponding spiritual vision would be a vision of plenitude in which each human being is a center and God a circumference, or "all in all," in Paul's phrase (I Corinthians 15:28). The proverb says that God's center is everywhere and his circumference nowhere, but in a human perspective the divine circumference would be everywhere too, as a center has no identity without a circumference.

The sense of allness, if there is such a word, transcends the totality of "all things," which suggests a number to be counted, however large a number, and is the basis for the conception of the spiritual world usually called pantheism. Traditionally, "all things" refers to the totality of created beings, as in Revelation 21:5 ("Behold, I make all things new"). "All in all" takes us further than statements of the "all is God" or "all is one" type, where the predicate "is" re-inserts the duality the statement itself attempts to deny. "All in all" suggests both interpenetration, where circumference is interchangeable with center, and a unity which is no longer thought of either as an absorbing of identity into a larger uniformity or as a mosaic of metaphors.

"More is the cry of a mistaken soul," said Blake: "less than all cannot satisfy man." Here the difference between "all" and "all things" is very clear. The world of all things, as we know it now, is the material world, and matter is energy congealed to the point at which we can live with it. In the spiritual vision we recover the sense of energy to the extent that we identify with the creating power, and have come from Yeats's polluted heart where all ladders are planted to the place where all ladders end. But where the ladder of progressive steps ends the dance of liberated movement begins.

CHAPTER SIX

Second Variation: the Garden

I

Let us now turn to the second or Jahwist creation myth, the one that starts in Genesis 2:4. This myth, like the P myth, has seven episodes, consisting of six acts and a final characterization. Not being explicitly fitted into the scheme of the week, they are not counted so frequently, but here they are:

1. Creation of a "mist" (Septuagint "fountain") out of dry ground. The earth and heavens seem to be already in existence, if in a still chaotic form.

2. Creation of the "adam" or soul-body human unit (not the proper name of a masculine being until later in the account). The body of the adam comes from the ground (*adamah*), and the soul (*nephesh*) is breathed in directly by God.

3. Creation of the garden and its trees, including the tree of life and the forbidden tree of knowledge.

4. Creation of the four rivers of the garden. Two of these are the Euphrates and the Tigris; the "Gihon" is traditionally identified with the Nile; the "Pison" is un-

known, but is identified by Josephus with the Ganges (GC 144).

5. Creation of the whole of the animal world (apart from human beings).

6. Creation of woman out of the adam's body.

7. Institution of the state of innocence ("naked and un-ashamed," Genesis 2:25).

The contrasts with the P account are more obvious than the similarities, which are few and minor. Two of the latter are that in both accounts the trees appear early, in the third episode, and that in both the fourth creative act brings the first one into familiar human conditions. On the fourth day in P the primordial light becomes the sun and other sources of human light; in the fourth episode of J the primordial "mist" expands into the great rivers. Both parallels could be accidents: according to Robert Graves, the trees appear early because they were the images of the first alphabet. It is the contrasts that concern us here.

First, in J the creation of human beings is emphatically separated from the rest of creation. As a male body implies a female one, the original adam must have been either androgynous or differently constituted sexually before the creation of Eve if the myth is to make any narrative sense at all. Such an androgynous adam-figure survives in kabbalism and elsewhere, though the Christian Fathers rejected it. Most Old Testament myths involve puns and popular etymologies, and the narrator of the J creation story, unfortunately, has two of these on his hands. The adam was formed from the dust of the ground (*adamah*), but the word *ish,* which is explicitly male, is also applied to him in order to etymologize the word "woman" (*ishhah*) as meaning "drawn out of man." We get two strains of tradition here. One is the mythical tradition that I am mainly concerned with in this chapter, and the other is

the rationalizing of the supremacy of the male which has produced, in English and other languages, the male metonymy.
That is, in English "man" or "mankind" means human beings
of both sexes, and "he" means in a great many contexts "he
and she." Probably the wisest course with such conventions is
to let them fossilize. Apart from human beings, the main emphasis in the J account falls on trees, rivers and the paradisal
garden: Adam and Eve are apparently assumed to be living on
tree fruits, and the animals are domestic pets.

   In the P account, we said, there is a strong emphasis on
differentiation, as the elements are created first, each in its own
sphere, and then a hierarchical order of existence is established
culminating in humanity. God's "rest" on the seventh day, we
said, implies that at the end of creation the cosmos became
objective to its creator, and remained so for man, a "Sabbath
vision" set up among other things for contemplation and study.
We spoke of the P account as a vision of nature as *natura naturata,* nature as a system or order. The J account is rather a
vision of *natura naturans,* the nature of vitality and growth.

   It is consistent with this contrast that the God of the P
account should have the whole design complete in his mind
before he begins, and that his creation should unfold ritually,
as the model for the rituals that are provided for man's response to it. The God of the J narrative, in contrast, has a
rather disarmingly experimental approach to his creation, and
seems to have little interest, at least at this stage, in wrapping
himself in omniscience. He assembles the animals and birds in
front of Adam and tells Adam to give them names: "to see
what he would call them" (Genesis 2:19). In *Paradise Lost* he is
even constrained to apologize for not being able to include the
fish in the gathering. The creation of Eve herself also seems to
be something of a second thought, a rectifying of an original
deficiency. The J account, though earlier than its predecessor,
comes nearer to our own sense of biological nature as a product of unconscious experiment.

Sexuality is of primary importance in this myth, and introduces the very intricate and tortuous problem of the distinction between symbolic and physical sexual identity. If we are right in suggesting that before the creation of Eve, the adam, the single human consciousness or living soul, can have been at best only symbolically male, then what was symbolically female before the appearance of Eve must have been the garden itself, with its trees and rivers. It seems to be a recurring feature of myth to think of nature as Mother Nature, and the pre-Biblical Near Eastern religions often centered on an earth-goddess representing this female figure, with her ambivalent womb and tomb imagery, the symbol of what is at once the beginning of birth and the end of death.

Clearly one intention in the Eden story is to transfer all spiritual ascendancy of the pre-Biblical earth-goddess to a symbolically male Father-God associated with the heavens. There is a trace of a potentially sinister earth-mother in the *adamah,* the grammatically feminine "ground" from which the body of the adam was made, and to which (or whom) he returns after the Fall (Genesis 3:19). This *adamah* appears to have been the primeval dryness irrigated by the mist which begins the J creation. The garden of Eden then became the adam's symbolic mate or bride, though not anything he or it could mate *with*. Next comes Eve, who, it should be noted, is the supreme and culminating creation in the J account. Her appearance is accompanied by a comment from God that it will become the normal human procedure for a male to leave his parents and seek a female. The comment indicates among other things that the sexual connection of man and woman is the seed, so to speak, of the human community, and so interposes the community between the individual consciousness and its environment.

At the center of the J myth is a series of transformations of a female symbol that occurs in many other myths. The typical form of the transformation is from the mother to the bride, as a result of either rejuvenation or special creation, as here. The pre-transformed stage is often a sinister or otherwise undesirable one. These statements should become more intelligible as we go on.

After Eve took the initiative in the Fall, the supremacy of the symbolically male is reflected in the supremacy of the sexually male in human society which God predicts will be the main result of the expulsion from the paradisal state. Theologians and commentators have been so anxious to emphasize this point that they have largely overlooked the central role of woman in the J account, and the fact that patriarchal societies are explicitly said to be the consequence of sin. Man falls as woman, that is, as sexual being, hence woman would have to be the central figure in the restoration of the original sexual and social state. According to Paul, Christ is a second Adam, reclaiming the Eden that Adam lost, and in traditional Christianity the Virgin Mary is a second Eve, bringing about the redemption of man by giving birth to the redeemer. Her entry into heaven at the head of human creatures completes the redemption of man as woman, and establishes the symbolic sexual imagery of the New Testament in which Christ alone is male, and the body or society of the redeemed is Jerusalem, the community in which all souls, whether with male or female physical bodies, are symbolically female (GC 140). There are parallel mythical themes in secular literature, the themes represented by Beatrice in Dante and by the *Ewig-Weibliche* figures at the end of *Faust*. These, however, suggest only that man is redeemed by or through woman, not that humanity is redeemed as woman.

The miraculous in the Bible, naturally, symbolizes an action of God cutting across the normal historical or natural sequence of events. The miracle of creation in J includes the counternatural creation of woman from a more or less male body, in deliberate contrast with the uniform procedure of nature (I Corinthians 11:12). It follows that redemption would be symbolized by another miraculous act reversing the perversion of sex at the Fall, which for the New Testament is the myth of the Virgin Birth, the begetting of God from a female body. The occasion for this myth is the prophecy in Isaiah 7:14 (see Matthew 1:23) that a "young woman" (*almah*) shall conceive and bear a son, "young woman" being rendered, in the Septuagint Greek translation that New Testament writers mainly used, as "virgin" (*parthenos*). There seems to be no support in the text of the New Testament for the continued virginity of Mary after the birth of the Messiah, much less for an Immaculate Conception.

The central place of the Virgin Birth in the Christ story is obvious enough if we have acquired the art of thinking mythically. Readers of Jung will have noted his insistence on the importance of the recent proclamation of the doctrine of the Assumption of Mary, as having transformed the Holy Trinity into a still more holy Jungian Quaternity, by adding a representative of humanity, specifically female humanity, as a fourth term. However far we follow this suggestion, it is at least an authentic example of mythical thinking, in contrast to the occasional announcements of church dignitaries that they can no longer believe in the Virgin Birth, with everyone assuming that the statement is heretical instead of merely illiterate. Meister Eckhart told his congregation that each of them was a virgin mother charged with the responsibility of bringing the Word to birth; but then Eckhart did understand the language of proclamation that grows out of myth, and its invariable connection with the present tense.

Of the many elements in the Fall myth, the one that concerns us here is the loss of sexual innocence. With the Fall Adam and Eve "knew that they were naked," and started trying to make clothes. D. H. Lawrence would call this sex in the head. As for the knowledge of good and evil, it is obviously wrong to equate this with knowledge in general. The answer to Satan's uncomprehending question in *Paradise Lost*: "Can it be sin to know?" must be an emphatic negative. Knowledge of good and evil seems to be a special kind of knowledge, dangerous in the wrong context, but genuine enough in the right one. Here it appears to be dangerous to God himself as well as to Adam and Eve.

In the pre-Biblical Near Eastern religions we often meet the theme of the gods feeling threatened by man's rapid advance, with a particular fear of his becoming immortal. The fear is curiously similar to the modern fear that machines may somehow acquire conscious wills and powers of reproduction and "take over." One of the Sumerian gods wants to exterminate mankind on the ground that they make too much noise at night and disturb his sleep, but human beings survive, partly because they are useful servants, relieving the gods from the need to work. In Genesis 3:22–23, where God seems to be addressing other gods in a spirit of something very like panic (GC 109), we seem to be back to this fear, associated this time with the mysterious "knowledge of good and evil" and, still more, with the fact that humanity may now reach for the tree of life. As the tree of life was not forbidden to Adam and Eve before, it seems to be only the possession of the new knowledge that makes it dangerous.

So we have to look more carefully into the nature of the knowledge acquired. What Adam and Eve seem really to have got, as a result of eating of the wrong tree, was a repressive morality founded on a sexual neurosis. The moral knowledge was disastrous when attached to a sense of shame and concealment about sex, and was forbidden because in that situation it ceases to be a genuine knowledge of anything, even of good and evil. Calling this moral and sexual repressiveness an eating of the fruit of a tree seems an unnecessary metaphor, except that such a tree is the demonic parody of the tree of life, and in the J account the tree of life looks as though it were the chief *axis mundi* image of the close connection with the world of the gods before the Fall.

The original adam, alone in his garden, was involuntarily virginal, and illustrates the theme of the virgin who has a peculiarly intimate relationship to an idealized natural environment. The term virgin is usually associated with females, but long before Genesis we have the pathetic story of Enkidu in the Gilgamesh epic, the wild man of the woods made by the gods to subdue Gilgamesh, but so feared by human society that they send a whore to seduce him. After she completes her assignment the link between Enkidu and the animals who once responded to his call was snapped forever.

The figure of Orpheus in Greece, if not strictly virginal, also has a magically close affinity with nature: he is a musician, and music symbolizes the harmony that holds heaven and earth in union on the paradisal level of existence. Female virgins, again, have been credited for centuries with magical powers over nature, including the taming of wild beasts, the attracting of unicorns, and an uncanny knowledge of herbs. The tradition is unchanged as late as William Morris's *Wood Beyond the World* (1894), whose heroine also possesses magical powers that disappear on the day of her wedding. In a slightly different but related area, one feels that Alice could hardly have held her Wonderland together if she had even reached the menarche, much less become an adult.

Latent in all this imagery is what we have identified as a metaphorical identity between a paradisal environment and a female body, or, in Genesis, between Eden and Eve, a metaphor in which Eve is to Adam what the garden of Eden was to the adam preceding Eve. There is no explicit image of a ladder or tower of love in the Bible, apart from the "tower of ivory" in the Song of Songs (7:4), but the metaphor in "fall" suggests a descent from a higher to a lower world, with the implicit suggestion of an ascent back to the higher one. We have to consider, therefore, the same three elements that we looked at in the previous chapter. First, the imagery of an ascent to and descent from a higher world through love. Second, the structure of authority derived from this, as the chain of being and similar authoritarian images were derived from the ladder of wisdom and consciousness. Third, the demonic parody of the situation, corresponding to the Tower of Babel in the previous group. One difficulty peculiar to this symbolism, once again, is that of distinguishing what is symbolically male or female from actual men and women. In English we badly need some such conception as the Chinese yang and yin, where images of male and female represent aspects of experience that often include the sexual but expand from it in various metaphorical directions.

We begin with the garden-body metaphor implicit in the J creation account, and strongly reinforced by the Song of Songs, especially in the verse "A garden enclosed is my sister, my bride; a garden enclosed, a fountain sealed" (4:12). Here the bride's body ("sister" is poetic diction for bride) is identified with the gardens and running waters of a paradise. In later Biblical typology this paradise would of course be the garden of Eden, and doubtless a parallel identification was there from the beginning. In any case the Song of Songs is a group of songs in a loose dialogue form with a chorus, celebrating a wedding, evidently of a rural youth and maiden, and intensely sexual in imagery. The imagery is of the expanding type already mentioned: sexual union suggests fertility, and the bride's body is metaphorically identified with vineyards, gardens, flowers and the awakening of nature in spring.

There is little more plausibility in ascribing the *authorship* of the poem to King Solomon than in ascribing it to the Witch of Endor; but King Solomon is certainly associated with the poem, and if the name "Shulamith" for the bride in 6:13 is a feminine counterpart of Solomon, the relation is very close. This association expands the imagery into a suggestion of a ritual wedding of the king with his fertile land, as personified in his bride. But it is an easy step from the symbol of the king marrying his land to God returning to his people. In the so-called Royal Psalms, notably 2 and 110, where the king is the "begotten" or chosen son of God, the bride of the king would be a kind of daughter-in-law, or bride of God once removed.

After kings disappeared from Israelite history, the expansion was sublimated still further, into the Jewish vision of the poem as representing Jehovah's love for his Shekhinah or presence, personified as feminine, and including Israel in the role of what Isaiah (62:4) calls "Beulah" or the married land (GC 155). The Christian view, symbolically almost identical, sees it as describing the love of Christ for his people or Church. Christianity being in origin an urban religion, the emphasis on the imagery of a fertile land is less prominent, but at the end of the Book of Revelation, the descent of the New Jerusalem bride (21:2) is followed at once by the restoration of the tree and water of life (22:1).

If we keep to the poetic structure, giving equal metaphorical weight to the bride and the garden, all these views become mythically concentric, as it were, planetary spheres surrounding the central sexual union, and expanding from it. If we adopt a critically deviant view, and say "The poem is not really about this but about that," the fertile promised land turns back into a desert.

Let us glance back to our suggestion that "the knowledge of good and evil" was a morality founded on sexual repression. Commentators infected with this repression cannot explicitly say that God ought to be deeply ashamed of himself for having instituted in human life what Sir Thomas Browne calls "this trivial and foolish way of union," but in practice that is much their point of view, and when they approach the Song of Songs they tend to treat it as a sublimated vision of the love of God for his people, where the meaning of every image is allegorical and never really refers to (ugh) sex. Bernard of Clairvaux, a very high-ranking medieval saint, preached eighty-six sermons on the Song of Songs to make this point: an impressive barrage, but not wholly successful in its aim, as the poem demurely continues to say what it always said.

Even the phrase in Genesis, "naked and unashamed," has

also been chewed by the rodents of prudery. A late pseudepi-
graph, "The History of the Rechabites," has an inhabitant of
the earthly paradise explain to a visitor:

> But we are naked not as you suppose, for we are covered with
> a covering of glory; and we do not show each other the private parts
> of our bodies. But we are covered with a stole of glory similar to
> that which covered Adam and Eve before they sinned.

The real issue involved here, however, is not one of simple
prudery, but of the difference between a poetic and metaphorical structure, founded among other things on the primary
concern of sex, and the transformation of this structure into a
form of ideological authority.

We should expect poets, on the whole, to have a better
sense of proportion about the great song: Spenser, for example, paraphrases from it at some length in his *Epithalamion,*
a poem celebrating his own wedding. What is more significant
is the way in which poets preserve and emphasize the metaphorical identity of the bride's body and the garden, which
enables them to associate sexual emotion with visions of a renewed nature. A study of the imagery of *Paradise Lost,* for
example, will show many subtle indications suggesting that
Eve is, so to speak, the incarnation of the garden itself in a
human form. The Lady in *Comus,* a musician like Orpheus,
also suggests an identity with a very different nature from the
forest in which she is lost.

In Marvell's "Garden" the poet enters a garden and becomes physically involved with it in a way strongly suggestive
of a sexual act ("Ensnar'd with flowers, I fall on grass"). The
progeny of this union, so to speak, becomes a creation of transcending worlds in his mind. Then his soul moves into what
his readers would recognize to be the tree of life, and becomes
a bird sitting in it, a bird of paradise awaiting the moment of
a "longer flight." The poet goes on to suggest that this mating

of the poet's body-mind-soul unit with the corresponding aspects of the garden was the real paradisal existence, before God spoiled it all by creating Eve, a malicious act that made the expulsion from paradise inevitable.

This latter aspect of the imagery recurs in Campion's well-known song "Cherry Ripe":

> Her eyes like angels watch them still;
> Her brows like bended bows to stand,
>   Threat'ning with piercing frowns to kill
> All that attempt with eye or hand
>   Those sacred cherries to come nigh.
> Till cherry-ripe themselves do cry.

The identity here is negative: like most mistresses in the love poetry of that period, the lady in this poem is not saying yes too soon, and is consequently identified with Eden after the Fall, when it was protected by a guard of angels against man's return. Such words as "sacred" and "like angels" dropped into the poem, no less than Marvell's reference to "that happy garden state," remind us that these are not just metaphors, but metaphors belonging to one of the organizing mythical frameworks of Western literature.

However, it is possible to recognize other approaches to the same metaphorical complex even when they are purely secular. Thus in D. H. Lawrence's *Women in Love* a man gets clobbered by his mistress with a paperweight, whereupon he goes into a wood, removes his clothes, and lies down naked, realizing that it was physical contact with flowers and leaves that he wanted, not contact with a woman. The metaphor is approached in terms of contrast, as it is in Marvell.

Romantic poets use the same metaphor. In Blake we have the conception of the "Emanation" or "concentering vision," the feminine principle that expands into the totality of what is loved:

He plants himself in all her nerves,
Just as a husbandman his mould:
And she becomes his dwelling-place
And garden fruitful seventy-fold.

In this symbolism "he" means humanity, whether the individuals are male or female, and "she" is the natural environment. The point is that the union with the environment, as it develops in the human attitude to nature, is not simple sublimation but an expansion of sexual emotions. Similarly in Shelley's *Epipsychidion:*

Let us become the overhanging day,
The living soul of this Elysian isle,
Conscious, inseparable, one.

We may compare the female figure in *The Sensitive Plant.*
In our day Jungian psychology has developed the conception of the anima, or feminine element in a male psyche, with symbolic affinities with nature. Before Jung clarified his conception, however, Rilke had produced a poem called "Wendung" (turning), where he says that he has internalized a large body of images in his earlier work, and that these images now form a single creature or "maiden within." We also referred earlier to one of Pound's final fragments, beginning:

M'amour, m'amour,
What do I love and
Who are you?

Part of the answer, at least, is the "paradiso terrestre" which, he says, the *Cantos* were an attempt to construct.
I have been dealing with the common tradition in which the poet is a male who begins with the expression of his love for a female, and expands from there into a vision of a sym-

bolically female nature. The sexual bias, however frequent, is certainly reversible, even if the history of literary imagery is not. I have said that there is no explicit ladder of love in the Bible, but there is one in Plato's *Symposium,* and there the object of love, on the primary level, is not female. A crucial, though not surprisingly often neglected, phase of the argument is the question about how far Socrates will go in bed with Alcibiades. The sublimating process starts from the beginning, but it goes in the same general direction, up to a vision of and ultimate union with the form of beauty.

II

Anyone coming to the New Testament from the outside may well wonder why we are presented in the Gospels with an incarnate god so hung up on sex that his followers claimed that his father was not his father and that his mother was a virgin, who went about the country accompanied by male disciples, of whom one is said to be "the disciple whom Jesus loved," whose last words to a woman were "Don't touch me," and who, when asked a question (admittedly a very unsympathetic one) about the spiritual world declared that there were no marriages there. There are equally obvious data in the Gospels that strongly qualify this impression. Jesus has many devoted women followers, and his relations with women seem to be uniquely enlightened for the culture of his time and place. His easy and relaxed friendship with Martha and Mary of Bethany, his willingness to talk to a woman who is both Samaritan and promiscuous, his realization that harlots are human beings, are features of this kind.

In the story of Mary of Bethany anointing his feet (John 12:3), Judas Iscariot objects to the expense involved, but even he does not question her right to be there. There is nothing in the Gospels resembling the episode of Xanthippe's entrance into Plato's *Phaedo.* Xanthippe is Socrates' wife, soon to become his widow, with all the terror and misery of widowhood in such a society waiting for her, but that seems less important than the incongruity of a woman's thrusting herself into a place where men are carrying on a serious discussion. Nonetheless it is true that the Gospel, the story of the virgin son of a virgin mother, is dominated by images of sublimation. The view of the Gnostics, and later of the Manicheans, that all sexual intercourse was foul and sinful—actual sin, that is, not simply rooted in original sin—might well have got control of Christianity, and Paul's attitude even to marriage is that of a workaholic, as we should call him now, confronted with demands by fellow workers for time off.

This point has in the first place a bearing on the role of the Song of Songs in Christian imagery. The central phrase, "a garden enclosed, a fountain sealed" (*hortus conclusus, fons signatus,*) is traditionally identified in Christian typology with the Virgin Mary, who is metaphorically a replica, in the form of an individual human body, of the original unfallen garden, with its "mist" or fountain, where God walked in the cool of the day. A verse or two further down (4:16) urges the north and south winds to blow upon the garden: these winds in Christian commentary represent the male impregnating spirit, the Holy Spirit, symbolically the wind in the garden. Again, this is a metaphorical replica of the breath of God in the garden that created a living soul out of Adam.

But if the whole poem is really about Christ's love for his bride the Church, where does the virgin mother stop and the bride begin? Are there two female figures or one? Some commentators have tried to make a second female out of the "little sister" in 8:8, but that raises more questions than it answers. And above all, what is all that sex doing in the poem, even symbolically, if the love described is really sexless?

In the New Testament there are two aspects of male-female imagery: one is concerned with the virgin mother and Jesus as a son, the other with the imagery of bridegroom and bride.

One aspect is linked to the first coming and the Incarnation, the other to the second coming and the Apocalypse. I have mentioned John's story of the wedding at Cana as a type of the second coming, and we notice that in it there occurs Jesus' curiously ambiguous remark to his mother: "What have I to do with thee?", as though he were looking over her head to a different structure of imagery. Paul's attitude to marriage and the sexual relation becomes more intelligible if its context is the assumption of an interval until the arrival of another event that can be symbolized only as some kind of hierogamy or sacred marriage. In the condensed form of pure metaphor, this would mean the rejuvenation of a mother-figure into a bride-figure, the mother of the Word into the bride of the Spirit. This conception fits no accepted doctrine, but is one that we can practically see happening in paintings of the Coronation of the Virgin.

Similar rejuvenation imagery, we suggested, lies behind the J account of creation, where we move from a pre-Biblical mother goddess to the bride figure of Eve. It seems involved too in the grain-cycle mythology of Demeter and Persephone, where the mother figure is linked to the old crop and the daughter to the new one. Psychologically, the rejuvenation of the mother is an internalizing and assimilating of a mother fig-ure; socially, it is an equalizing of a figure of authority. Both of these elements are included in, for example, Shelley's *Prometheus Unbound,* where the Earth-Mother of the first act becomes the sister-bride of the third.

Mother, bride, virgin: no Council ever decided that these were different persons of the same substance, and that anyone who confounded the persons or divided the substance was, etc. They are only female figures after all. Hence there has been little effort, to my knowledge, to put into critical lan-guage the mythical and metaphorical relations of the tradition-ally female symbols of the Bible. Those we have tried to consider here include: (a) woman as one of the two human

sexes, (b) woman as the representative of human community,
(c) woman as symbol of the fact that humanity cannot be redeemed in isolation from nature. Some sayings ascribed to Jesus
outside the New Testament seem to suggest that his spiritual
kingdom returns to the total fusion of male and female on
equal terms that is suggested in Genesis by the adamic body
that contained both sexes. But they are too muddled to be of
much use:

> Jesus said to them, "When you make the two one and make the
> inside like the outside and the outside like the inside and the above
> like the below, and that you might make the male and the female be
> one and the same, so that the male might not be male nor the female
> be female . . . then you will enter" [i.e. the spiritual kingdom].

The ladder of love in Plato's *Symposium* is accompanied,
like Jacob's, by ascending and descending angels. But it is not
a vision of ascent to a higher world through sexual union: that
gets by-passed in a process of self-realization beginning with
the love of beauty in a world where love inheres in a physical
subject and beauty in a physical object, and rises into a world
of forms, culminating in the identity of the two. We get a
glimpse, developed in later poetry, of a polarizing of two principles, one associated with energy, desire, love, heat and the
symbolic male, the other with form, response, beauty, light
and the symbolic female. But, as noted, the connection of the
symbolically female with women is tenuous. We notice too
the figure of Socrates' female teacher of the art of love, Dio-
tima, one of a line of maternal figures including Beatrice and
the Philosophy who comes to console Boethius in prison. Such
figures are emblematic of a Sophia or wisdom, often called a
virgin daughter of God. Her manifestations include the "Sap-
ience" who appears in Spenser's *Hymn of Heavenly Beauty*. In
the authoritarian form of the ascent-of-love image, it is inevi-

table that the foreground female figures should suggest maternal authority.

Thus, just as the hierarchy of the chain of being was reproduced in the social hierarchy of monarchies and aristocracies, so the Father-God and virgin mother of Christianity were reproduced in a priesthood of fathers and a mother church, with celibate orders of brothers and sisters completing a structure of incest taboos. The Song of Songs tells us (8:6) that love is as strong as death: the love it speaks of is clearly rooted in sexual love, and the Septuagint renders the word love as *agape*. But in the New Testament the *agape* Paul speaks of is God's love for humanity and the human response to it, and the sexual and erotic aspects of love seem to be given terms that are either pejorative or imply simply gregariousness (e.g. *philia*).

The word *eros* does not occur in the New Testament, nor is there any connection of the erotic with the ecstatic, such as we find in the Greek Dionysian cults. We have to look briefly therefore at the poetic tradition that accepts the parental imagery, with the structure of authority that accompanies it, and the literary and erotic rebellions against it. A remarkable (though unfinished) poem to the Virgin by Hölderlin speaks of her as the central symbol of a traditional age of authority, law and the absence of the gods, before the return of all the gods, Christian as well as Classical, which he prophesies in other poems. But the scene still appears to be dominated by the tree of knowledge with some kind of tabooed primal scene in its top branches.

The love poetry in Western literature shows a spectrum extending from complete sublimation, where all sexual imagery "means" or points away from sex to religious experience, to a more directly erotic form where sexual experience is the central focus. The mystics are of particular interest here, because of the place of the Song of Songs in their imagery. St. John of the Cross, for example, combines the theme of the bride seeking her lover at night in Song of Songs 3 with the ascent of the soul toward God up a "secret stair" (*secreta escala*) in the darkness of spiritual negation.

A very beautiful English example of a religious poem based on the Song of Songs is Henry Vaughan's "Regeneration," the poem that stands first in his book *Silex Scintillans*. Here the narrator begins by ascending the wrong mountain, at the top of which he sees a scale measuring pleasures and pains. Then he is transported to a garden, a "virgin soil" or "Jacob's bed," where there is a large company of people, some awake and some asleep, awaiting the spirit or wind in the garden. Song of Songs 4:16 is quoted at the end.

In St. John of the Cross and Vaughan the main imagery is of ascent; images of descent are often connected with the common arrangement that puts the male above and the female below, and consequently associates the sky with the male and the earth with the female. The imagery of *Paradise Lost* is full of passages associating Adam with rain and Eve with flowers. One central theme in this imagery is that of the descent of the Word to the Virgin, as in the exquisite medieval poem:

> He cam al so still
> Ther his moder was
> As dew in Aprill
> That falleth on the grass.

We noted that according to Herodotus the great temples of Babylon and Ecbatana had a chamber at the top where the bride of the god was placed to await the descent of her divine lover. Students of mythology connect this with the story of Danaë, imprisoned in a high tower but wooed by Zeus in the form of a shower of gold, or metaphorical sunshine. Hence Danaë could be a type of the Virgin, as she is in Francis Thompson's poem "Maria Assumpta":

> I am the four Rivers' Fountain
> Watering Paradise of old;

Cloud down-raining the Just One am
Danaë of the Shower of Gold.

In his Fourth Canto Ezra Pound follows a reference to Danaë with an account of carrying a medieval picture of the Virgin in a procession, thereby identifying the two on his principle of metaphor by juxtaposition (GC 56). On the other hand, the line in Tennyson's *The Princess,* "Now lies the earth all Danaë to the stars," takes us all the way back to a primordial myth of a male heaven and a female earth.

The remarkable convention usually called, with whatever accuracy, Courtly Love, also shows a spectrum ranging from the sublimated to the more candidly erotic. In its sublimated form, the lover attaches himself to a mistress who commands his utter and unquestioning devotion, but without any sexual contact and with no relation to the lover's marriage. Dante's Beatrice and, in a modified form, Petrarch's Laura did most to establish this pattern. The central aspect of the theme in both poets is the triumph of love over death, as the lover continues an undiminished love after his mistress dies. A similar relationship, in what seems a father-daughter context, appears in the fourteenth-century English poem *The Pearl.*

But there was also a good deal of relatively unsublimated poetry of love, and *The Romaunt of the Rose,* for example, concludes with an assault on a tower so explicit in its general tone that a Victorian translator suppressed what the poem says in favor of a more muted conclusion. In fact it may be said that it was the medieval poets who insisted on adding Eros to a cultural tradition that might have preferred not to have it: they drew mainly on Virgil and Ovid, and on Plato after his love dialogues had been explored by Ficino and others in the fifteenth century. Erotic and ecstatic themes in English cluster around the Elizabethans: we mentioned Donne, whose "Extasie" is about the clearest example we have of the paradox inherent in erotic poetry, the fusion of two bodies into one flesh spoken of in Genesis 2:24, and their eventual separation into two bodies again. The sexual union is often referred to as "death" in the poetry of this period, and a similar death in Shakespeare's "Phoenix and the Turtle" occurs according to the voice of Reason, though the reader may suspect that something other than ordinary death is involved.

Shakespeare's two birds are red and white, copulating (or whatever) presumably on St. Valentine's Day. Parallel imagery (reversing the colors) appears in alchemical literature, where one climactic process is the sexual union of a red king and a white queen. I do not profess to understand much of what is going on in alchemical literature, but the emphasis on a "mysterium conjunctionis" seems clear enough, and survives in various disguised forms. For example, Lewis Carroll's *Through the Looking Glass* ends by asking the reader whether the story is the Red King's dream about Alice or the dream of Alice, the rejuvenated White Queen, about the Red King. We also referred above to the powerfully erotic song in Tennyson's *The Princess,* where the opening line is "Now sleeps the crimson petal, now the white."

The J account of creation, we are saying, suggests a ladder of love and beauty, like the one explicitly mentioned in Plato, between this and a higher world. The story goes on to speak of a fall or descent into a lower world of morality and sexual self-consciousness. One of the features of this fall, we said, is the instituting of a patriarchal society ("He shall rule over thee"). Another is the descent from a paradisal form of life to an agricultural one. Then again, of the many ramifications of the sexual imagery of the Bible, two concern us at present: that in which the individual is symbolically male and the community symbolically female, and that in which the center is symbolically male and the circumference symbolically female.

A clear example of the former is the portrayal of the Christian people, the redeemed community and the Christian form of Jerusalem or Israel, as the bride of Christ. In the Old Tes-

tament too Israel, though usually a son of God (Exodus 4:22),
is sometimes a bride, or, as in Hosea and Ezekiel 16, an un-
faithful harlot to be forgiven and restored (GC 141). In this
relationship there would be no difference between a wife and
a daughter, following the theme in the Eden story in which
Eve is not only the archetypal wife but extracted from the
adamic body. Milton has Adam address Eve as "Daughter of
God and Man." It is also Milton who gives us the famous, or
notorious, line: "He for God only, she for God in him." This
would be a quite accurate description of the relation of Christ
to his redeemed Bride, and apparently Milton felt that Adam,
before his fall, would be in the same position toward Eve and
perhaps also toward the unfallen Adamic family that never
materialized.

The imagery of center and circumference is clear in the
final vision of the Apocalypse, where the Bride is the city of
the New Jerusalem with the Bridegroom as the temple in the
middle of it, except that now there is no place called the temple, but only the body of Christ. Similarly with the restored
garden and the tree of life in the midst of it.

Other images of the same type may have been concealed
by editing. In John's account of the Resurrection in Chapter
20 Peter and another disciple, apparently John himself, run to
the tomb of Christ and find it empty. This episode looks very
like an insertion, perhaps from the same writer who added
Chapter 21, and who shows the same anxiety to mention Peter
and a beloved disciple evidently identified with John. If it is an
insertion, then the four accounts of the Resurrection all speak
only of women as gathering at the tomb on the first Easter
morning as the seed, in our previous image, of the later community as Bride. When in verse 15 Mary Magdalene speaks to
Jesus "supposing him to be the gardener," the pattern of imagery we have been tracing suggests that her supposition was
correct, she herself being part of the garden.

Admittedly, when we begin reading the Bible at the open-

ing of Genesis, and find a symbolically male God creating an
apparently male human creature, then extracting a female from
him in a reversal of all other births, then prescribing male rule
over females because Eve took the lead in following the serpent's advice, we seem to be confronted with patriarchalism
gone mad. There is also the historical context to be considered, if the assumption is right that Genesis represents in
part a patriarchal reaction against the earth-goddess cults that
probably preceded it. But in the perspective of the whole Bible
things begin to look rather different.

We start with the fact that the Fall was from a paradisal
into what eventually became an agricultural way of life. In *The
Great Code* I drew up a table of apocalyptic imagery in the
Bible in which trees and water, the imagery of the oasis, belonged to a paradisal category of existence, and imagery of
harvest and vintage to an agricultural one. The imagery associated with the bride of the Song of Songs is oasis imagery;
for harvest imagery we should turn to the Book of Ruth, where
so many of the major Biblical themes relating to women are
brought into focus.

In this story the Israelite woman Naomi follows her husband
into Moab, loses two sons there, and returns forlorn and
childless to her original home near Bethlehem. Her daughter-
in-law Ruth, who is Moabite, insists on accompanying her: an
act of quite exceptional courage and loyalty in the circum-
stances. Ruth "gleans" in the field of Boaz, a local farmer who
is a kinsman of Naomi's: gleaning was a resource for the
destitute permitted by Israelite law. Boaz is at once attracted
by Ruth, and, to make a short story even shorter, eventually
marries her. In the course of time she becomes the great-
grandmother of King David, so that this book is linked to
David as the Song of Songs is to Solomon, though much more
tenuously.

The fertility imagery surrounding the harvest seems more
concrete and closely related to human situations, however, than

the imagery of the Song of Songs. When Boaz lies down drunk on the harvest field, and Ruth comes to sleep beside him and asks him to cover her with his cloak, there seems to be a displacement of a more primitive custom of copulation on the harvest field as a fertility rite. The close relationship to fertility myth and ritual is a part of the cultural evolution of such a story, not necessarily a sign of direct historical descent from it (GC 35). Still, it does suggest a more primitive type of story in which the female seeks out her lover, though the main thrust of the story we have is in the opposite direction. In one of his letters Keats speaks of the simple pleasure in discovering that Helen was a rogue, Cleopatra a gypsy, and Ruth a "deep one." The pleasure comes partly perhaps from glimpsing a simpler and earlier form of the story underneath its accommodation to a more male-dominated culture.

One theme involved in the story of Ruth is the custom of levirate marriage, prescribed in the Mosaic code as a means of protecting widows in a patriarchal society. A dead man's brother or other close relative was obliged to marry a widow in the family to enable her to retain her status as, in the expressive French phrase, a *femme couverte*. The most famous story illustrating this custom is that of Tamar (Genesis 38), the daughter-in-law of Jacob's son Judah, the eponymous ancestor of the tribe of that name. Tamar's husband, whose name was Er, was, we are told, so wicked that God killed him; she was then married to the next son Onan, who has given the word "onanism" to the language because of the method he took to show his disapproval of the whole procedure. However, God approved of it, so Onan lost his life too. Tamar was then to be married to a third son, but the arrangement lapsed, perhaps because by that time she seemed an unlucky bride. She then disguised herself as a (temple) prostitute to attract the attention of Judah himself. Judah responded, though on learning later that Tamar had acted as a harlot, he ordered her to be burnt, in accordance with the comfortable double standard of his age.

Tamar then revealed her plot; her disguise was justified by the levirate law, and she became a legitimate wife to Judah, thereby placing herself, like Ruth later, in the direct line of succession to King David.

Boaz clearly feels some levirate responsibilities of this kind to Naomi, and transfers them to Ruth, marrying her only after he has cleared a possible prior claim of a nearer kinsman. His motive in doing this was apparently to give Ruth full status as an Israelite widow instead of merely a foreigner. The relevance of the situation to the Tamar story is brought out by the comment of the community: "May your house be like the house of Perez, whom Tamar bore to Judah" (4:12).

A second theme in the Ruth story is that of late childbirth, where a woman too old to bear a child naturally is allowed a son as a special favor (there seems to be no record of a comparable desire for a daughter). Examples are Isaac, Sarah's son by Abraham, Samuel, born to Hannah after many prayers, and, in the New Testament, John the Baptist, a similar latecomer to Elizabeth (Luke 1). Sarah is so incredulous at the idea of becoming a mother at her age that she laughs, and her son is given a name suggesting laughter; Elizabeth's husband Zechariah inquires of the announcing angel "How shall I know this?", and is punished by being struck dumb until the son is born. (A few verses later the angel Gabriel tells Mary that she will have a son though she is a virgin; she inquires "How shall this be?", but nothing untoward happens. Evidently there are differences of temperament among angels.)

Ruth is a young woman, but when her son is born the neighbors express their congratulations in a curious phrase: "A son is born to Naomi" (4:17). One aspect of the story, then, is the sequence of affliction, exile, return and rehabilitation in the life of Naomi, whose story becomes that of Israel itself in miniature. In an undisplaced form of the story Ruth herself would be a rejuvenated Naomi, a mother growing younger and becoming a bride. In fact every story of a miraculous late birth implies some displaced theme of rejuvenation.

A third theme is the removal of some stain on the bride's character, actual or implied. Tamar is accused of adultery and narrowly escapes death by fire, Susanna is successfully defended by Daniel against the slanders of the elders, and a similar theme lurks in the background of the Virgin Birth (Matthew 1:19). Ruth's Moabite nationality practically amounts to a moral stain in the ambivalence about mixed marriages in the Old Testament. In the time of Ezra and Nehemiah all the returning Jews married to foreign wives were compelled to get rid of them, and it has often been thought that the story of Ruth is making a political and more liberal point by placing her in the line of David. Moses and Joseph both married foreign women; even Rachel, the symbolic mother of Israel, stole what seem like very non-Israelite household gods from her home when she married (Genesis 31). But Moses' marriage was condemned by those around him, and one of the pseudepigrapha whitewashes the marriage of Joseph to the Egyptian Asenath by supplying her with a miraculous conversion beforehand. There was always the horrific example of Solomon, whose wives persuaded him to build temples to Moloch and other false gods. Psalm 45, which apparently celebrates a wedding between an Israelite king and a Tyrian princess, earnestly exhorts the princess to forget everything Tyrian in her ancestry.

The Moabites, along with the Ammonites, ranked very high even in the interminable list of peoples that the Israelites hated, being excluded from the Israelite community for seven generations (Deuteronomy 23:3). There is a parody of the levirate theme in the story of the incestuous union of Lot with his two daughters (Genesis 19), unions which produced the Moabites and the Ammonites. So Ruth's Moabite nationality appears to be making a very subversive point, although after the book became canonical, the inevitable commentators arose to explain that the Deuteronomic law did not apply to women.

In the Song of Songs itself, some of the statements made by or associated with the bride seem difficult to account for except on some assumption of foreignness or something else undesirable by the standards assumed. One wonders, for example, about her statement "Mine own vineyard have I not kept," and her dream of being beaten by watchmen as she goes in quest of her beloved. She says she is "black but comely": that may mean only that she has been out in the sun a good deal, and has thereby acquired, so to speak, a patina of fertility. It is also dimly possible that "black but comely" actually means "black but comely," and is intended to suggest a southern origin for her. In the Solomon dimension of the poem there has always been some association of her with the Queen of Sheba, the "queen of the south" as Jesus calls her. In Numbers 12 Moses' wife Zipporah is said to be a "Cushite," usually meaning an Ethiopian (and so rendered in the AV), whether it means that there or not.

The theme of foreign ethnical origin symbolizing some kind of moral stain links with that of the forgiven harlot I have elsewhere mentioned (GC 142). In the genealogy of Jesus with which the Gospel of Matthew opens, the name of Boaz' mother, not elsewhere recorded, is given as Rahab (Matthew 1:5). If this is, as many commentators think, the celebrated harlot of Jericho, she is twice spoken of approvingly in the New Testament as a pattern of faith and good works (Hebrews 11:31; James 2:25). In *Paradiso* ix, Rahab appears in the circle of Venus, at the limit of the earth's shadow.

The reverse of this theme is that of the Israelite woman who defeats the enemies of Israel. The best-known story of this type is that of Esther—the queen, or more probably a concubine, of the king of Persia—who delivers her people from the threat of genocide and triumphs over her enemies. The story of Judith, and by extension of Jael, in the song of Deborah, represents cruder if pictorially more interesting versions of the same type of story.

Secular literature, from folktales to our own time, is full of themes of rejuvenation or the removal of some undesirable feature connected, as a rule, with the heroine. The *Wife of Bath's*

Tale in Chaucer is a familiar example, and the same principle accounts for the fact that Shakespeare's *Taming of the Shrew*, for all its preposterous sexist ideology (never taken very seriously, of course, even in its own day), is still sure-fire drama. The Greek New Comedy theme of the heroine who can marry the hero because she is not really a prostitute-slave or a shepherd maiden but was abandoned by or kidnapped from a noble family is one I have often reverted to: it is central in *The Winter's Tale*. But I think a still more important aspect of such motifs is concealed in Hannah's song of triumph when her son Samuel is finally born:

> The Lord maketh poor, and maketh rich: he bringeth low, and lifteth up: he raiseth up the poor out of the dust, and lifteth up the beggar from the dunghill, to set them among princes . . . (I Samuel 2:7–8).

This theme recurs in the Magnificat (Luke 1:52–53), which is partly modeled on Hannah's song (GC 183).

What we have here is the suggestion that the themes brought together in the Book of Ruth and elsewhere, themes connected with the position of women in Biblical history, such as levirate marriage and miraculously late births, have a dimension in which woman expands into a kind of proletariat, enduring, continuous, exploited humanity, awaiting emancipation in a hostile world: in short, an Israel eventually to be delivered from Egypt.

The emphasis on levirate marriage, and the frequency of references to widows, reinforces the suggestion that the widow is in part an image of Israel in exile (Lamentations 1:1) or, more universally, of humanity in history. Figures of lonely and threatened women, in constant danger of being deprived of protection, run through the Bible from Hagar in Genesis 21 to the woman crowned with stars in Revelation 12. In both these instances the life of the son is also in imminent danger. This revolutionary aspect of the sexual relations of men and

women suggests that patriarchal ascendancy eventually reverses itself, not into a matriarchy but into a society where
love makes everyone equal. The body-garden metaphor continues to be appropriate here, for nature is also exploited, fruitful
and patient.

I referred earlier to the question asked Jesus by the Sadducees about marriage, which is really a question about levirate
marriage in the spiritual world. Suppose a woman has been
married to seven husbands: "In the resurrection, therefore, to
which of [them] will she be wife? For they all had her." Jesus'
answer is "When they rise from the dead, they neither marry
nor are given in marriage, but are like angels in heaven" (Mark
12:25). Three points may be noted here. First, the Sadducees
say there is no resurrection, and their skepticism is obviously
regarded with disapproval; yet, as Jesus is still alive, they are
quite right according to the Christian doctrine which says that
there was no resurrection until the one achieved by Jesus. Perhaps the writer of the Gospel has a conception of resurrection
that the doctrine has not grasped. Second, it is possible that
the kernel of Jesus' answer is a refusal to accept the assumption in the word "had." Third, while many would feel that
the inference was obvious that angels are asexual—"barren
angels," as Donne would call them—the inference is not inevitable.

In *Paradise Lost* Adam asks Raphael outright whether angels have any sexual love or not, and although Raphael blushes
and hurries off without answering, it seems clear that neither
Adam nor Milton himself is convinced of the barrenness of
angelic life. As according to the same poem spirits can change
sex whenever they please (i, 423), and as there seem to be
young and old angels (iii, 636), it sounds almost as though
some such arrangement as the one in Ursula Le Guin's *Left
Hand of Darkness* was close to the surface of Milton's imagination. Blake, perhaps thinking of some speculations or visions
in Swedenborg, remarks sardonically that in eternity

Embracings are comminglings from the head
    even to the feet,
And not a pompous high priest entering by a secret place.

There are parallel speculations in Yeats, as well as a delightful poem called "Solomon and the Witch," based on the premise that a perfect act of sexual intercourse would restore the Golden Age. However, something seems to be still imperfect, and the last line is the queen's cry: "O Solomon! let us try again." There are two things to notice here. One is that we see the same divergence of vision here as elsewhere between those who include and those who exclude the sexual experience from the ladder of love. The other is that Blake's remark, at least, suggests that he thinks of spiritual sex as closer to the polymorphous than to the genitally centered.

This last in turn borders on the theme of the ascent of love as a return to a childlike state of ecstatic union with the mother, or, in more traditional religious language, as a nostalgia for the lost paradise of Eden. In Vaughan and Traherne, and even more notably in Wordsworth's *Ode on the Intimations of Immortality,* we encounter the theme of childhood as a state of innocence closer to the Edenic than we ever reach again in adult life. We remember that Dante, climbing up the mountain of Purgatory, is traveling backward in time, toward his own childhood as a child of the unfallen Adam. A modern poem using a parallel convention is Dylan Thomas's "Fern Hill," where, in view of the images we have been dealing with, we are not surprised to hear echoes of the Annunciation and Magnificat, the Song of Songs, and of course the Eden story itself. It may take a fairly attentive ear to catch the echoes of Luke 1:28 and Song of Songs 2:5 in the line "And honored among wagons I was prince of the apple towns," but the echoes are there, "wagons" being a rhyme with the "flagons" of the AV rendering of the Song of Songs verse.

So one consistent form of the quest of love appears to be

the journey to identity with the god of love as child, whether
the infant Jesus in the arms of his mother or the infant Cupid
frolicking around Venus. As early as Socrates we are told that
Eros is the youngest as well as the oldest of the gods. I have
elsewhere considered (GC 156) the implication that the Oedipal quest is the tragic version of the Christian one: a view that
underlies much of the symbolism of Yeats. The Oedipus who
kills his father and possesses his mother sexually is the contrasting figure to the Christ who appeases the Father and res-
cues a bride who is symbolically very close to the mother, as
we have just seen.

III

The contrast of Christ and Oedipus raises another dimension
of sexual imagery. We saw in the previous chapter that Jacob's
ladder and parallel images of a connection between earth and
heaven had a demonic parody in the Tower of Babel. This
latter turned out to be the cycle of rising and falling empires
that later ages portrayed as the wheel of fortune. The ascent to
love and beauty also has its demonic parody, the sado-
masochistic cycle, in which the female may tyrannize over the
male or vice versa. Here again the metaphorical link between
nature and the female is usually preserved.

In this book and its predecessor it is suggested that God is
symbolically paternal in the Bible partly because Nature is
symbolically maternal, and the mother is the parent we must
break from to get born. When the mother is mother nature,
we have an earth-goddess cult indicating a human society in
an embryonic state, imprisoned in nature's cycle of life, death
and rebirth in a different form. When Adam falls he returns at
least halfway to the cycle of nature, and two episodes in the
Genesis story point to this: the cursing of the ground (*adamah*)
from which the adam was originally made, and the cursing of
the serpent, whose ability to shed its skin makes it an admirable emblem of the cycle of death and renewal.

Robert Graves's *The White Goddess* outlines the imagery of the cyclical earth-goddess cult as he reconstructs it from Classical sources. In a poem closely connected with it, "To Juan at the Winter Solstice," the "true king" is chosen by the white goddess, who mates with him in the spring. By the fall he is abandoned and turned into a sacrificial victim, whereupon the white goddess renews her youth and virginity over the winter and erases her memory of the previous year, ready for a new love in the following spring. The basis for the myth is evidently the continuity of the fertility within the earth in contrast to what temporarily grows out of it, which is cut down in harvest and vintage.

The great royal marriage poems, like the Song of Songs, belong, for Graves, to one episode of this cycle; poems about elusive and tantalizing sirens belong to another; poems about cruel mistresses who kill their lovers with neglect, like Barbara Allen in the ballad or fairy tales with sinister stepmothers, belong to still another. Elizabethan love poetry is very largely a chorus of complaints about the cruelty and disdainfulness of mistresses, some of whom spread their elusiveness over the whole of time, or the whole available time, like Marvell's "coy" mistress. Some of these mythical praying mantises even collect dead lovers, like the mistress addressed in Campion's song "When thou must home to shades of underground." The most haunting portrayal of such a figure in the literature of that period, perhaps in all literature, is Shakespeare's Cleopatra, whom we finally see apparently dead with her infant serpent at her breast, but perhaps only asleep and ready to "catch another Antony."

Romantic and later poets are also preoccupied with *femme-fatale* figures: Medusa in Shelley and Salome in Oscar Wilde and elsewhere, the latter holding the severed head of John the Baptist, dramatize their castrating proclivities. Keats's "La Belle Dame sans Merci," which takes its title, though not its theme, from a fairly harmless medieval poem, presents us with an inferno of damned lovers in the setting of a bleak landscape of exhausted fertility. The dark and gigantic females in Baudelaire assimilate the figure to the vast unconsciousness of the natural environment. Gérard de Nerval's poem "Horus" takes us back to Graves's mythological context: the goddess Isis, finding herself in bed with an old king, flings away from him and goes to look for a younger partner. As we should expect, the *femme fatale* is sometimes associated with Eve after the Fall: such an association turns up in Valéry's long poem *Ébauche d'un serpent* (it is also one of the strands in the complex weave of *La jeune Parque*). Once again, it will not do to write these off as individual psychological quirks of misogyny.

The white goddess often appears in a threefold form representing fatality, like the Greek Fates and the Scandinavian Norns who are identified with the past, present and future of time. In space she covers, as Keats says, heaven, earth and hell, as the "Triple Will," in Graves's phrase, who is Cynthia the moon, Diana the virgin huntress of the forest, and Hecate the queen of hell. Her colors are the red and white of love and the black of death. In English literature, one very haunting evocation of the "triple will" is Tennyson's poem *The Hesperides,* which he omitted, to his later regret, from his collected poems, perhaps because he was frightened of it. Here three sisters are guarding a golden apple, in company with a dragon and a "Father Hesper," from some Eastern invader who is apparently linked to some advance in human enlightenment. The sisters are terrified that if the apple is stolen "the world will be overwise," and exult in the mystery that keeps the human race in subjection:

> The world is wasted with fire and sword,
> But the apple of gold hangs over the sea.

But the light that seems to be moving steadily from the east fills them with dismay.

Blake calls the white goddess the "female will," and a somewhat different cycle from that of Graves, more closely geared to a cyclical view of history like Vico's, appears in his poem "The Mental Traveller," which deals with the series of cycles of civilization under the imagery of a male figure representing humanity and a female one representing nature. They go through what looks like a mother-son, a bridegroom-bride, and a father-daughter relationship, the male growing older as the female grows younger; but none of these relationships is genuine. The mother-figure is an old nurse, called Tirzah in the prophetic books: she is the natural mother, the aspect of nature that sets such narrow limits to human perception that birth in this world might be described as a mutilation. The bride-figure is not a bride but is merely "bound down" for the hero's delight in a vague parody of the Song of Songs; the daughter-figure is a changeling springing from the hearth. At that point the female figure breaks the cycle, and the male one goes in quest of another, who brings the cycle around to the beginning.

The mysterious second half of this poem may be partly understood from the more detailed treatment in the prophetic books. Blake saw not only that the exploitation of human labor was morally wrong; he also saw that the unlimited exploitation of nature was wrong, and that the same master-slave paradoxes operated there as well. The more man achieves "mastery" over nature, the more he becomes a slave to an enclosing natural order which eventually will, in Blake's phrase, "him to infancy beguile," and start the whole elusive and frustrating cycle over again. In Yeats's "Blood and the Moon" an Irish round tower becomes a kind of phallus pointing at an unstained moon, which remains out of reach of a cycle composed of the blood-stained power of the warrior, who so often dies in mid-life, and the wisdom which is "the property of the dead."

Closely linked to this mythical complex is the theme of the heroes who are betrayed or brought to disaster by a woman.

Samson betrayed by Delila is the great Biblical example. The mythological reason for this convention is that the heroes lack some essential quality of maturity that the woman-inspired disaster symbolizes. Hercules and Achilles both have episodes in which they fall under the domination of women, and Achilles' curiously childlike dependence on his mother Thetis is explicit in the *Iliad*. Shakespeare's most "macho" hero, Coriolanus, is similarly mother-dominated. Aggressiveness in war seems to go with a weakness in love that sooner or later turns destructiveness into self-destructiveness, the Valkyrie or chooser of the slain hidden behind the battlefield.

However, the sado-masochistic cycle is readily reversible, and if we have Delila and Deianeira, we also have Iphigeneia and Jephthah's daughter, women sacrificed to what it seems fair to call male whims. The conclusion of the episode of Jephthah's daughter (Judges 11:40) tells us that her grave became a cult site for women lamenting her yearly—a significant social expansion from a stock rash-vow story. Male-dominated as the Western literary tradition has been, it is still strewn with heroines whose lives have been betrayed and blighted by callous lovers. Their reactions range from the ferocity of Medea to the quiet self-obliteration of Ophelia.

Modern literature seems on the whole to confirm the conclusion of Kierkegaard's brilliant analysis of Mozart's *Don Giovanni,* that the aesthetic-erotic is locked in to some inherent limitation, that the sexual quest as an end in itself seems to aim at possession rather than union, and so inevitably to collapse on the sado-masochist cycle. The proposal of some Freudians (though not Freud) to return to the state of innocence by throwing off the sense of guilt about the sex act seems a trifle simplistic, the sense of the inadequacy of the sexual relation as an end in itself being more deeply rooted than such a remedy implies. The Song of Songs tells us that love is as strong as death, but immediately adds that jealousy is as cruel as the grave, and sexual relations in themselves appear to be inseparable, according to the testimony of the poets, from the tension of egos, the sense of ownership and possession, the panics of status.

In the myth of love, as in the myth of wisdom in the previous chapter, we have three elements. One is demonic parody, the possessive cycle of jealousy dramatized in all the cruel mistress or *femme fatale* conventions, where women usually tyrannize over men, at least when men write the poems. Another is the ideological adaptation of the myth, taking traditionally the form of a social institution dominated by incest-taboo imagery and metaphors of paternal and maternal authority, where as much spiritual activity as possible is withdrawn from physical sex. What sexual life is permitted is regularized by strict monogamy and is regarded as existing primarily for the begetting of children (although sometimes the remarkably repulsive phrase "for the relief of concupiscence" is included). The primary concern of our present variation is of course the sexual one, and from the point of view of that concern the sexual experience itself is what is really important, the begetting of children being an incidental by-product. That leaves us with the authentic myth symbolized by the hierogamy or sacred marriage, which has several distinguishable aspects.

The first of these is the hierogamy of Adam and Eve in Eden, for each of whom there was, naturally, no one else. In the Gospels Jesus sets up this lifetime permanent commitment as the mythical model for human marriage (Matthew 19:6). Such a model distinguishes casual sexual liaisons founded on pure mechanical reflex and sexual unions which individualize both lovers. In actual life sexual unions depend mainly on chance, and the ideal that every marriage must be a sacred marriage strains the laws of chance intolerably—at least, that is more or less the basis of Milton's argument in favor of divorce. In literature the monogamous model survives in the conventional assumption of old-style comedies that young lovers will remain permanently attached to each other after surviving the troubles of the comic action itself.

The real New Testament hierogamy, however, is one in which the risen Christ is the Bridegroom and his redeemed people the Bride. In mystical literature this relation is intensely personalized, like the monogamous relation. The writings of the saints and mystics of divine love have a powerfully erotic quality, a fact which gives a special poignancy to those who happen to be female. When Freud's impact was still new, this erotic quality was widely thought to devalue the experiences in some way, instead of establishing the principle that spiritual love expands from the erotic and does not run away from it. Here the union symbolized by the one flesh of the married state (Genesis 2:24) has expanded into the interpenetration of spirit.

In the Book of Revelation, however, the symbolism is different: the Bridegroom has any number of brides, male and female, Christ the Bridegroom being the principle of unity or individuality, and the Bride the principle of community. The Old Testament type is Solomon's love for the Shulamite, attached to a historical Solomon involved with a thousand and one women—seven hundred wives, three hundred concubines (I Kings 11:3) and the Queen of Sheba. The reason for including earlier in this chapter some light-hearted poetic speculations about sexual unions in the spiritual world was to indicate the fluidity of personality in such a world, where the paradox of Donne's "Ecstasie," of two bodies striving to become one flesh and never succeeding, no longer applies. The love of children or youths, as a part of the community, is an essential aspect of this, what is relevant here being not simply their care and fostering but their education, or integration into the group. Socrates' seeking out of the youth of Athens is part of an educational ideal, but the erotic impulse in his search is clear enough.

Behind the hierogamy of individual and community is the bride-garden metaphor in which the Bridegroom represents humanity and the Bride nature. Some of the complexities in this conception of nature await us in the next two chapters. Here we are concerned with the oasis-paradise of gardens and fountains that derives from the Biblical Eden and the Song of Songs. It may be an impossibly idealized vision of a very tame aspect of nature, especially when in Isaiah it extends to a world in which the lion lies down with the lamb (11:6 ff.). But it is the imaginative kernel of a nature that should be loved and cherished, and the beginning of a sense that exploiting nature is quite as evil as exploiting other human beings. Admittedly, the Bible itself has done a good deal to promote the conception of nature as something to be dominated by human arrogance, for historical reasons we have glanced at. Contact with some allegedly primitive societies in more modern times, with their intense care for the earth that sustains them, has helped to give us some notion of how skewed many aspects of our traditional ideology is on this point. But even in the Bible the bride-garden metaphor works in the opposite direction of associating nature and love, and I doubt if it is an accident that feminism and ecology have moved into the foreground of social issues at roughly the same time. The "Introduction" to Blake's *Songs of Experience* centers on a female "Earth" who is called a "lapsèd Soul" because she includes the first adam as well as the garden of Eden. Elsewhere in literature there are romance-patterns in which a male hero delivers a female figure who sometimes, as in the sleeping beauty archetype, has fertility associations. There is also a sequence of myths, including the story of Isis, in which the redeeming power is female. Our male-dominated tradition has something to do with the pervading association of the sky with the male and the earth with the female which we noted in *Paradise Lost*. This tradition is partly an accident of a specific culture: if the Western Semitic peoples had had a mythology that began, as Egyptian mythology did, with a female sky and a male earth, the conventions would perhaps have differed accordingly.

Another symbolic aspect of hierogamy is based on the fact that Eros is the creator of all the arts, and man's procreative power has been associated with his creative powers for centuries. The convention called Courtly Love, already mentioned, adopted the monogamous ideal of the New Testament but (at least in its earlier stages) separated it from marriage. The Courtly Love mistress in this model is the focus of all creative effort, the flowering of love into the energy and labor of creation, as in a famous passage in Chaucer:

> The lyf so short, the craft so long to lerne,
> Th'assay so hard, so sharp the conquerynge,
> The dredful joye, alwey that slit to yerne:
> Al this mene I by Love.

The ladder of love, like the ladder of wisdom, leads up to a world which is neither the objective world of science nor the subjective world of psychology, though it interpenetrates with both. The cosmos of love is a cosmos that reminds us of the etymological link with "cosmetic": that is, it contains the categories of beauty and ugliness. These categories are, once again, not objective and cannot be quantified, but they are not subjective either, as in the facile axiom that beauty is in the eye of the beholder, an axiom that overlooks the role of social consensus in this kind of order. As Matthew Arnold remarked, many things are not seen in their full reality until they are seen as beautiful. To which Ruskin and Morris added that much of human civilization—especially, for them, Victorian civilization—could not be really seen until it was seen as ugly.

The term "beauty" is always subject to heavy ideological pressures, and is constantly being confined to the superficially attractive in subject matter, to things which remind us of what is pleasant or conform to fashionable standards. The progress of criticism has a good deal to do with recognizing beauty in a greater and greater variety of phenomena and situations and works of art. The ugly, in proportion, tends to become whatever violates primary concern. Even then, of course, we have to make some elementary distinctions: a starving child is not ugly, but starvation is. There are other such categories of the imaginative cosmos—a sense of humor, for example, is also part of a sense of reality—which will not line up with any subjective-objective antithesis. A still wider perspective opens out in Kant's *Critique of Judgment,* which links together the experience of beauty and that mysterious sense of the teleological, the intuition of a purpose in the creation, which we cannot demonstrate but which keeps nagging the mind with a sense of something left out. Such a purpose cannot be reduced to function, which can be demonstrated, although the twentieth century has been making various ill-advised attempts at such reductions. Kant's formula of "purposiveness without purpose" seems to apply to all works of art, as distinct from the applied arts: perhaps the ultimate resolution of the question is the identity of beauty and purpose.

The perception of a hierogamy in which the Bridegroom is love and the Bride beauty, in any case, leads us to the discovery of the reality of beauty. However incongruous it may seem to apply the word beauty to a work of art, a field of flowers and a pretty girl in a bikini, the fact remains that beauty is something that, in Wordsworth's phrase, we partly perceive and partly create, something belonging both to art and to nature. And while the central link of descent in our conceptions of love and beauty is Platonic, there are remarkable glimpses of such a world of beauty in Old Testament prophets and the Gospels (GC 76). As with other myths, we soon find ourselves expanding from the Bible to the great recognition scene of myth that lies behind the totality of human creation. We remarked earlier that gods, personalities who are also natural forces, were among the first of human creations, and that they were banished from the Bible because man projected them into external powers. But they survived in the arts, and are ready to return at any moment with renewed ways of extending the expression of our energies and vision. At their head will be Eros, oldest and youngest of gods, whom in Apuleius' story the human Psyche drove away, but who is still and always present when the time of the singing of birds is come.

CHAPTER SEVEN

Third Variation: the Cave

I

We have been looking at two major aspects of the relation of this world to a metaphorically higher world of intensified consciousness and experience. One of these aspects puts the emphasis on wisdom and the word, the other on love and the spirit. The relation as a whole is represented by some form of *axis mundi,* one of the metaphors that inform and arrange reality around primary human concerns. We have now to consider the images of the relation of this world to a lower world. Here again we shall find both an enlarging and expanding of consciousness, corresponding to Jacob's ladder, ideological adaptations of it like the chain of being, and demonic parodies of it, corresponding to the Tower of Babel.

We also connected our two types of higher-world ladders with the two creation myths in Genesis. In the story of the fall of Adam and Eve in the J account, the metaphor in "fall" suggests a descent of the wrong kind. In looking at the contrasting images of Jacob's ladder and the Tower of Babel, we saw that the latter modulated into a cyclical vision of history, later called the wheel of fortune. In medieval literature, tragedy was thought of as primarily the falling of a hero from the top of fortune's wheel, or similar height. The image persists, with little if any essential mythical change, as late as William Golding's *The Spire*. Climbing mountains and towers, usually with the object of falling off them, is also a central theme in Ibsen from the early *Brand* to *The Master Builder, John Gabriel Borkman* and *When We Dead Awaken*. Such tragedy is a repetition, according to Chaucer's monk, of the original fall of Adam (more strictly Lucifer, a different theme to be examined in the next chapter). What man fell into was a cyclical world in which every life ends in death, life being renewed only by metamorphosis in some other form.

Descent themes, from New Testament times to the eighteenth century, have the difficulty that their full metaphorical exploitation in literature is hampered by the ideological derivations, the chain of being and the like, which provide little if any place for a creative descent. Descent themes, as we have them in Dante and Milton, are simply descents to death and hell.

The post-mortem hell of eternal torments developed by Christianity, eternal meaning endless in time, has largely disappeared from our metaphorical cosmos by now, though some desperate rationalizers insist that it is still there even if no one is in it. We should think rather of hell as a human construct on the surface of this earth, within which most human history takes place. Like Dante's hell, it has some relatively comfortable, if spiritually lonely, suburbs, but in ironic literature even these disappear. Such a hell is below primarily in the sense that it falls so far short of the world that we could be living in.

Sartre says that hell is other people, and Blake that it is being shut up in the prison of unsatisfied desires. The two statements are not incompatible: they relate to the social and individual aspects respectively of the same state. Hell is the world of the lonely crowd, or, in a more virulently hellish form, the mob. There are other people but there is no community; there is solitude but no individual space. Milton's Satan falls downward to a world which he knows to be hell because of the presence of other rebel angels, but at the same time he falls inward to a claustrophobic state of what Kierkegaard calls shut-upness. He refers to this when he says "myself am hell." Once we realize that hell is the world we live in when we are compelled to do so by our own perversity or the folly and cruelty of others, the way is opened for creative descents that take us much deeper than hell. There are two main varieties of such creative descents, again the social and the individual.

A standard work on pre-Biblical Mesopotamian religion remarks that the two most prominent mythical themes in that period seem to be the sacred marriage and the descent to the lower world. The lower world is the world of the dead, but not of simple death: there is always some sense of a surviving and continuous form of existence, a *kingdom* of the dead, however vague or insubstantial. In the Old Testament there is a similar lower world called Sheol, usually translated "grave," although it is a much broader conception than that. It resembles the Greek Hades more closely than the hell developed later in Christian theology.

The summoning of Tiresias from Hades in *Odyssey* xi has a Biblical parallel in the story of the invoking of Samuel by the Witch of Endor at the behest of King Saul (I Samuel 28). The contrast with the Homeric scene is more striking than the resemblance. The witch is clearly accustomed to the vague entities that drift through her world, ready to claim any identity suggested to them, and there is a sardonic humor in showing how demoralized she is by seeing real "gods" or spirits rising from below the earth, including what appears to be the authentic ghost of Samuel.

In the prophets we have powerful scenes of the great kings of the heathen world entering a world of shades, mocked by those already there for having become "as weak as we" (Isaiah 14:10), and in the penitential Psalms (e.g. 69) the speaker is represented as being in a subterranean or submarine world which is really a state of alienation from God. This Sheol is also identified with the "great fish" that swallowed Jonah (Jonah 2:2).

One of the most famous of the Mesopotamian lower-world myths tells how the goddess Inanna descended wearing all her queenly regalia, part of which was removed at each stage of descent, until she arrived in the realm of death helpless and naked. One of the many elements in this haunting myth is the fact that one can possess nothing in such a world. This anticipates the theme later known as the *katabasis* or *danse macabre,* a genre based on the conception of death as a total leveler in which all social distinctions are obliterated. In Lucian's afterworld satires, particularly, we meet people with great possessions or privileges in the upper world, who, once become shades, beg and plead to be allowed to go back to them even for an hour. The Cynic Menippus, the hero of most of these satires, is the only one without worries, as he possessed nothing when alive. The *katabasis* theme contains a latent revolutionary motif that is one of our main themes at present.

We quoted Yeats as saying that all ladders are planted in the "foul rag-and-bone-shop" of the human heart, which is an excellent metaphorical foundation for ladders. But Jacob's ladder appears to have been planted in Jacob's dreaming brain, and hence it extends into a world below the stone under his head, the world of the "sub"conscious or suppressed (i.e. pressed down or under) energies. By consciousness, to start with, I mean more or less what we think we possess when we wake "up" in the morning. The fact that we wake up indicates that the consciousness extends into "lower" elements in the individual psyche, such as dream and fantasy. We can perhaps visualize this more clearly if we think of the image of the *axis mundi* as a world-tree. The trunk extending from the surface of the earth into the sky is nourished by roots below, and the intensifying of consciousness represented by images of ascent is unintelligible without its dark and invisible counterpart, which diversifies and broadens consciousness with other psychic activities.

Creative descents to worlds of dream go deeper than hell, which is, as just said, on the surface of the earth. For that matter they go deeper than the relatively shallow graves of death, and they are far older than any existing religion. If we look through a collection of folktales like that of Grimm, we see how thickly such tales cluster around a "lower" world of dream, fantasy, wish-fulfillment, and hidden powers of nature. Helpful or grateful animals or ghosts of the dead solve impossible tasks like those assigned to Psyche in Apuleius' story, or provide directions for journeys into the unknown. Magical objects assist good people or are perverted by bad ones. The links of memory break, as a man forgets his wife or the like, and the link is restored by some talisman of recognition, birthmark or what-not. Something precious is lost in the ocean, an obvious symbol of dream and unconscious memory, and is then recovered, sometimes by catching a fish that has swallowed the object. Mysterious beings, benevolent or malignant, lurk in another such natural symbol, the forest. Occasionally we get a glimpse of more primitive world-pictures: thus treasures of gold or heroes with golden hair may reflect in a blurred form a vision of the sun passing through the lower world on its way from west to east.

The most remarkable Biblical example of a descent romance is the story of Tobit and his son Tobias. Tobit is struck blind by accident after burying an Israelite martyr, and the angel Raphael accompanies his son on a journey to another city, where Tobias's affianced bride Sara lives, a sleeping-beauty figure beloved by the demon Asmodeus, who has already killed a previous series of lovers. It has long been recognized that Raphael belongs to the common folktale theme of the "grateful dead," and probably in an earlier version of the story was the ghost of the man Tobit buried. Tobias and Raphael are accompanied by a dog, a common lower-world image. The demon is driven off by the smell of frying fish, exiled to Egypt, a very low world indeed in the Bible, and Tobias and Sara are united at the same time that Tobit is cured of blindness, brought from darkness into light again. The frying-fish theme sounds a trifle grotesque, but the efficacy of smell and taste and magic food and drink in recalling memories and performing similar miracles runs all through literature. Magic cakes may make Alice in Wonderland grow larger or smaller, and a cake with no magic except its connection with time may transform Marcel the dilettante into Proust the novelist.

In most descent myths there is some formidable enemy— Minotaur or dragon or demon like Asmodeus—to be fought and overcome, and frequently this enemy is blocking the goal of the descent. The goal is often, in popular romance especially, a treasure of gold or jewels, as in *Treasure Island* or *Tom Sawyer* or Poe's *Gold Bug*. The same theme turns up in Conrad's *Nostromo,* and, in a context of demonic parody, in the first book of *Paradise Lost.* The type of society that searches for such treasure is an intensely selective one. In popular literature the searchers may be boys or anti-social groups (pirates and the like) that boys find it easy to identify with. The standards of admission often reverse those of more conventional societies. The opening chapters of *Moby Dick* are full of images of descent, as Ishmael joins the highly selective community of whalers who hunt for the submarine treasures of the sperm whale. The turning point in his initiation is the forming of his friendship with Queequeg, who according to Ishmael's social standards before the story begins was hardly a human being at all. The whaling quest, of course, is deflected by Ahab's obsession with a different kind of quest, of a type we shall meet later. Often, however, the dragon-guarded hoard is a metaphor for some form of wisdom or fertility that is the real object of the descent.

The traditional fall of Adam deprived him of immortality, and made death the one certain and inevitable condition of human existence. But there is also the temporary death in which we "fall" asleep and wake "up," where there may be imaginative rewards not afforded by the waking consciousness. The most remarkable of these is the increased control over the experience of time that dreaming seems to bring with it, or at least represents.

The emphasis on dreams and the sense of an increased control over time comes out in the story of Joseph and of how he brought Israel into the then-more-fertile Egypt. The patriarchs in Genesis are often spoken of not only as conversing or communicating with God, but also as being in a dream or trance state. Their successor Joseph was a dreamer of a different sort. His were aggressive and self-promoting dreams of ascendancy over his brothers; he was tactless enough to tell them his dreams, which failed to increase his popularity with them; they plotted to kill him and threw him into a deep pit. The scene changes to a prison in Egypt, where Joseph turns inside out, as it were, from a dreamer into an interpreter of dreams. One of the dreams he interprets for the Pharaoh suggests adapting the Egyptian food supply to the seven-year cycle that was prominent in Near Eastern life. Much later, Daniel performs a similar service as dream interpreter for Nebuchadnezzar of Babylon, accompanied by extended prophecies of future history.

This enlarged view of the future occurs also in the major prophets, who are often surrounded by a hostile or at best an indifferent environment, where predictions of disaster or martyrdom are almost self-fulfilling. I have observed elsewhere that knowledge from "above" is usually associated with daytime and the present moment; knowledge of the future normally comes from a "lower" world associated with the darkness that usually surrounds the dream. Examples of the latter are the *nekyia* or summoning of Tiresias from the shades in *Odyssey* xi; the descent of Aeneas in *Aeneid* vi; the revelation of Michael in *Paradise Lost;* a summary of future history as set forth in the Bible; and the fact that the people in Dante's *Inferno* know more of the future than they do of the present.

In the New Testament the Incarnation, though it is from our point of view a descent from a higher world (*descendit de coelis*, in the creed's phrase), is in fact a descent to a lower one for Christ himself. Both the infancy stories read like a dream sequence: we notice the themes of treasure and wisdom in Matthew's wise men, coming from far-off countries with costly presents, and the sense of the opening up of time, and a change in the direction of history, in the prophecies of Simeon and Anna. The traditional Old Testament type of the journey of the Magi to Christ is the visit of the Queen of Sheba to Solomon, and the mythical Solomon is pre-eminently a magus figure, with a possession of magic, wisdom and knowledge of the mysterious aspects of nature unparalleled in the Old Testament.

The waking consciousness is considerably more docile than the more repressed forms of awareness, and consequently most structures of authority tend to focus on it and try to make sure that repressed impulses remain repressed. As usual, there are resistance movements among poets. We spoke of the Courtly Love or Eros convention in medieval poetry as evidence of the determination of medieval poets to maintain an imaginative tradition of their own, whether officially approved or not. Another such convention is that of the dream vision. The medieval dream journey is not always to a lower world, but it turns up (or down) so often as to give the impression that the poets of the time regarded dream and fantasy as an essential part of the imaginative cosmos they were safeguarding. They drew also on a largely repressed oral literary tradition, repressed because the art of writing was controlled mainly by more official authority.

In the period of Shakespeare and the drama contemporary with him, two other themes of descent and return are prominent. One is the society that forms around lovers in most forms of New Comedy, which remains submerged under parental arrogance throughout most of the story, but emerges newly born at the end. The other is the theme of demonic ascent, represented by the ghosts in *Hamlet* and *The Spanish Tragedy,* who come up from the lower world of the dead screaming for vengeance. Such a ghost is a literary parallel to a Freudian repressed consciousness, which has been thrust into a lower world in the hope that it will stay there, but refuses to do so.

In the fall of Adam there is another type of potentially creative descent that is more social and political than psychological in reference. Adam's fall was primarily an exile, a matter of being turned out of his natural place or home. The theme of exile is repeated by his son Cain, the symbol for the development of the heathen kingdoms that surrounded Israel. A move from Israel to Egypt or Babylon would clearly be a descent, and such kingdoms are regularly associated with monsters or dragons, but the buried treasure—whether wealth, wisdom or fertility—to be found there might be genuine enough. Isaiah, praising the tolerant policy of Cyrus, has God say to him: "I will give thee the treasures of darkness, and the hoards of secret places" (45:3). Ezekiel speaks of the original splendor of Tyre when "every precious stone was thy covering" (28:13); and at the time of the Exodus the Israelites "spoiled" the Egyptians, to their own great profit, with some co-operation from them (Exodus 12:25–6).

Under Joseph and his Pharaoh Israel becomes, apparently, a relatively happy and prosperous community within Egypt; eventually, however, we have a Pharaoh "who knew not Joseph," and Israel entered a state in which it was, as later in Seleucian Syria, threatened with persecution or genocide or was under pressure to assimilate with other religious customs. Two strains of imagery follow from these contrasting situations. One, the more prophetic of the two, views Israel as a kind of microcosm of humanity. We saw the significance of Ruth's Moabite ancestry in the previous chapter, and Jonah, with its suggestion that Nineveh is as much under the eye and care of God as Israel, belongs also in this group. One particularly fascinating vision, apparently coming from a time when Judaism was thought of as having an active mission to the Gentiles, is this:

In that day shall there be a highway out of Egypt to Assyria, and the Assyrian shall come into Egypt, and the Egyptian into Assyria, and the Egyptians shall serve with the Assyrians.

In that day shall Israel be the third with Egypt and with Assyria, even a blessing in the midst of the land:

Whom the Lord of hosts shall bless, saying, Blessed be Egypt my people, and Assyria the work of my hands, and Israel mine inheritance. (Isaiah 19:23–25)

In the other tradition Israel is thought of as isolated from all the societies around it, and the resistance engendered by this is seen in the rigidly exclusive view of Ezra and Nehemiah, already mentioned. Isolation makes Israel a kind of proletariat, or group excluded from the benefits of society at the bottom of the social order. In times of persecution, a conspiratorial body may form, or, in different social conditions, a resistance band of guerrillas like those who gathered around the Maccabees. Or perhaps it is even reduced to a "saving remnant" whose survival makes the transition from total disaster to the next turn in fortune. Most of the Old Testament prophets assume an Israel in exile or under the domination of a foreign power and speak of its eventual restoration; as time goes on, prophecy turns into apocalyptic, where an oppressed and persecuted group emerges triumphant after a sudden overturn of social power.

In this situation we are at the other end of the dream spectrum, the nightmare of imprisonment, sometimes life in a hell from which the only release is death. The proletarian archetype, however, is based on the assumption that whatever is excluded or pushed out of the social order will sooner or later return. The original descent is complemented by a creative ascent, in the form of the revolutionary release of repressed elements, whether political or psychological. The exploration of repressed worlds, and the study of techniques for releasing them, are, of course, what make Freud and Marx such portentous figures in the contemporary world. In the Old Testament the central image of this emancipating revolt is the Exodus; in the New Testament it is the Resurrection, Christ's escape from death as well as hell. The Resurrection is presented in the individual context of Christ alone; later legend added the Harrowing of Hell, the release of a community from the lower world. This legend was in turn an allegory of the revolutionary tactics of the Christian Church in history, which in the course of centuries overthrew the officially pagan Roman Empire.

II

The same revolutionary movement appears in a larger historical rhythm, as the social values and scientific projections of the old four-level authoritarian mythology began to disappear in the eighteenth century. To, say, a medieval mind the heavenly bodies were the images of all that was left of God's original and unfallen creation: they were made of quintessence, a substance purer than the elements; they revolved in perfect circles (or at least there were strenuous mathematical efforts to make them do so); they manifested the intelligent art of God at the creation; they were immune to change and decay. As these notions began to fade away after Newton's time, the movements of the starry heavens began to look increasingly mechanical, which left the organism, the living body, as the "highest" entity in the visible cosmos.

In this climate of metaphorical opinion the older God, who is thought of as a governing providence in the skies, comes in for a good deal of abuse from the poets. We have Blake's Nobodaddy, rejoicing over the cruelty and repression in France, Shelley's Jupiter, "the tyrant of the world," Mallarmé's *vieux et méchant plumage,* Emily Dickinson's "Burglar—Banker—Father," Housman's "brute and blackguard," Hardy's semi-idiot who, echoing Genesis, regrets that he ever attempted creation in the first place. In short, the sky-world has changed, for these and many other poets, from a symbol of heaven to one of alienation. This leaves us with the two inner worlds of the older cosmos, the worlds forming the order of nature as previously understood, and an altered relation in the two levels of the garden-order and wilderness-order has to be our next theme. There are no new myths, but when an ideology loses its imaginative ascendancy it may be replaced by a new emphasis on a complementary myth. This, of course, inevitably creates a new ideology.

Garden and oasis, images of a nature most obviously assimilated to human needs and tastes, and to human conceptions of art, predominate in the Bible and through most of the Christian centuries. The more wild and untamed side of nature, with its destructive moods and its enthusiasm for copulation, was usually confined to specific conventions, like the convention of the "vernal frenzy" in Milton's Fifth (Latin) Elegy, where the poet identifies with the revival of natural energies in spring. With the eighteenth century, however, the duality represented by the words "sublime" and "beautiful" began to include in the cosmic picture an aspect of nature that might be austere, forbidding, even alienating to a degree, but nevertheless representing something that complemented human nature with an aspect of nature that humanity could not wholly dominate. Such a nature would include "the weeds and the wilderness" celebrated by Hopkins along with the mountains and the sea.

A famous tag of Horace tells us that if we expel Nature with a pitchfork, she will always return; and what began to return in the eighteenth century was a feeling for a more autonomous aspect of *natura naturans,* which had been subordinated and distrusted for so many centuries. The sky metaphors, we saw, became mechanical, and organic metaphors superseded them. We have here a historical example of the principle of exclusion and return just mentioned.

In Rousseau's early essay on whether the arts had improved or corrupted human life, and his following treatise on the origin of inequality, it was suggested that civilization was full of the corruptions engendered by the ostentation and luxury of an over-privileged class. Whether or not art is man's nature, in Burke's phrase, the arts are full of what is profoundly unnatural. No one had ever denied this: what was new were the suggestions that the natural came from man's setting in physical nature, that reason was not a faculty separating man from this nature, but one uniting him with it, that man should recover the perspective in which he was a child of nature as well as a child of God, and that the old upper level of nature to be reached by virtue and religion and the benefits of civilization was not really a fulfillment of nature, as it claimed, but an impoverishing of large elements of it. By the time of the *Social Contract* (1762), this thesis had expanded into a revolutionary program on both political and psychological fronts.

In the terms of the present book, Rousseau is a herald of the collapse of the old dominant four-level structure, the ideological adaptation of the symbolism of a world "up there," and the coming into being of a more revolutionary cosmos where the driving energy comes from below, and thrusts upward from suppressed elements in man's nature. Among these suppressed elements is a natural society embodied in a "general will" which is blocked by most existing systems of government; psychologically, traditional hierarchies produce a narrow and arid rationalism, which, as the word suggests, does little except to rationalize their own domination.

The true, or repressed, human society contains, for Rousseau, both aspects of nature: nature as a structure or system and nature as the energy of growth and development. In *Émile* particularly, where the theme is education, or the development of the child's character out of his nature, we meet the suggestion that the creative and recuperating powers of nature are not simply around but below, in the sense of having been subordinated in the past. However, the superiority of the organic over the mechanical, and the ascendancy of *natura naturans* over all systematic and hierarchical approaches to nature, is marked not only in Rousseau but in many other Romantics: we find it also in Coleridge, for example, who could hardly be less of a Rousseauist.

The political part of Rousseau's construct was consolidated eventually in Marxism, where, in a revolutionary context, traditional civilized values are seen to be possessed, with a show of legitimacy, by an ascendant exploiting class, who derive their privileges and power from the repression of an alienated working class. The psychological part of the structure took longer to develop, and it was not until Freud that such conceptions as repression, censorship, a superego, and similar shadows of the Hapsburg monarchy began to be generally recognized as existing within the psyche.

Marx and Freud are only the best known and most followed examples of a mythical pattern that stretches over the whole nineteenth century. In Schopenhauer we have a world-as-representation (*Vorstellung*) on top, which is a distinctively human world, and a world-as-will underneath it, which embraces not merely the natural environment but the natural origin of man. Here the creative power of civilization that produces the represented world floats like Noah's ark on a troubled sea of existence that continually threatens to destroy it.

In Darwinian thought, as expressed in such essays as Huxley's *Evolution and Ethics*, there is also a human and moral order that has developed out of the process of natural evolution, but must remain aware of its limitations as an order precariously on top of this process. The evolutionary force is competitive, the organizing of human morality co-operative, but if co-operation goes too far, it will overcrowd the world and find the competitive rhythms of nature forcing their way back. This is the Malthusian element in Darwinism that was so condemned at a certain stage of Marxism. In Kierkegaard, a more revolutionary thinker than Schopenhauer, the aesthetic and metaphysical human structures of thought and imagination again float on a sea of existential "dread." In Nietzsche there is a "will to power" which at first shows affinities with Schopenhauer's world-as-will, but Nietzsche eventually reversed Schopenhauer's pessimistic attitude and made his will to power a transcendental force enabling man to surpass himself.

I am sorry if these bald summaries of complex thinkers sound glib, as they are bound to do to some extent. I am not suggesting that they are all saying the same kind of thing: what I am concerned with is the similarity of the underlying mythical and metaphorical shapes, and it is difficult to discuss mythical shapes without making what the cliché of academic tunnel vision calls sweeping generalizations. All our present mythical shapes seem to cover two levels of nature, an upper one carrying the traditional historical human values, and a lower one allied more closely to physical nature, or to whatever in human nature is subordinated in the traditional structures. This applies mainly to the *natura naturans* side of nature, its aspects of fertility and sexuality. The old simplistic moral ascendancy of human over physical nature, deriving directly from the divine creation at the beginning, is gone. The two levels interact in very different ways for the different thinkers, but, as a rule, the initiative comes from below, especially in revolutionary thinkers, and the response to it is normally a journey of exploration downward. We notice also that our list of thinkers exhibits the whole range of emotional response to the lower world, from revolutionary optimism to the pessimism in Schopenhauer and elsewhere.

William Blake, from the point of view of this book, was the one who hit this particular cultural bull's-eye. I was originally attracted to him because he was, so far as I knew and still know, the first person in the modern world to see the events of his day in their mythical and imaginative context. He realized that the old mythical universe, in its ideological form as a rationalizing of traditional authority, was dead, and that it was time for a new emphasis in mythology that would accommodate the revolutionary movements he saw rising all around him. Being a poet and not a dialectician, Blake also understood better than most others the metaphorical shape that the new construct would have. Many people were wondering with Rousseau why man should be born free, and yet be everywhere in chains, and wondering why oppressed man should put up with so much tyranny when, in Shelley's phrase, he knows quite well that "ye are many; they are few." Blake saw that as long as man lives within a hierarchical myth without really knowing it, his whole behavior will be conditioned beyond the point of resistance: a rebellion against one hierarchy will merely set up a second one.

Blake begins with the categories of innocence and experience. Innocence he associates with children, not because of any moral superiority in the child, but because the child assumes a world that makes human sense, and was in fact probably created for his benefit. The child grows into an adult, and learns that the world is not like this at all. What then becomes of his childhood vision? The answer is simple enough to us now, but nobody really hit on it before Blake. The childhood vision is driven underground into what we now call the unconscious or subconscious, or some other metaphor meaning underneath, where, in proportion as the sexual life grows in intensity and insistence, it becomes a furnace of frustrated desire, just as Egypt became for Israel a "furnace of iron."

Human life thus takes the form of a force of experience, that is, of compromise with "reality" (ascendant ideology), sitting on top of a human desire that has no real outlet. These two elements in Blake's mythology are called respectively Urizen and Orc. Urizen means, among other things, "horizon," the sense of the limitations of human power when bound by its own ideological assumptions, and Orc means, among other things, Orcus or hell, hell being precisely the condition of human life under interminable frustration. Orc squirms under Urizen like a Titan under a volcano, getting some revenge every night in dreams, and periodically exploding in revolutions. Thus the Urizen-Orc relation has a psychological aspect that anticipates in mythical outline the Freudian picture of the psyche, and a political aspect that anticipates in mythical outline the Marxist picture of society. Blake sets out this view of human life most clearly (though without using the names Urizen and Orc) in *The Marriage of Heaven and Hell,* engraved in 1793, but perhaps written earlier, just after the fall of the Bastille. At around the same time he was writing poems celebrating the American and French revolutions.

Blake has two versions of this Urizen-Orc relationship, one in which youth and rebelliousness remain perpetually polarized against age and reaction, and one in which the same individual form of life (as in "The Mental Traveller") changes as it grows older from one to the other. The spirit of rebellion itself, which Blake came to call Luvah (identical with Orc, but stressing the sacrificial aspect), which cyclically rises and is repressed again, thus comes to symbolize the continuous martyrdom of man under the miseries of war and the evils that go with war.

However wrong-headed he may have been in details, Blake's importance as a pioneer of modern imagination was potentially far greater than Rousseau's, and I wonder if there is a parallel anywhere in history to so momentous a discovery being so totally ignored. In the bitter line from *The Four Zoas:* "Wisdom is sold in the desolate market where none come to buy." Not only was Blake ignored in his own time, but very few people even today understand how much of what has happened in the last two centuries was an effect of a change in man's mythological and metaphorical picture of reality.

One thing of particular interest to us here is that Blake's outlook is as solidly Biblical as that of his predecessors. The assumption that the Bible supports only established authority overlooks the central importance of the Exodus and the Resurrection. I have spoken elsewhere (GC 183) of the theme of *culbute* or social overturn associated with a miraculous birth, as in Hannah's song and the Magnificat, and there are several elements in the Gospel teachings, such as the parable of Dives and Lazarus, linked to the same theme. The end of history, called the "Day of the Lord" in the Old Testament and the Apocalypse in the New, is a repetition of this type of social reversal.

Blake's adherence to the Bible in fact isolated him in many

respects from other champions of the new mythology. Because he laid such stress on human creativity, the imaginative assimilating of nature, he regarded the "natural religion" proclaimed by the Savoyard vicar in Rousseau's *Émile* as a red herring. One can learn from nature only what is natural, and Blake distrusted any attitude to impressions received from an external nature that might lead to passivity and intensify the old submissiveness. Hence although he hailed Rousseau in his early poems as a fighter for freedom, he denounced him in the later work, and he sharply disagreed with Wordsworth on the question of the "influence of natural objects." He saw, in short, an ambivalence in the conception of nature that many of his contemporaries failed to see.

The disappearance of the sky-god from the metaphorical cosmos of so many poets leaves humanity and its natural environment as about all that remains. But in what we call nature there are still many ambiguities. For Wordsworth, who had no thought of breaking with any established body of religious belief, humanity is surrounded by its own civilization, but within, and at a deeper level, the individual can commune with a nature which is other than himself, yet also complements his own nature: a nature that contains, for Wordsworth, aspects of both the sublime and the beautiful that we discussed above.

But what does Wordsworth's gentle goddess who never betrayed the heart that loved her have to do with Tennyson's nature red in tooth and claw, with its ferocious and predatory struggle for survival? Even more, what does she have to do with the narrators in the Marquis de Sade, who, after some particularly nauseating orgy of cruelty and violence, appeal with equal confidence to nature to justify their pleasure in such things? Are there two natures, and if so are they separable? It is obvious that Wordsworth's teacher-nature is an intensely humanized nature, even the Lake country and the Alps being dominated by human artifice. And yet one feels that it would be oversimplifying to call Wordsworth's nature a mere projection of human emotions on nature, even though there often seems to be more evidence for de Sade's view of nature than for his.

What we are back to here is the Pauline contrast between the natural or soul-body and the spiritual body. Wordsworth's nature has a genuine otherness, but it is an otherness of the spirit rather than of the objective environment. The fact that man starts out as a child of nature means that he is equipped with what has been called the selfish gene, aggressive, competitive and predatory. He derives his power to create and live in hell from the same source in nature that he derives his creative and imaginative abilities, or at least appears to. But the traditional view of nature seems right to the extent that man does not live directly in nature like the animals—there are no noble savages of that kind—but within a cultural envelope that conditions his approach to nature. What Wordsworth is talking about is a reconstructed paradisal myth of nature. In order to reach it at the bottom of the mind we must make a still deeper creative descent to circumvent the hell that is also within nature.

In several Romantic poets the myth of Atlantis is used to symbolize this deeper paradisal nature hidden within humanity. Atlantis appears in Blake, for whom it is the world of imagination sunk under the "Sea of Time and Space," and in Shelley, where it suddenly turns up at the end of *Prometheus Unbound* as soon as Prometheus is freed and the tyranny of Jupiter overthrown. In Wordsworth's famous fragment called "The Recluse" Atlantis is described as not "a mere fiction of what never was," but as something that ought to be "A simple produce of the common day." I have given other examples elsewhere. Blake's "Sea of Time and Space" echoes the symbolism of sea monsters in the Bible (leviathan, Rahab, tannin, etc.), who metaphorically *are* the sea, the chaos from which the original creation was separated. In the new creation of the Apocalypse there is no more sea (Revelation 21:2), which means no more death (GC 146). In Dylan Thomas's "Ballad of the Long-Legged Bait" a girl thrown overboard from a ship brings up the whole sea with her, and the poem ends with an echo of the Revelation passage and a vision of "nothing but land." Such imagery reminds us of many primitive creation myths that begin with a bit of earth taken up from the bottom of the sea, which expands into an entire world.

What is beginning to emerge here is a four-level cosmos that is very like the older one upside down. Again a table may be useful:

Alienation imagery of "outer space," usually thought of as dead or mechanical.

Human civilization, with its built-in injustices and absurdities along with its positive achievements.

Something subordinated, neglected, or underestimated in power which is excluded from the thought or material benefits of civilization, yet is dangerous to ignore. This something is usually some aspect of nature that complements human nature, but may be also a part of human society with a similar complementary role.

A point of identity where human creation and imaginative power start, often symbolized as under the earth or sea, like Atlantis.

Two poets in English literature give us this four-level cosmos most clearly and completely, Blake and Shelley. In Blake it has as its two middle orders the cyclical repression and rebellion against repression which are the worlds of Urizen and Orc respectively. Below Orc is Los, the creative spirit of prophecy and the hero of Blake's later poems. Above Urizen is the alienating sky-god of outer space, Satan the death-principle.

In Shelley's *Prometheus Unbound* the sky-god Jupiter corresponds to Blake's Satan; below him is Prometheus, the enslaved spirit of humanity, and Earth his mother. Below them again is the cave of Demogorgon, a mysterious Titan who is Jupiter's son, but who, at the appointed hour, rises from the fourth level to the first one and dethrones Jupiter, destroying all hierarchies of tyranny as he does so.

Jupiter, who of course is identical in Shelley with the Greek Zeus, pretends to be a father-god, but, in spite of the "piter" part of his name, he is really a usurping son, dethroned in turn by his son. He thus belongs in the Oedipus sequence mentioned earlier. Another theme we have already encountered is that in the course of the final emancipation Mother Earth is rejuvenated into a sister-bride. Still another is the fact that the deliverance of Prometheus takes place in a moment of expanded time. Prometheus complains of the endless passing of hours all exactly alike in the pain and misery they bring, but is confident that eventually one of these hours will detach itself and bring about a gigantic mutation in time. This is what happens: Demogorgon rises from his cave into the sky to dethrone Jupiter as "The Car of the Hour arrives." This "hour" is a moment of *kairos* or expanded time coming from below, an event like the Incarnation moving the opposite way.

Atlantis is a somewhat specialized conception for so crucial a role, and we need a few supplementary images to round out this myth of an inner paradisal spiritual core of human and physical nature. We spoke of the "treasures of darkness" of heathen kingdoms, most remarkably displayed in the immense treasures placed in the tombs of dead Pharaohs in Egypt; and we also spoke of the buried treasure as a romance theme, which seems to symbolize, if not always simply treasure, at any rate something well worth the perils of descent to get. The Romantic movement around which the new cosmology took its form saw the beginnings of archaeology and the rising of one buried civilization after another into the light.

The paleolithic paintings discovered a little later bring us still closer to our buried-world theme. When one considers the skill and precision of these works, and the almost impossible difficulties of positioning and lighting surrounding their creation, we begin to grasp something of the intensity behind them to unite human consciousness with its own perceptions, an intensity we can hardly imagine now. Magical motives, such as maintaining a supply of game animals by picturing them on the cave walls, seem utterly inadequate: for one thing, many of the figures are evidently human beings in animal skins. In any case such caves are the wombs of creation, where conscious distinctions have no relevance and only pure identity is left.

Later cave-paintings in Etruria, Anatolia, India and elsewhere, and the frescoes of the cathedrals, seem to indicate some affinity between painting, the ghostly two-dimensional representing of a three-dimensional experience, and a kind of unborn world. However that may be, the verbal equivalents to such a world are harder to define. It was, we said, in the Romantic period and its *Sturm und Drang* predecessors in England and Germany that poets and other students of literature discovered the primitive quality of poetry, and began to realize that whenever a society is reduced to the barest primary requirements of food and sex and shelter, the arts, including poetry, stand out sharply in relief as ranking with those primary requirements.

At the bottom of the primitive in literature is a totally metaphorical world with no consistent distinction of subject and object. Space in such a world is, like dream space, anywhere but nowhere in particular. As for time, we noted the sense of enlargement of time associated with dreaming in the Old Testament, and saw the same theme returning in the "Car of the Hour" that delivers Prometheus in Shelley's poem. Blake's Los is also a prophet of enlarged time, having constantly to subdue a fellow-worker named the Spectre of Urthona who represents the terror and despair inspired by ordinary or clock time.

The verbal unit of this Atlantean world is the oracle, which is usually thought of or employed objectively as the voice of a god or a god's agent giving advice, usually about the future, such as we have in Apollo's oracle at Delphi or Jehovah's at Jerusalem (II Samuel 21:1). Such oracles have a curious double-edged quality: they are supposed to be accepted uncritically, and yet contain a riddling, teasing quality as well, with an element of a bad joke in it, as when Croesus is told that if he attacks Cyrus he will destroy a great kingdom, meaning his own. One has only to look at *Macbeth* to realize how malicious such jokes can sometimes be.

It is obvious that there must have been much more to Delphi than the mere handing out of formulas of advice in verse by a more or less stoned priestess. The motto of Delphi was "Know thyself," which suggests that the self intended was a conscience far below the ego with its anxieties of self-interest, far below all social and cultural conditioning, in short the spiritual self. For that self to "know itself" would constitute the unity of Word and Spirit in which all consciousness begins and ends. Such a spirit could produce its own oracles, and they would be not only genuinely prophetic but genuinely witty. *Finnegans Wake* is the only book I know which is devoted entirely to this hidden intercommunion of Word and Spirit, with no emergence into the outside world at any point, but of course the creative energy involved has produced all literature.

III

I have spent so much time on the Romantic mythological revolution mainly because the impact of myth and its cosmologies on history has been so little studied, and this is perhaps its most conspicuous historical impact. Of course customary metaphors do not drop out of the language when their original reference becomes obsolete, but last as long as they seem convenient. We do not stop using such phrases as "hanging fire" or "a flash in the pan" merely because we no longer shoot with flintlock muskets; we continue to speak of sunrise and sunset without committing ourselves to a geocentric solar system, and similarly in religious language God is still above us in the sky in innumerable traditional phrases which are as intelligible as they ever were. But ideologically it is fairly evident that a new kind of alliance with nature, cemented two centuries ago, has shifted the conception of man from a primarily reasoning or conscious being, who creates in imitation of God's creation, to a primarily willing being whose creations are allied to natural energies like the mutations of evolution.

There being no new species of myth, the Romantic myth re-emphasized the myth that its own existence dramatized, the myth of death, disappearance and return familiar from pre-Biblical cultures. Descent and ascent metaphors are as frequent as ever, even if there are fewer ladders. In its commonest form this myth is cyclical, and as such often has the same sinister or pessimistic aspects of other cyclical myths studied in the two previous chapters. It also has a revolutionary form, thrusting up from a lower world into a higher one, and liberating long repressed or imprisoned energies as it does so. Some of the confusions of the cyclical and the revolutionary aspects of the myth have already met us, and others are to come.

Our previous "variation" was based on the sexual concern and its sublimations and extensions into the spiritual world: it may seem startling to say that the present one has, for its metaphorical kernel, the concern of food and drink. But if we look at the sequence of decline, disappearance and return we can see that the emotional focus comes in the interval between the last two, and that this goes back to a time when, in agricultural societies particularly, so much emotional energy was focused on the reappearance of the food supply in spring or autumn.

The cycle of the order of nature, the cycle of descent and return, death and new life, the passing from winter to spring and from darkness to dawn, dominates all the "dying god" mythology that is so central in so many cultures. Some scholars think that the cycle of the moon, with its crucial three-day period of waning, disappearance and return, provided the metaphorical kernel of the three-day ritual in which a god associated with vegetation is usually put to death on the first day, is buried, disappears and his absence mourned on the second, and rises again on the third. For agricultural people the continuity of this cycle is what is important. Proserpine is kidnapped by Pluto and taken off to the lower world; the world turns barren as her mother mourns and searches for her; eventually she is released, and her re-appearance (the rising of the corn-maiden or anodos of Kore) is an occasion of great rejoicing. But she must go back to the lower world again, otherwise there will be nothing to eat next year.

In the Old Testament deluge the whole world is sunk under water, and when it emerges an agricultural cycle of seed-time and harvest is established, with God himself guaranteeing its permanence. The main agricultural products of Biblical countries are grain and wine, and Noah celebrates the occasion by discovering wine, with predictable results. There must have been however an agricultural cycle before this, as Cain's offering of first-fruits shows. The "cursing of the ground" between Cain's murder of Abel and the end of the deluge (Genesis 4:12 and 8:21) perhaps points to an earlier and more hazardous food-planting economy. The promises of regularity in the annual cycle, however, do not exclude frequent famines, including the one that drives Israel into Egypt at the end of the Book of Genesis.

We suggested that the buried treasures of popular romance may be metaphors for other motives for descent, notably oracular wisdom, or a source of fertility. In Ruskin's tale "The King of the Golden River," the rumor of gold lures two wicked brothers to their death, while for the good brother the real gold turns out to be a fertilizing river. Buried fertility appears in some Celtic myths of cauldrons of unlimited food and drink, which some scholars have tried to connect with the Grail romances: in any case the cornucopia is an ascending spiral of life, as the maelstrom or whirlpool of death is the opposite. This theme of the inexhaustible vessel of food or drink appears in parody in the Holy Bottle in Rabelais, where the word "oracle" links the descent, also of course in parody, to that of descent for wisdom or secret knowledge.

At the lowest point of descent there is likely to be a crucial turn from death to new life, when a threatening monster is killed or a similar crisis passed. The sunrise and the release of the life-giving waters of rain in the spring are often connected with victories over sinister powers that try to prolong darkness or winter, like those who "curse the day" in Job 3:8. There is a beautiful if slightly grotesque example in *Beowulf*, where the hero goes under water to kill Grendel's mother and the poison from her blood melts his sword, an event at once associated with the image of icicles melting at the coming of spring. The descent to obtain renewed fertility is not the theme of the story, but the imagery is closely related.

The rhythm of the natural cycle has provided a great many mythical analogies to human life. We have cycles in history, of empires rising, declining and being succeeded by new empires; we have cycles of authoritarian regimes followed by revolutions, which are followed by a new form of authority; we have the cycles of conversion and similar reversals of movement in the individual psyche; we have images of the natural cycle acting on human beings, in the way that the awakening spring gets Chaucer's pilgrims out on the road to Canterbury. The human cycles in history are much more irregular and unpredictable than the natural ones, though Yeats's *Vision* draws what are alleged to be very precise ones from the phases of the moon.

However, the thought of Yeats's *Vision* is not the real mythical thinking of Yeats's poetry, but an obsessive distortion of it, and I think Nietzsche's "eternal recurrence" notion is similarly an obsessive distortion of his myth of the Superman. In any case, for most religions and ideologies, the notion of human life as totally dominated by cyclical repetition is a blankly pessimistic one, to be counteracted by some belief in or hope for some mitigation of what Yeats, again, calls "the crime of death and birth," a phrase evoking conceptions of karma and reincarnation. Of our three versions of myth—the demonic parody, the ideological adaptation and the authentic myth—the unending cycle, as in the other variations, appears to be an element of the demonic parody.

On the other hand, the continuity of the vegetable cycle is the basis of the ideological adaptation of the myth. The anxiety to continue eating our daily bread expands into the anxiety to survive, to preserve a consistent identity up to or even beyond death. This in turn expands into the vicarious continuity of social institutions or ideological causes that will survive the individual. Here the assumption is that all the deeper forms of human dignity and self-respect are bound up with an identification of the individual with a church, a nation, a social revolution, the advancement of learning, or whatever seems to connect the past with the future, or realize Burke's contract of the dead, the living and the unborn. Social senility results from forgetting the traditions of one's cultural heritage; repudiating one's obligations to posterity is generally felt to be irresponsible.

The metaphorical kernel of all this in food and drink includes two significant features. One is that eating is a much more immediate form of identity with nature than the bride-garden sexual myth just examined, but not one that leads directly to the love of nature. It points rather toward the integration of society, and makes a good deal of the pun on "body" that expresses both individual and social unity. And while there are many social bodies not directly connected with food, the etiquette of eating together in human societies, as among many animals and birds, is very strictly regulated, and seems central to the fact that human beings are social animals. Even the most exalted flights of Platonic philosophy rise from banquets.

Hence, while this part of the *axis mundi* is, like its predecessor, a ladder of love, the emphasis falls on *philia* rather than *eros,* on the friend, neighbor, leader or (usually small) community rather than the sexual partner. Negatively, one of its central genres is the elegy on the lost friend (*Lycidas, Adonais*) that descends historically from the lament for Adonis.

The hypothetical ritual studied in Frazer's *Golden Bough* may be vulnerable enough in various anthropological contexts, but as a mythical structure it is as solid as the pyramids. Here a king regarded as divine is put to death at the height of his powers, for fear that his physical weakening will bring a corresponding impotence to the fertility of the land he rules. The motive for the ritual, therefore, is anxiety about the food supply as well as about the need for strong leadership. When sacrificed, the divine king is immediately replaced by a successor, and his body is then eaten and his blood drunk in a ritual ceremony. We have to make a rather violent effort of visualization to see that there are now two bodies of the divine king, one incarnate in the successor, the other concealed in the bellies of his worshipers. The latter causes the society to become, through eating and drinking the same person, integrated into a single body, which is both their own and his.

In the pre–Biblical Mesopotamian poem *Enuma elish,* we are told that mankind was formed from the blood of the god Kingu, killed as a traitor because he took the wrong side in the cosmological Marduk-Tiamat conflict (GC 146). This aspect of the creation myth is omitted from the Genesis account, though it has profound analogies to the Christian myth in which

Christ has to die to redeem the world he created in the first place. There are similar myths elsewhere (e.g. the story of Ymir in the Prose Edda), but in the Old Testament the theme is replaced by the emphasis on the continuity of the society of Israel. It reappears however in the center of the New Testament, where its connection with the renewal sequence of reaped grain, buried seed and new grain seems clear enough.

Certainly it was clear enough to the New Testament writers, who are emphatic about the analogy between the passion of Christ and the seed which is buried and rises again. It seems important even to insist on the death of the seed (John 12:24; I Corinthians 15:36). Then again, Christ is constantly associated with the miraculous provision of food. Miracles of feeding large multitudes with very small amounts of food are recorded in all four Gospels, sometimes more than once, and such miracles are explicitly antitypes of the provision of manna in the wilderness (John 6:49–51). The imagery of eating Christ's flesh and drinking his blood meets us in the Gospels even before the institution of the Eucharist. That Christ's body is an unfailing source of food and drink is asserted on both physical and spiritual levels (the "daily [*epiousion*] bread" of the Lord's Prayer might also be regarded as "supersubstantial" bread). The body of Christ is not only "to be eaten, to be divided, to be drunk," in the words of Eliot's "Gerontion," but is the source of the continuity of the life of his people, hidden within their bodies. It was so in Old Testament times too, according to Paul, who says that the Israelites in the wilderness all ate the same spiritual food and drank the same spiritual drink, the latter from a rock which was Christ (I Corinthians 10:3). The Resurrection accomplishes what in the primitive Frazerian eucharist is impossible: the God-Man who has been buried within his community suddenly reintegrating, reappearing and turning his society inside out into a single body.

The successor who follows the dead king would be metaphorically or spiritually his son, and sometimes we have the sacrifice of a son to prolong the life or fortunes of the father (GC 184). In Classical mythology there seems to be no father who has himself no father. Zeus, father of gods and men, is a son of Cronos, who was a son of Ouranos, and some mythographers know of still further parentage. In Yeats, Oedipus—killing his father and living in incest with his mother—is the central symbol of a tragic and heroic period (or rather phase) of history, followed by a more reassuring Christian period where Christ appeases his father and reconciles his mother with his bride-church. That Oedipus is to tragedy what Christ is to comedy is an insight of great profundity, but I think Yeats misunderstood the real contrast of Christ and Oedipus, partly because of the carpet-knight in him that led him to idealize the heroic and tragic, and partly because of the vagueness of Christian doctrine on the point. The theologians say that Christ offered himself as a sacrificial victim to appease his Father's thirst for vengeance on the first Adam. What Jesus tells his disciples is rather more coherent: he speaks of the day when he can tell them "plainly of the Father" (John 16:25). His mission is not to do anything to or with his Father, but to reveal him as the figure who, because he is the power who began the old creation, is also the power that can end it in a new one.

In the Gospels Jesus speaks of being succeeded by a figure later identified with the Holy Spirit. This forms part of a pattern that runs from the beginning of the synoptic Gospels to the first two chapters of Acts. In the Incarnation the Spirit is the father of Christ; the Word descends and the Spirit, having accomplished his mission, goes up. At the end of the Gospel story in Acts is the Ascension, where the Word goes up, followed by the descent of the Spirit, who is now a "son" or successor of the Word. This succession is differently interpreted by different bodies within Christendom: for our purposes it is enough to say that the Word, which points toward a spiritual understanding of itself, can be succeeded only by the spiritual form of itself.

If the king in any society is actually a leader, it can hardly be practicable to assimilate social to mythical patterns so rigorously: such a king would have to have genuine abilities, and to the extent that he has these, it would be very unsettling to society to get rid of him at the height of his powers. Hence the rise of substitute figures who do not threaten the continuity of the sequence, such as prisoners or criminals, who are given divine-king privileges for a brief time before execution. Or the king may simply have his power renewed each year, in a ceremony reaffirming the power and protection of his god, as apparently in several of the psalms. So the conception of the rightful king or "Lord's anointed," whose person is sacred as long as his natural life extends, replaces the supposed earlier conception. This is already established in the Old Testament: Saul is killed in battle and is succeeded by his son-in-law David, but it is most important to make the point that David has nothing to do with Saul's death.

The ideology of the Lord's anointed continues in the Tudor mystique of royalty that is so central in Shakespeare. *Macbeth,* for example, is not primarily a play about murder, even the murder of a king, but about parricide and sacrilege. When the king dies naturally, then, in all societies accepting the mystique, it is essential that there should be a smooth transition to the rightful heir. Shakespeare's most remarkable treatment of this is the close of *King John,* where the rascally John, who was the king only because he had got the rightful heir Arthur out of the way, is peacefully succeeded by the infant (and eventual weakling) Henry III, while the one real leader, Falconbridge, abstains from taking over. A generation or two later than Shakespeare, however, the English did execute a lawful king, and King Charles's head was the mythological palladium that helped to keep England in the forefront of the world for over a century. After that, the ideology of divine right gradually shifted its center of gravity to the will of the people and the democratic process, and the *de jure* leader is now the elected one, in contrast to the dictator coming from the only social area where supreme authority is still appropriate, the army, and ruling by martial law. We note that the divine king, so far as his divinity or *de jure* status goes, is not supreme over his society but their shared possession. He is primarily a victim-figure, and Jesus is an archetypal divine king because he is not even recognized to be a king, except in mockery.

The Old Testament records the divine command to substitute animal and vegetable offerings for human sacrifice (GC 183); the New Testament introduces the Eucharist, the bloodless communion in bread and wine, which are still spiritually the body and blood of Christ. Both of these assimilate the myth to the cycle of time, though always with some element that evades the pure cycle. Another part of the demonic parody, the opposite of the fertility god whom we eat and drink, is the demon who eats and drinks us, the figure of death who lurks behind all the cannibal giants and gobbling sea-monsters of so many myths and folktales. He appears in a different kind of parody in Rabelais, where most of the characters disappear into the body of Pantagruel at the end of Book Two, and in a more serious form in the Satan of the *Inferno*. The journey of Dante through hell is displaced, but it is not hard to see the more condensed metaphorical structure in which the whole of hell is the body of Satan, with Dante entering by the mouth (as Jesus does in paintings of the Harrowing of Hell), traversing the bowels, and emerging from the anus. The kind of harvest and vintage that represents the wrath of God, like the treading of the winepress in Isaiah 63, repeated in Revelation 14, is a Biblical example of the same reversal of imagery.

IV

There are two great organizing patterns in the Bible, as in imaginative literature generally. One is the pattern of the natural cycle, the other the pattern we have been calling apocalyptic, the final separation of life from death, where the revival of spring from winter does not simply start another cycle leading to another winter, where death is not simply followed by the birth of someone else. Easter is a festival assimilating the Resurrection to the cycle of time, but the Resurrection itself is not a cyclical event but the beginning of the apocalyptic separation. As no such separation becomes visible in the physical world, the apocalyptic consciousness becomes a hope for something in the future, whether a historical future or a personal after-life. In the New Testament itself the apocalypse is thus projected into a future, however close at hand (Revelation 1:3), a second coming taking the form of a revolution when the present social order is overturned and a now-oppressed minority will be exalted. This kind of reversal-language is used a good deal in the Gospels (e.g. the parable of Dives and Lazarus), as well as in the Book of Revelation and the later legend of the Harrowing of Hell. The general assumption is that those removed to the world of permanent life are a very carefully selected lot—heaven being, like a tourist resort, unspoiled because not too many other people like ourselves are present. Visions of an imminent end to history as we have known it have inspired social and religious movements at intervals ever since. Sometimes, as in Virgil's Fourth Eclogue, a vision of a new age still has a continuing cycle in its background which for the moment is disregarded.

The earliest generations of Christians obviously thought of a second coming as an event in the near future which would be a final awakening from the nightmare of history. As the twentieth century has seen so many similar visions so cruelly betrayed, it is perhaps worth considering the possibility that focusing so intensely on the future represents an incomplete form of mythology. In the New Testament Christ descends to the lower world in his death and burial, returns to the surface of the earth at the Resurrection, ascends the higher ladder to the sky in the Ascension, and descends from there at the Apocalypse. The entire *axis mundi* is traversed in this quest, and any second coming after that can be only an enlarged vision in ourselves of what is there now.

We noticed that the Frazerian rituals included a custom of appointing a temporary ruler or mock king: such a figure is sometimes associated with a licensed carnival period, and the main mythological point about a carnival is that it recalls an original Golden Age of freedom and equality, like the reign of Saturn in Roman myth. In the Saturnalia itself, the best known of such carnivals in the ancient world, the vision of a society in which slaves are made equal to their masters explicitly appears. Again, Jesus is not only a victim-king of the line of David, as the "King of the Jews" inscription on the cross says, but a mock or carnival king, with a crown of thorns, yet promising a paradise to the repentant thief in the teeth of the secular powers. If we ask why the mock king or so-called interrex should be associated with a Golden Age, the answer may be that he represents the break in the anxiety of continuity, the hope for the end of dependence on the natural cycle and of an eventual transformation of human life in time. Once again, the cyclical ritual cannot wholly exclude the apocalyptic hope, the hope of the revolution that will reverse but not again revolve.

It may seem tactless to bring up the image of excretion when discussing apocalyptic visions, but excretion is a part of the food concern, and I suspect that it is the metaphorical kernel of the ultimate separation of heaven and hell just mentioned. The philosopher who said that dirt is matter in the wrong place did not make a very exhaustive analysis: the snow that falls on one's sidewalk in winter is matter in the wrong place, but the difference between clean and dirty snow is something else again. Dirt always has some psychological connection with excretion, and is linked to whatever we want to separate ourselves from. This is the point of Jesus' remark

(Matthew 15:11) that man is defiled by what comes out of him and not by what goes into him—a remark one wishes that those who put so much faith in censoring and banning books and other works of art would pay more attention to. People with unusually silly prejudices against social groups different from their own have a strong attachment to the word "dirty." The ambiguity of sexual attitudes that we traced in the previous chapter has much to do with the inter-relation of sexual and excretory organs in the body, and the consequent notion that the sexual act is "shameful," which is a modulation of "dirty," as we see in, for example, the hysterical term "filth," so frequently used by the allegedly moral to describe the sexually explicit. Many religions, also, develop patterns of the ritually unclean in order to set up excluding barriers which help to define themselves on the primitive basis of nausea. Just as the Eucharist in Christianity is founded on the metaphorical basis of food and drink, so baptism becomes the physical image of spiritual cleanliness, the separating of the true individual from the excreta of original sin.

Excretion has also a close mythical connection with death, the dead body being for most mythologies what Blake calls the "excrementitious husk," something to be cast off and left behind. Many of our euphemisms for death, such as "passed on," contain a suppressed excretory metaphor. As death happens to everyone, it often seems the only principle we know that is utterly fair and without respect of persons. Hence the popularity, already mentioned, of the form known as the *danse macabre,* where the same end visits king and beggar alike. It is for a closely related reason that scatological and excretory imagery is so essential to literature, more particularly satire. Much has been said, for instance, of Swift's excremental vision, and Swift certainly had an excremental vision: nobody has any business setting up as a major satirist without one. But Swift's vision was of a leveling kind: excretion equalizes humanity just as death does, and the phony idealism that tries to ignore it is for Swift a form of the sin of pride. In the notorious "Ladies' Dressing-Room," for example, with its "Celia shits" conclusion, we may feel that Celia is being despised for having functions that no organism in the human or animal world does not have, and hence that there must be some kind of kink in Swift himself. But I suspect that the real ridicule falls on Celia's lover Strephon for trying to surround his beloved with a dream of a purity and refinement of a type that cannot co-exist with human life. Naturally the desire for such purity can be genuinely imaginative too: one thinks of Marvell's exquisite poem on the drop of dew, which falls into a polluted lower world and is eventually exhaled back into the purer world it came from. But Marvell is not, in this poem, writing satire.

The types of myth examined by Frazer include many of the "carrying out death" type, where some figure or symbol identified with death is driven away or "killed." The paradox of the death of death rests on what may well be something of a virgin soil in the human mind, the feeling that, in spite of the totality of evidence to the contrary, death is not really inevitable, but is always caused by somebody or something. To kill death is to bring to life, and to drive out a scapegoat is another ritual expressing a hope of a permanently new unity in life, where death is excluded, or, again, excreted.

If we look at a detective story of the older-fashioned puzzle type in vogue a generation or two ago, we start with a death that conventionally cannot have been due to natural causes, but presupposes a murderer—an assumption that some primitive societies make about all deaths. Once the death principle has been identified at the end of the book, a new social group among the characters is formed with the murderer outside it, a scapegoat or killed-death figure. If the story is well constructed, all kinds of parenthetical comments and episodes that had apparently no point at the time take on a new and portentous significance.

The detective story also makes use of the device technically called *catastasis,* the plausible but false solution offered, usually by the police, just before the great detective arrives to straighten everything out. E. T. A. Hoffmann's "Mademoiselle de Scudéry," which must be one of the first detective stories ever written, includes a fully developed example. This device is also in Biblical imagery, where the catastasis is the convincing but ultimately false vision of the power of Babylon and Rome. When it is expelled, its opposite, the *apocatastasis* or restitution of all things (Acts 3:21) can take its place, after the last enemy, as Paul calls death, has been destroyed.

Not only does the myth of the Passion in the Gospels include the fertility cycle celebrated in Easter, but in Luke's account of the Nativity, with its shepherds and its manger, including the traditional ox and ass, the theme of a renewed intensity of contact with nature is present. Nevertheless the Resurrection is an upthrust from a lower world into a higher one, and is quite distinct from fertility themes like those of Adonis, where the new lives of spring are different from those of the previous year. It is this upthrust that is completed by the second coming or Apocalypse. The Resurrection narratives in the Gospels are kept deliberately placid and serene, full of the unearthly quiet of a spiritual event. But in the background there is the power of a God infinitely stronger than any Samson or Hercules tearing himself loose from all the stink of death and with his face grimy from the smoke of hell.

The next step is to examine what he brings up with him. In the traditional Harrowing of Hell, the rising community consists only of those who are mentioned in roughly favorable contexts in the Old Testament (plus John the Baptist). But a glance at the larger pattern of Biblical imagery shows a more comprehensive outlook. We mentioned the significance of Ruth's Moabite ancestry and of God's concern for Nineveh in the Book of Jonah, and in the New Testament much is said about the welcoming of the lame, the halt and the blind, of calling sinners more urgently than the righteous, of prodigal sons returning, of Jesus' friendship with publicans and sinners, of Zealots (political extremists) among his disciples. A disciple is expressly ordered to journey into the desert to baptize an Ethiopian eunuch (Acts 8), and Paul speaks of the obliterating of all differences of social, sexual or religious status (Galatians 3:28). It looks as though a fair-sized proletariat is included as well as the conventional pre-Christian heroes: so large a body, in fact, as to suggest that the Resurrection represents the release of everything that has been unjustly or needlessly repressed, whether in society or the human mind.

We need one more structural principle to pull all this together, and to find it we must return to descent themes in romance.

The great majority of such descent themes include some variety or mutation of two motifs in particular: amnesia and doubles or twins. A descent into a world below consciousness involves some break in the continuity of conscious memory, or some annihilation of the previous conditions of existence, corresponding to falling asleep. The lower world is often a world of greatly enlarged time, where a few moments may correspond to many years in the upper world. The twin motif is an aspect of the immensely complex theme of the double or Doppelgänger, which runs through all folklore, literature and comparative religion, but had a particular literary vogue in the Romantic period between Hoffmann and Dostoevsky.

One aspect of the double of particular interest is the relation between the self as dreamer and the self as—well—dreamee, the main character in the dream. This follows the pattern of an observer and an actor within the same psyche of which other forms are the myths of the conscience, of the guardian angel, of the daimon of Socrates, and the like. In the literature of this century we have the relation between Finnegan in Joyce, the dreaming giant-man who is all men, and HCE, the same man as the hero of the dream, who goes through a cyclical experience of history. Any duality deriving from a feeling of conflict within oneself can take a Doppelgänger form: the soul-body one, the good-evil one, the conscious-unconscious one, the subjective and objective side of the personality being a few examples. In American literature Poe and Mark Twain were especially fascinated by double themes. Huck Finn and Tom Sawyer are related rather like Esau and Jacob in Genesis, the hairy man of the wilderness and the smooth man of the establishment, but in the final episode of *Huckleberry Finn* Huck not only acts under Tom Sawyer's orders but assumes his name. In more complex literature Thomas Mann's *Transposed Heads,* Graham Greene's *Ministry of Fear,* and Patrick White's *Solid Mandala* will give some idea of how varied and yet recurrent the double theme can be.

The simplest image of the double is the mirror-double, which can extend to shadows or portraits like Wilde's picture of Dorian Grey. I have noted elsewhere that we can objectify our own existence in time and space only by looking at the face of a clock or at our own face in a mirror. The frequency of clocks and mirrors in, say, Poe indicates a world where the distinction of subject and object has gone so far that the subject itself has turned into an object. Or the doubles may represent a moral contrast, like the good and evil angels of Marlowe's *Faustus.* Poe's "William Wilson" story and Stevenson's Jekyll and Hyde are familiar examples. Science fiction has also contributed various forms of doubles, notably the doubles created by traveling in time and those created by the conception of parallel worlds. Both these forms were anticipated by Henry James. In James's unfinished *Sense of the Past* a twentieth-century man goes back a century or more in time, while his double moves from the earlier period into the hero's twentieth-century setting which is the double's future. In "The Jolly Corner" an American who has spent his life in Europe returns to America to confront himself as he would have been if he had stayed on that side of the Atlantic.

It seems clear that most double stories are concerned with

what we described earlier as the quarrels of what are called the
soul and the body, the conflicting demands of consciousness
and something that eludes consciousness. In such stories each
aspect of the double is necessary to the other one, and, as in
Poe's "William Wilson," to destroy the double is to destroy
oneself. In Hoffmann's *The Devil's Elixirs* we have a saintly
monk with a double who involves him in rapes and murders.
If we are not committed to the religious assumptions in the
story, or at least to the assumptions of the characters in it, we
may feel that the hero's austere and celibate life is one more
effort to expel nature with a pitchfork, with the inevitable results.

Such a divided state of life could be symbolized by a head
separated from the rest of the body and living on in a discarnate existence. In one of Poe's stories, "A Predicament," we
read of a woman caught in a clock tower where one of the
hands cuts her head off, both head and trunk being convinced
that they are the real psyche (the woman calls herself Psyche).
In Yeats's play "The King of the Great Clock Tower" there
are again a clock tower and a severed head. The presence of a
clock suggests again that the gap between the conscious and
subconscious has much to do with the way we observe time.
This last aspect of the situation comes out in several poems
and stories that reflect the curious nineteenth-century fascina-
tion with the story of Salome, Herodias, and the severed head
of John the Baptist. In one of the most condensed poems ever
written, Mallarmé's "Cantique de Saint-Jean," the image of
the severed head is linked with the position of the sun in the
zenith, suggesting the paradoxical timeless moment that never
quite exists.

Not all double themes are so ironic, however, as Otto Rank
shows in his study of the motif: the most metaphorically condensed form of the myth is that of immortal and mortal aspects
of the same identity, the grain as the double of the seed. The
theme of a higher and lower self appears in a variety of moods:

a fairly light-hearted one is in Hoffmann's story about the painter Salvator Rosa, in which a miser is cured of his miserliness and lechery by seeing his double on the stage, the part of the double being enacted by the painter. In another Hoffmann story, "The Golden Pot," a young poet is in love with a girl who wants to marry a Councillor (Hofrath), but is also involved with a mysterious snake girl associated both with Atlantis and a paradisal garden. The surface narrative of the story appears to tell us that the poet, retreating to his own world of imagination, eventually chooses a fairy girl, while the other heroine, remaining in real life, marries someone else who becomes a Councillor instead. But the conception of the double is flexible enough for us to feel that the same man may actually get both heroines, one in his imaginative and the other in his everyday life.

The French dramatist Jean Giraudoux wrote a play called *Amphitryon 38,* meaning that the myth it is based on had been dramatized (at least) thirty-seven times before. In Greek mythology Amphitryon's wife Alcmena strongly attracted Zeus, who assumed the form of Amphitryon and lay with her. A similar story is told about the parentage of King Arthur. Alcmena produced twins, the immortal Heracles, the son of Zeus, and the mortal Iphicles, the son of Amphitryon. In Plautus' adaptation of the story (and Molière's) there are twin servants as well as the doubled divine-human figure. The double twin theme recurs in Shakespeare's *Comedy of Errors,* where the uncanny atmosphere seems closer to *Amphitryon* than to the *Menaechmi,* its more frequently cited source.

In the New Testament the father of Jesus is the Holy Spirit, not Joseph, but Jesus is said to have had a brother, whose father would have been Joseph, and early Christian legend associated Jesus also with a twin figure called "Jude Thomas," identified both with the apostle Thomas (whose name means twin) and with the author of the Epistle of Jude. Legend also ascribes the founding of Rome to the twins Romulus and Remus, who were fathered by the god Mars on a vestal virgin. Here both twins seem to start out with the same status, though before long Remus is obliterated. A closer example of the double as immortal self is Heracles in the *Odyssey,* who is said, in an interpolated verse which fascinated Yeats, to be simultaneously a shade in Hades and an immortal spirit among the gods.

We are approaching here a form of double imagery in which a central figure rises into the higher world as an integrated spiritual body. This may be a sexual double, involving a hierogamy like that of the previous chapter, where only the setting is different. Two lyrics in Blake's *Songs of Innocence,* "The Little Girl Lost" and "The Little Girl Found," tell us of a child named Lyca who is carried off by a guardian lion to a protected cave. The prelude to the first poem indicates that the story symbolizes the interval until the awakening of a female earth who is united with her creator and transformed into a paradise. The prelude is followed by the narrative, where the first line contains the phrase "southern clime," recalling the "southern wild" of "The Little Black Boy" in the same book, and perhaps suggesting that Lyca is actually a little black girl, which would link her both with the lower-world Proserpine and the black heroine of the Song of Songs. In any case she represents an inner vision of a regenerate Nature waiting to enter her rightful kingdom. Lyca is also linked to the dark Earth of the "Introduction" to the *Songs of Experience,* already mentioned, the "lapsèd Soul" who is neither Adam nor Eve but a female entity containing them both and much else besides, who is urged to stop turning away into the dark every night and to emerge into the eternal world of light.

Here we skirt the fringe of the theme of male and female united in a single androgynous being. In Dylan Thomas's "A Winter's Tale" a female bird, red and white like the phoenix-turtle of Shakespeare's poem, descends on an old man dying in winter, uniting with him at a point where death, the consummation of a sexual union, a new birth, and the transformation of winter into spring are all the same event in the same place and time. Other examples range from the displaced romantic comedy of *Twelfth Night,* where brother-sister twins cement a double marriage, to the condensed and explicitly metaphorical form of the central figure of Balzac's androgynous *Séraphita.* In a context of parody, the sterile unions of Eliot's *The Waste Land* are observed by the androgynous Tiresias, "old man with wrinkled dugs," as Eliot calls him.

The more ironic double themes converge on what we may call the prison of Narcissus, the beautiful youth paralyzed by the mirror-reflection of himself and hence unable to love. Mythologists very early made Narcissus a type of the fall of Adam, as Adam, like Narcissus, identified himself with his own parody-reflection in a lower world. Paul's conception of Christ as the second Adam makes Christ the double of the Narcissus-Adam who delivers the original one from what Lacan calls the *stade du miroir* and Eliot a wilderness of mirrors. Buber's *I and Thou* tells us that we are all imprisoned in an "It" world which is really a reflection of ourselves. The world of "It" includes nature and the physical environment, but it also includes the social world, "he" and "she" being really aspects of "It" in this context. Creation, in this view, is intelligible because it reflects our minds; the world is beautiful because it reflects our emotions. Only a "Thou," who is both another person and the identity of ourselves, releases the ability to love that gets us out of the world of shades and echoes (Echo was the mistress of Narcissus, and his aural counterpart) into the world of sunlight and freedom.

CHAPTER EIGHT

Fourth Variation: the Furnace

I

We have been outlining three groups of images of the *axis mundi*. Two of them, so far as they relate to the Bible, seem to be linked to the P and J accounts of creation respectively. The third, the imagery of descent from the surface of the earth, begins with the story of the fall of Adam and Eve attached to the J account, where humanity descends into a cyclical order of nature and a political cycle of oppression and revolt. The political cycle begins symbolically with the murder of Abel and the exile of Cain. There seems to be a missing quadrant, an imagery of fall attached to the P account. This does not appear in what would seem its appropriate place, the first chapter of Genesis, and if it did it would contradict the tone of God's general satisfaction with his creative efforts. However, such a story very soon develops as the narrative proceeds. This is the story of the rebel angels, the war in heaven and their expulsion: the story incorporated by Milton into *Paradise Lost* as he reconstructed it from Biblical allusions.

A demonic fall, as Milton presents it, involves defiance of and rivalry with God rather than simple disobedience, and hence the demonic society is a sustained and systematic parody of the divine one, associated with devils or fallen angels because it seems far beyond normal human capacities in its powers. We read of ascending and descending angels on Jacob's and Plato's ladders, and similarly there seem to be demonic reinforcements in heathen life that account for the almost superhuman grandeur of the heathen empires, especially just before their fall.

Two particularly notable passages in the Old Testament prophets linked to this theme are the denunciation of Babylon in Isaiah 14 and of Tyre in Ezekiel 28. Babylon is associated with Lucifer the morning star, who said to himself: "I will be like the Most High"; Tyre is identified with a "Covering Cherub," a splendid creature living in the garden of Eden "till that day that iniquity was found in thee." In the New Testament (Luke 10:18) Jesus speaks of Satan as falling from heaven, hence Satan's traditional identification with Isaiah's Lucifer and his growth in legend into the great adversary of God, once the prince of the angels, and, before being displaced, the firstborn son of God. The superhuman demonic force behind the heathen kingdoms is called in Christianity the Antichrist, the earthly ruler demanding divine honors (GC 95).

Much of this demonology is late: it is not until the very end of the New Testament (Revelation 12) that we are explicitly told about a war in heaven and a revolt by a third of the angels. The Book of Revelation thus seems to be not merely a coda to the Bible, but a recognition scene, in which the mysteries latent in earlier imagery come to light. Later legend, in its efforts to reconcile Genesis 1:27 and 5:1 with the J account, developed the figure of Lilith, Adam's first wife and the mother of demons (GC 140). Again, the cursing of the serpent in the J account, who is there presented simply as a serpent, is accounted for by a later assumption that the serpent was the mouthpiece for Satan.

The beginnings of the demonic story, however, come very early in Genesis. First we have the account of the progeny of

Cain in Genesis 4: the descendants of Cain established arts, notably music, metallurgy and other elements of urban life, along with a renewal of Abel's pastoral world. But the Lamech episode at the end of the account seems to indicate the working out of a strain of evil that began with Cain's murder of Abel. Another starting point is the mysterious passage in Genesis 6:1-4 which tells how the "sons of God" were attracted by the "daughters of men," descended to the earth and begat on them a race of giants. These giants seem to have been a factor in provoking Noah's flood, yet they seem to have survived the flood, as their descendants continued to terrify the Israelites on the very borders of the Promised Land (Numbers 13:33). We pass on to "Nimrod the mighty hunter" and the vast project of Babel in Genesis 10-11.

One thing that we seem to have in these Genesis passages is a Biblical parallel or contrast to the age of heroes in Hesiod (though Josephus makes a comparison with the story of the Titans). In the account of the origin of giants God is represented as saying rather wearily:

My spirit shall not abide in [AV "strive with"] man for ever, for he is flesh, but his days shall be a hundred and twenty years.

Among the many things this could mean, one is perhaps that God is rejecting the Greek myth of the hero, the being of mixed divine and human origin with (usually) a divine father and a human mother. Nothing comparable to such a race of semi-divine heroes is recorded in Genesis, though in *Paradise Lost,* in the first two books, Milton is obviously associating many aspects of Classical heroism, as we find it in Ajax, Odysseus and Achilles, with the rebel angels.

The Genesis passage was the basis for the Book of Enoch, which expands to great length the story of the fall of the lecherous spirits. The Book of Enoch had some influence on the later and more decadent books of the New Testament (Jude

14 and II Peter 2:4). Perhaps that influence is reflected in the Book of Revelation too. We noted earlier the statement in Revelation 14:4 that the redeemed of the earth, said to be 144,000 in number, are all male celibates who have never been "defiled with women." One way to make sense of this phrase is perhaps to take it as an antitype (GC 79) to the angels who were so defiled in the Enoch account, although the superficial meaning of the passage seems to be only more patriarchal overkill.

The Classical parallels to the Enoch story, the descents of the gods, notably Jupiter, to various luscious females, the god being usually in some animal disguise, have been a popular feature of Western literature, as well as painting and music. Naturally these stories are more playful in tone than the Enoch story, though because of the inequality in the sexual partnership they create little affection for the gods. We can see why when we look at more humanized versions, like the *droit de seigneur* theme in *The Marriage of Figaro,* which brings out very clearly an underlying resentment against the over-privileged. Another step takes us into the almost proto-Marxist class antagonism of Lope de Vega's extraordinary play *The Sheep Well,* in which villagers rise in revolt against noblemen who make free with their women.

Clearly the hero with one divine and one human parent, even if the divinity is only an angel, has no place in a strictly monotheistic religion such as Judaism, or, much later, Islam. It was therefore something of a scandal, a relapse into Hellenizing mythopoeia, as it were, for Christianity to present a Christ begotten by God on a human mother. The New Testament story however suggests a more positive aspect to the Enoch myth. The Classical hero is normally a tragic figure whose divine and human intermixture tears him apart; the mixed parentage of Christ points to, at least, a reconciliation of the divine and human, and is therefore comic (in Dante's sense of Christianity as a *commedia*). Yeats's mythology, previously referred to, includes a cyclical conception of history in which

a tragic and heroic civilization is followed by a comic and social one. Each cycle begins mythically with the conjunction of
a divine bird and a human woman: Leda and the swan for the
Classical cycle, the Dove (Holy Spirit) and the Virgin for the
Christian one. A third cycle beginning in Ireland is prophesied
in his play *The Herne's Egg*. After Yeats's death a popular mythology with a similar shape arose with stories of chariots of
gods at the beginning of history and of flying saucers at the
present end of it. What concerns us here is the fact that the
Genesis myth amplified in Enoch has a positive and creative as
well as a sinister aspect.

The world of titans, primeval giants and devils has usually
been regarded as simply evil, and the word "demonic" is normally used, as it has been in this book, to mean a death-cen-
tered parody of human life. But what we are looking for now
is an area of *axis mundi* imagery that has creative as well as
destructive aspects, like the other three. In literature there is
an ascent and descent from and to the lower worlds that is evil
and sinister, and we may retain the word demonic for it. There
is also however a creative descent and ascent, and for this I
shall use the word "titanic." The imagery of the titanic takes
us into the lower depths of the imagery of descent and return
that we traced in the previous chapter, and brings us down to
the origins of human wisdom and power.

The Bible, as we indicated, is not very friendly to the heroic or the tragic, much less to the titanic, and the Bible's
ascendancy in our culture is the main reason for the tradition
of identifying the titanic with the demonic. Taking a more
inclusive view, there is no reason for making such a contrast
between the daimon of Socrates and a Christian guardian angel, or between what Wordsworth felt when he spoke of "huge
and mighty forms" in nature and what a Greek would have
felt when he thought of Dionysus or Artemis. Even the titanic
powers that raised Egypt and Babylonia to world-empires are
obviously regarded with a good deal of respect by the Old
Testament prophets.

Each of our axial surveys may be linked to a god or informing presence: the presiding deity of the ladder of higher wisdom, outlined in the fifth chapter, is Hermes the psychopomp, of the ladder of higher love, Eros; of the descent and return theme of lower love (i.e. fertility), Adonis. Our present hero of lower wisdom is Prometheus, the titan who created man, in some accounts, and the defier of the gods, who overthrew (or reduced to absurdity) the cult of sacrifice, and brought to man the fire that made his civilization possible. Traditionally, God creates man and his Word becomes flesh; in the Promethean context man creates his gods, and his flesh becomes word: that is, his body or created bodies develop consciousness. Such a Prometheus is a patron of the attitude, which has sporadically appeared in literature ever since Lucretius, of ignoring the gods on the ground that even if they exist they can only be alien beings unconcerned with human life. Goethe's poem on Prometheus has him say that he forms men in his own image to be like himself, to grieve and rejoice and above all to ignore the gods, just as he does:

Hier sitz ich, forme Menschen
Nach meinem Bilde,
Ein Geschlecht, das mir gleich sei,
Zu leiden, zu weinen,
Zu geniessen and zu freuen sich
Und dein nicht zu achten
Wie ich!

However, our most familiar picture of Prometheus is of the crucified titan tortured by a malicious sky-god, in other words a tragic figure like the Jesus of the Passion. The Bible rejects the conception of the larger-than-life hero, and it largely passes over the aspect of imagination we call tragedy, where a hero's struggles may meet with disaster not only in spite of his greatness, but often because of it. The tragic hero raises too many disturbing questions about the moral virtues of the gods and the irreconcilable conflicts within not only human but divine nature. Greek tragedies, on the other hand, were part of a Dionysus cult, and Dionysus, with his sufferings of death and dismemberment, is another form of the Promethean power behind what we are calling titanic creative energy.

It is Dionysus rather than Prometheus who is the central figure in Nietzsche, with his self-transcending Superman, his *Herrnmoral* with its celebration of heroic and aristocratic pride, and his final self-identification with Dionysus, whom he considers an "Antichrist" figure. The preoccupation with Dionysus develops out of his early *Birth of Tragedy*. Yeats also contrasts pagan and Dionysian ideals with Christian ones, with marked preferences for the former. But he is less rigorously anti-Christian than Nietzsche: in fact he is buried in a Christian churchyard.

As for Nietzsche, he may have believed or tried to believe that the perpetually dying Dionysus was a life-affirming figure, and that the Christ of the Resurrection was a life-denying one. But this hardly makes Nietzsche an Antichrist, who is described in the New Testament (II Thessalonians 2:4) as someone who "as God sitteth in the temple of God, shewing himself that he is God." This figure combines the statue or heathen presence profaning the Holy of Holies (Matthew 24:15) with a kind of demonic Narcissus who claims to be God himself. Such a figure has little to do with Nietzsche, but a good deal to do with Hitler and such fictional prototypes of Hitler as the Kurtz of Conrad's *Heart of Darkness,* whom we shall come to in a moment.

Blake had previously sketched the outlines of another kind of Antichrist in *The Marriage of Heaven and Hell,* where he contrasted good as "the passive that obeys reason" with evil as "the active springing from energy," and promised a "Bible of hell" that would explain this. In the later *Everlasting Gospel* he also contrasts the true Jesus who acts with "honest, triumphant pride" with the "creeping Jesus," the real Antichrist, who comes to terms with passivity and mediocrity. There are parallels with Nietzsche here, in the suggestion of *Herrnmoral* associated with Jesus, though Blake is well aware that rebellions against conventional morality are quite different from actual evil, and that he is not attacking the authentic Christian myth, but the institutional distortion of it that Kierkegaard called "Christendom."

The fact that Prometheus and Dionysus are tragic figures raises all the ambivalent aspects connected with tragedy, the one we are concerned with now being the duality within nature, discussed in the previous chapter, the contrast between Wordsworth's nature and de Sade's. This duality is what links together the titanic and the demonic. A cat knows when it is warm and well fed; if we add human consciousness to that feeling, we may get the beginnings of a Wordsworthian view of nature. A weasel is a ferocious predator, and if we add human consciousness to its ferocity we may get the beginnings of malice and a psychopathic pleasure in cruelty. This would be a fusion of reason and nature on a genuinely demonic level, of the sort that Gulliver's Houyhnhnm master suggests:

Although he hated the Yahoos of his country, yet he no more blamed them for their odious qualities, than he did a bird of prey for its cruelty. . . . But when a creature pretending to reason could be capable of such enormities, he dreaded lest the corruption of that faculty might be worse than brutality itself. He seemed therefore confident, that instead of reason, we were only possessed of some quality fitted to increase our natural vices.

In *King Lear*, the presence of Lear as king, whatever his human frailties, sustains what for Shakespeare's audience would be a "natural" society, in which authority and loyalty are functioning virtues. With Lear's abdication, a lower level of nature opens up, a parody of a natural society in which the leaders are predators, and which is set up primarily for their benefit. The great rush of animals into the imagery, and the feeling that the animal world symbolizes the total breakdown of human life into something subhuman, as in Albany's

> Humanity perforce must prey upon itself
> Like monsters of the deep (IV, ii, 52–53)

indicates a demonic descent that goes much further down than any animal, as the scene of the blinding of Gloucester shows. In demonic worlds there is a curious combination of the deliberate and the automatic: thus as soon as Duncan is murdered, Macbeth finds himself on a treadmill of evil, having to kill more and more people to make himself feel secure.

With *Macbeth* we move from demonic descent to demonic ascent, in other words to tyranny, the placing of evil in a position of supreme social power. Twentieth-century writers are, as we should expect, profoundly interested in this theme, and Conrad studies it in almost all of his major works. The Kurtz of *Heart of Darkness* is a particularly notable example, as he is the prototype of all the tyrant figures who have made the twentieth century perhaps the ghastliest in history.

The tyrant draws his strength from social hysteria, and this is what gives him the aura of possession by a supernaturally evil power. Conrad's Kurtz would like to "exterminate all the brutes" around him, without realizing that this is a perverted way of going native, of absorbing the darkness of which he has become the heart. The darkness is not the society of black people, but a fusion of that society with the "mean and greedy phantoms" of the white world and the ivory trade, the imperial tyranny that debases itself along with its victims. Kurtz also develops the paranoia inevitable in his situation, forming vast and grandiose plans and attracting fanatical devotion (one of his admirers remarks that he would have made a wonderful leader of a political party, as long as it was an extreme one). Such a man seems to be immune from death, like Big Brother in *1984*, and when he does die the fact is announced with contempt.

We can, up to a point, understand motivated evil, but unmotivated evil has something bafflingly inscrutable about it. When Iago is asked why he deliberately destroyed the lives and happiness of Othello and Desdemona, who had trusted him and never done him any harm, he replies only with obstinate silence. He doesn't know why himself, for one thing. True, at one point in a soliloquy, he suggests that Othello may have cuckolded him with Emilia, but he does not believe that: he is simply trying to poison the minds of the audience against Othello. More imaginative villains sometimes give us a sense of being imprisoned in an illusion which still implies an absence of self-knowledge. When Bosola is asked at the end of Webster's *Duchess of Malfi* how Antonio came by his death, he says:

In a mist: I know not how:
Such a mistake as I have often seen
In a play.

For Shakespeare or Webster to suggest devilish inspiration for their villains, whatever they or their audiences may have believed about devils, would be a dramatic cop-out. Christianity has never come up with anything much better than the metaphor of "lost soul" to explain the Iagos of the world: something essential to humanity is simply missing from such people, and nothing more can be said about the matter.

The modern conception of *Angst* or dread, however, does at least give us a name for the mystery. Kierkegaard defines the demonic, in *The Concept of Dread,* as "dread of the good," and good for Kierkegaard is connected with what he calls ethical or constructive freedom. In this kind of freedom the antithesis between freedom and compulsion vanishes: with a creative artist, for example, what he wants to do and what he has to do are the same thing. But Adam in paradise, the same book suggests, was in a state of abstract freedom separated from compulsion, and in such a state there is only one thing man can do with his freedom, and that is to throw it away. Gide's conception of *acte gratuit* is another approach to the paradox of abstract freedom: anyone who is in this state, or thinks he is in it, is like a man deprived of atmospheric pressure. Dostoevsky's *Dream of a Ridiculous Person* supplies a parallel with Kierkegaard's argument, in a parable that shows us how, confronted with a paradisal situation, man can only act the role of the serpent and destroy what is there. Aldous Huxley's *Island* makes a similar point, if much less incisively.

In tragedy the titanic and demonic appear in the context of a self-destructive or anti-social impulse, of the kind expressed in Greek tragedy by the word *hybris,* the excessive action which is both conscious and mechanical, the result of a *hamartia* or "flaw," which is not a moral defect but a situation so maladjusted that prudent or temperate action is impossible. The reason for the maladjustment is often simply the presence of heroism itself, which by definition is too big to fit the situation it is in. The primary response to a tragic action is not sympathy with or condemnation of the chief characters, but a recognition of the inevitability of the action. This is not the same thing as a sense of fatality, though closely allied to it, and often confused with it. It is however the lurking connection with fatality that helps to keep the Bible aloof from tragic themes: even in Job the tragic action employs Satan as a kind of lightning rod deflecting the divine will.

In the Romantic period the tragic vision modulated to a different though related theme. There is a series of potentially tragic figures in the Old Testament (GC 181), Cain, Ishmael, Esau, Saul, who seem to be first in line for a divinely ordained inheritance, but are passed over for younger successors, often for mysterious or inscrutable reasons. We find a renewed sympathy for such figures in Romantic literature: examples are

Byron's *Cain* and the narrator Ishmael in *Moby Dick*. But the type is also very common in Victorian literature with no explicit Biblical connections, where the "lost heir" plot is a standard device, the story of the rightful successor returning to claim his inheritance.

In the fifth book of *Paradise Lost* we see the passing over of Lucifer by God the Father in honor of the newly begotten Christ. This story is of course not in the Bible, but it fits very well into the Biblical mythical pattern we are noting. Romanticism included a movement of diabolism which made Lucifer into a heroic and sympathetic figure, or even the true God. Many examples can be found in Mario Praz's *Romantic Agony*, which traces various subsidiary trends like the reversal of good and evil in followers of de Sade. The feeling is usually directed against the sky-god of authoritarian Christianity, and idealizes a figure who partakes of human nature, including its evil aspects, on the ground that the moral conformity demanded by the sky-god deprives humanity of its essential creative energies.

Some of this half-Biblical titanism in the Romantic period is nostalgia for a vanishing aristocracy, but there is more to it than that. To return to the story of the origin of giants in Genesis, amplified in the Book of Enoch: there is a spirited resistance to the uniformly demonic reading of this story in Charlotte Brontë's *Shirley*, in a chapter called, ironically, "The Blue-Stocking." This chapter contains an essay purportedly written by Shirley as a French exercise, which treats the encounter of angel and woman as the encounter of Genius and Humanity, in other words as a titanic spiritualizing of human beings, specifically female beings.

Shirley had previously spoken of the Eve of Milton's *Paradise Lost* as insipid, and asserted that the real mother of mankind must have been an awe-inspiring goddess figure much more like the traditional Lilith. The character of Shirley is often thought to be partly modeled on Emily Brontë, though, as Shirley has more money and a higher social position than her prototype, she would find it easier to speak her mind in ordinary conversation. Byron's *Heaven and Earth* also deals with the same Genesis passage, but naturally (being Byron's) contains no feminist enzyme. Charlotte Brontë seems, on whatever level of consciousness, to have reconstructed the full reversal of the Enoch story, in which "man," in the form of woman, is reunited to his (her) divine nature. In the Enoch story itself and its Classical counterparts, the subordination of the female partner is the sign of a turning of the wheel of time, not a movement out of it, hence Yeats's use of the bird–woman union as an image of historical cycles.

Themes of descent often turn on the struggle between the titanic and the demonic within the same person or group. In *Moby Dick,* Ahab's quest for the whale may be mad and "monomaniacal," as it is frequently called, or even evil so far as he sacrifices his crew and ship to it, but evil or revenge are not the point of the quest. The whale itself may be only a "dumb brute," as the mate says, and even if it were malignantly determined to kill Ahab, such an attitude, in a whale hunted to the death, would certainly be understandable if it were there. What obsesses Ahab is in a dimension of reality much further down than any whale, in an amoral and alienating world that nothing normal in the human psyche can directly confront.

The professed quest is to kill Moby Dick, but as the portents of disaster pile up it becomes clear that a will to identify with (not adjust to) what Conrad calls the destructive element is what is really driving Ahab. Ahab has, Melville says, become a "Prometheus" with a vulture feeding on him. The axis image appears in the maelstrom or descending spiral ("vortex") of the last few pages, and perhaps in a remark by one of Ahab's crew: "The skewer seems loosening out of the middle of the world." But the descent is not purely demonic, or simply destructive: like other creative descents, it is partly a quest for wisdom, however fatal the attaining of such wisdom may be. A relation reminiscent of Lear and the fool develops at the end between Ahab and the little black cabin boy Pip, who has been left so long to swim in the sea that he has gone insane. Of him it is said that he has been "carried down alive to wondrous depths, where strange shapes of the unwarped primal world glided to and fro . . . and the miser-merman, Wisdom, revealed his hoarded heaps."

Moby Dick is as profound a treatment as modern literature affords of the leviathan symbolism of the Bible, the titanic-demonic force that raises Egypt and Babylon to greatness and then hurls them into nothingness; that is both an enemy of God outside the creation, and, as notably in Job, a creature within it of whom God is rather proud. The leviathan is revealed to Job as the ultimate mystery of God's ways, the "king over all the children of pride" (41:34), of whom Satan himself is merely an instrument. What this power looks like depends on how it is approached. Approached by Conrad's Kurtz through his Antichrist psychosis, it is an unimaginable horror: but it may also be a source of energy that man can put to his own use. There are naturally considerable risks in trying to do so: risks that Rimbaud spoke of in his celebrated *lettre du voyant* as a "dérèglement de tous les sens." The phrase indicates the close connection between the titanic and the demonic that Verlaine expressed in his phrase *poète maudit,* the attitude of poets who feel, like Ahab, that the right worship of the powers they invoke is defiance.

It is Verlaine too who portrays, in his poem "Crimen Amoris," a poet with a strong resemblance to Rimbaud, who arises from a group of devils engaged in the seven deadly sins with the Luciferian cry that he will become as God ("O je serai celui-là qui sera Dieu!"). He proposes the union of Christ and Satan in a love that will transcend the antithesis of good and evil, and burns hell up with a torch. He is then destroyed by the sky-god because his love is not of the kind that the sky-god approves. This gives us the reverse side of Rimbaud's own attitude when he was writing his poetry, his realization that for a genuine *poète maudit* the reprobate state is also the regenerate one. Rimbaud, however, escaped from his "season in hell" by abandoning, and eventually repudiating, his poetry altogether, and by the end of his life he had perhaps come around to the masochism of Verlaine's vision.

A more thoroughgoing "dérèglement" than Rimbaud attempted is recorded in Gérard de Nerval's *Aurélia,* the first part of which is an almost clinical account of a mind descending into a world of primordial forces coming through dream and fantasy that are at once illuminating and destructive to it. Much of it covers territory we have previously glanced at: the double, the stream of ancestors, the "layers" (*couches*) of buried civilizations. In the second and perhaps more recognizably sick part, there is more confusion in the imagery, but a still determined effort to penetrate to some kind of source of psychic wisdom and energy that will give some definite function to both dreaming and waking worlds.

At the beginning of *Aurélia* de Nerval refers to his predecessors in vision: they include Swedenborg and Apuleius, besides Dante. Swedenborg, with his hypnagogic visions of a hell below and a heaven above the middle world of ordinary consciousness, is a major influence on literature in the 1750–1850 period, although he seems to have been able to remain a detached observer, not taken over by the demonic powers he glimpsed. Apuleius records a descent to a lower state of being symbolized by metamorphosis into an ass, from which the narrator is rescued, or rather redeemed, by the goddess Isis, who also appears in de Nerval. The Cupid and Psyche story in Apuleius is not a mere inserted episode, but a counter-vision of the real relation between love and the soul, the relation obliterated by the evil enchantment pushing the narrator into the hell of brutality that the ass endures.

If Dante's *Inferno* stood by itself, we should lack the key to it, the *Vita Nuova* with its focus on the Beatrice figure who, naturally, is not to be found in hell, but reappears at the end of the *Purgatorio*, preceded by Lucia and Matelda. Similarly, the key to *Aurélia* is the lovely pastoral idyl *Sylvie*, the song of innocence preceding the later song of experience. In *Sylvie* the male and female elements are stabilized on a pre-sexual, brother-sister basis; in *Aurélia* the extrusion of the female figures, who appear in judgmental and disapproving roles, is mainly what makes the descent so destructive to the narrator. *Sylvie* begins with both a reference to Apuleius and the phrase "ivory tower" (Song of Songs 7:4), which is used here as a symbol of ascending vision, a long way removed from the vulgar and stupid cliché that it has since become.

Close to de Nerval is the theme of a quest for the wisdom that more mysterious realms in the psyche may reveal to consciousness. We do not know what the underworld wisdom was for which Odin lost an eye, but we can read the directive issued to Keats's Endymion at the bottom of the sea, and the cipher that Poe's Arthur Gordon Pym finds at the bottom of the world (i.e. the South Pole). Inner quests are of course exposed to all the perils of the demonic: they may simply take one into the hell of James Thomson's *City of Dreadful Night*, or into the dark tower of Browning's "Childe Roland" poem, but there seems a compulsion to make such journeys nonetheless.

George Macdonald's *Phantastes* also deals with an inner quest: the hero's name is Anodos, but his adventure is really a *kathodos*, a descent to what a post-Freudian reader would immediately recognize as an Oedipal situation in which the hero resigns the possession of the heroine to a father-surrogate. It is hardly surprising to find infantile elements in such descent narratives as *Phantastes* or the second part of *Aurélia*, in view of the central importance of childhood experiences in forming the structure of the unconscious. But the infantile tends to block off the quest for the renewal of wisdom and energy which is the real object of the descent, and substitute for it a renewal of dependence on parental projections.

In many of these descent narratives, as well as in most tragedies, one of the most persistent conventions is the use of omens, portents, or some image that anticipates the later catastrophe. The ominous, however malignant, indicates the presence of something that participates in human concern. Man apparently cannot do without some sense of meaning directed toward himself: if the feeling that the world was created or designed for him fails, he will settle for a belief that he is uniquely accursed, the scapegoat of creation. It is the feeling that there is nothing at all outside himself aware of his existence that drives him up the wall—that is, drives him up the ladder of the *axis mundi* in search of something that conforms to his paranoia.

So far we have been speaking mainly of a descent into the individual psyche, a quest which, like death itself, must be carried out alone. There is a still more radical creative descent to examine to make this type of imagery fully intelligible.

What did God make the world from, or out of? The orthodox answer is "out of nothing" (*ex nihilo*), with its corollary that nothing is co-eternal with God. Milton protests in the *De Doctrina Christiana* that there must be something wrong with this formulation, because the product of anything and nothing is still nothing, and it makes more sense to think of creation as having been produced from God (*de Deo*). The *ex nihilo* doctrine is even more puzzling when we realize the extent to which the conception of creation is a metaphor drawn from a human process, as clearly human beings cannot create out of nothing.

Apart from the "no thing" aspect of the word, which is an accident of the English form of it, we are confronted first of all by the double meaning of nothing as meaning both "not anything" and "something called nothing." The latter is normally spelled with a capital N, to distinguish the non-existent from a negative existent. For something called nothing is still something, whatever it is called. So if we say that nothing is co-eternal with God, we make a very innocuous, not to say tautological, statement, but if we say "Nothing (nothingness, something called nothing) is co-eternal with God" we are making a very different statement, and to many people a most disturbing one. Bergson's "Existence is a conquest over Nothing" needs the capital, otherwise it means that there is no conquest at all. "Dread reveals nothing" says that dread, whatever it is, can hardly be very important; Heidegger's "Dread reveals Nothing" means the exact opposite, and gives a central significance to dread. Or we might put it this way:

A. There is nothing to be afraid of.
B. Wrong. There is Nothing to be afraid of.

This shift from zero as nothing to zero as the basis of number has been incorporated into various philosophical and literary contexts. Of those in the Christian theological tradition, perhaps Boehme is the most thoroughgoing in showing that the conception of God is essentially connected with nothingness, that the presence of God appears in an *Urgrund* from which all conditions and attributes of being have been withdrawn. Boehme's vision of the creation anticipates Hegel in speaking of a negating of negation, a transforming of God from nothingness to an infinite something, which left the nothingness behind as a kind of vacuum suction, drawing everything within its reach into non-being. The abandoned nothingness is the principle of evil, the Lucifer or light-bearer which turns into the adversary of light, or Satan, after the light or Word has freed itself. This may sound difficult, but Boehme is difficult. The essential point is the association of nothingness and divine creation, an association that fascinated Yeats, who refers to Boehme in his play *The Unicorn from the Stars,* in which the climactic phrase is "Where there is nothing, there is God."

In Eliot's "Burnt Norton" the influence is St. John of the Cross rather than Boehme, but there too we are urged to descend far lower than death or hell, into a world described purely in negatives, though one in which the presence of God is still to be found. A more ironic version is in Henry James's *The Beast in the Jungle,* a story about a man to whom nothing has ever happened, although he is obsessed by the notion that some overwhelming experience lies in wait for him. The obsession causes him to ignore the significance of everything that actually does occur, and he is finally destroyed when Nothing happens to him.

We mentioned Hegel, who tells us that every affirmation, simply because it affirms, contains its own negation as a part of itself, a negation that is negated again and turned into a positive. As usual, the literary counterparts of negation are not as carefully studied, but are all there to be studied. There is the ordinary use of the words myth, fiction or fable as stories about nothing that ever really was. There is Theseus' conception of imagination as seeing things that are not there. There is the fact that characters of fiction have no existence, which compels us, as remarked earlier, to consider what is physically nothing as what is spiritually true. And there is the nothingness of time and space, with their dimensions that never quite seem to exist. All of this is familiar to us by now.

In the second part of *Faust* we are told that Faust himself, without help from Mephistopheles, must descend to the realm of the "Mothers" to bring up the deeper mythical archetypes, such as Helen of Troy, that eventually expanded into the Classical Walpurgis Night. No details are given about Faust's journey, but the phrases used about it are interesting, especially his hope of finding the All in the Nothing: "In deinem Nichts hoff' ich das All zu finden." We notice the close connection of the word "All" with the theme of the negating of nothingness. In the conversations with Eckermann, Goethe surrounds his "Mothers" with some mystification, and perhaps, if one may say so with all due reverence, he may not have had a very clear idea of what he was talking about himself. It has been pointed out that "Mütter" and "Mythe" form practically a pun in German, and perhaps the world of the "Mothers" is also the world where the stories that are about nothing, verbal energy without content, take shape on the threshold just below consciousness. To the extent that they have content it is a content of otherness, an evocation of mysterious powers and forces so remote from human control that it seems appropriate to place them in some metaphorical setting below the subjective and objective worlds.

The human poet does not create out of nothing; he creates out of his previous experience of literature. But he stares at nothing, so to speak, and negates himself as a subject as well as negating the objective environment. He is in the position of Wallace Stevens's observer looking at "The Snow Man," who is "nothing himself," and sees both "Nothing that is not there and the nothing that is." Hence, like Donne's geographer painting a map of the world on a globe, he "can quickly make that which was nothing, all," or at least potentially all. It is also Donne who introduces the theme of negating nothing, in an alchemical context, in his "Nocturnal upon St. Lucy's Day." Mallarmé, who was fascinated with such words as "aboli," is pre-eminently the poet of the nothingness of the world the descending poet enters. The celebrated poem usually called the "sonnet in yx" describes how Dread or Angst (L'angoisse) inhabits a deserted room, deserted because its master has left for the lower world ("Styx"), taking with him "ce seul objet dont le Néant s'honore," a "ptyx" which could mean fifty things and also means nothing.

In *Igitur* the central character descends a staircase, commanded by his ancestors to take a candle with him which he blows out at midnight, recalling the "chapel perilous" image of medieval romance, then throws (or perhaps merely shakes) dice, and lies down on the ashes of his ancestors, described as the "ashes of stars," for the stars seem to keep recurring in Mallarmé with a Dantean persistence. In *The Ancient Mariner* a throw of dice accompanies the victory of Life-in-Death over Death; in Mallarmé the dice represent a world where, in Yeats's phrase, choice and chance are one. Throwing dice is a commitment to chance that does not abolish chance, but is in itself a free act, and so begins a negating of negation that brings something, perhaps ultimately everything, into being again. A connection has been suggested between Mallarmé's word "Igitur" and the Vulgate text of Genesis 2:3, *igitur perfecti sunt coeli.* This has been discredited for lack of evidence, but it is a most penetrating comment nonetheless. For Mallarmé was also preoccupied by the opposite of his "Néant" world, speaking of a kind of definitive book that would contain the entire verbal cosmos and would be in literature what the "Great Work" was to "our ancestors, the alchemists." We shall return shortly to this metaphor of alchemy.

Looking back to the suggested connection between "Mütter" and "Mythe," I have long been fascinated by the opening and setting of William Morris's *Earthly Paradise*. The prelude to this collection of tales in verse tells how two groups of wanderers meet together on a lonely island in the midst of the Atlantic Ocean after having visited several societies that tried to make them into kings or gods. Once on their island, they proceed to tell stories, two for each month of the year, one story Classical and the other Northern in origin. Whatever one thinks of the level of poetic ability displayed in the telling of these romances, something of far-ranging importance for the theory of criticism is bound up with them.

Morris showed all his life, as a poet, a tendency to translate or otherwise retell every standard story in literature, and the sense of the great stories as forming a complementary Classical-Northern shape reminds us of Goethe and the way in which the Classical symbolism of the second part of *Faust* complements the Northern setting of the first part. There is a rather relaxed and dreamy quality about Morris's setting (he calls himself "the idle singer of an empty day") that makes it sound curiously pointless and ineffectual for so vigorous a writer. But perhaps the suggestion is that we are at the bottom of the human creative mind, watching the great narrative shapes emerging, with their vast latent powers as yet unused.

Morris is, of course, following Chaucer and many other writers in using the device of a group or society of story-tellers, each contributing a story to a series. With a controlling mind at work, this gives the sense of myth expanding into mythology, a body of stories corresponding to a latent and embryonic social body, and forming the outlines of a cultural tradition. The title "Earthly Paradise," too, suggests something considerably more positive than a mere retreat of old men to a lonely island. It suggests in fact the goal of a journey of creative ascent.

The three elements of this variation, the demonic parody, the ideological adaptation and the authentic myth, should be reasonably clear by now. The demonic parody is the descent into nothingness, and may involve only an individual life or a whole society. Antichrist can descend to hell, even harrow it, but what he brings up is only a hell to earth. The ideological adaptation to this is the realization that power always corrupts, but that nothing can be done about the ascendancy of such corrupt power in human society. Defenders of the doctrine of the divine right of kings said that if the king were a ferocious tyrant God was punishing his victims through him, and even the revolutionary Milton has Michael explain to Adam that tyranny is inevitable because the victims of the tyrant are tyrants to themselves. The creative descent to a lower wisdom is a descent to the sources of genuine human power, and the ascent from there is the authentic myth that we shall be concerned with in the remainder of this chapter. We are told how difficult and heroic a quest this ascent is by the Sibyl in Aeneid VI, in one of the most frequently quoted passages in all literature:

facilis descensus Averno:
noctes atque dies patet atri ianua Ditis;
sed revocare gradum superasque evadere ad auras,
hoc opus, hic labor est. (126–9)

In a poem of Robert Frost, "West-Running Brook," there is a dialogue between a male and female speaker taking place on a mountain watershed where all the brooks are flowing toward the east except one that has decided to go in the opposite direction. Despite its originality, however, it is still flowing downward toward the sea, like all brooks. But then the man notices an eddying movement in its current that arrests the flow downward and seems to be standing up against the current. He sees in this a figure of the imagination itself, the human consciousness born from nature and yet resisting nature with its own natural energy:

It is from this in nature we are from.
It is most us.

We conclude by pursuing the theme of creative ascent suggested by Frost's brook, which, like the river of Eden, divides into four streams: the purgatorial, the technological, the educational and the Utopian. These correspond to the four main aspects of Prometheus: the tormented champion of mankind, the bringer of fire to man, the god of forethought (the traditional meaning of his name) and the ultimate creator of humanity.

II

Let us start with the technological imagery, of which there is a surprising amount in the Bible, beginning with the account of the descendants of Cain in Genesis 4. Cain was a farmer, but his name could suggest smith, and, as we saw, his descendants developed urban as well as pastoral modes of life, including metallurgy. There is always a good deal of ambivalence about technological developments, both inside and outside the Bible, partly because a great deal of such development is inspired by war, and consists in improving lethal weapons. Milton was following a well-established theme of his time when he represented the devils as inventing gunpowder and artillery during the war in heaven. The same principle of destruction being the mother of invention recurs in our time, when so many scientific developments have to take second place to military demands.

Even what seem obviously progressive inventions are often resisted by conservatism. Thus when the god Thoth, at the end of Plato's *Phaedrus,* proudly displays his invention of writing, he is merely told that he has discovered a means of destroying the human memory. The "sin" of Prometheus in transmitting to mankind the primary means of technology, fire, also aroused the greatest anxiety among the Olympians. We are told in the Book of Enoch that the fallen angels, having become devils, then taught mankind the arts, so that we are hardly surprised to find that the book's response to their culture is a horrified what's-the-world-coming-to. The release of titanic powers in man through invention is feared and dreaded at every stage in history, partly because of the intertwining of the titanic and the demonic, and partly because technology, having no will of its own, is readily projected as a mysterious, external and sinister force. Thus the primary invention of the wheel suggested the symbolism of the wheels of fate and fortune.

So metallurgy readily acquires a dubious reputation in the symbolism of the ancient world, more particularly the working in iron, which comes fairly late. In the Old Testament the building of altars to God is sometimes accompanied by taboos on the use of iron in constructing them (Joshua 8:31), not merely because iron was new, and religious conservatism rejected it, but because the overtones of "iron age" suggest a debasing of culture.

Similarly, the smith in mythology often has a sinister reputation: the swords and shields he makes often have magical properties, and the lurking menace of magic clings to them. Smiths, including Hephaistos and the Anglo-Saxon Weyland, are often lame, perhaps recalling a custom of hamstringing slave-smiths to prevent them from wandering to other masters. The implication is that smiths, whatever the view taken of them, were rare and very useful artisans, and when the Philistines, and later the Babylonians, occupied Israel (later Judah), they carried all the smiths away to their own centers (I Samuel 13:19; Jeremiah 24:1).

The smith often represents a destructive force, as apparently in Zechariah 1:20. In this verse the AV reads "carpenters": in Biblical Hebrew it is sometimes difficult to distinguish the worker in wood from the worker in metal except by the context. But just as there can be benevolent carpenters, like the New Testament Joseph and traditionally Jesus himself, so there can be creative smiths, like the forger of the new Jerusalem in Isaiah 54:16. This smith, who creates a new city glowing with gems and gold, represents perhaps the closest Biblical parallel to the symbolism of alchemy, and is the Biblical basis for Blake's conception of his culture-hero, the blacksmith Los working with his furnaces.

The image of the furnace may be used for either the negative or positive aspects of the lower world. The negative or demonic world is the traditional hell which is a furnace of heat without light. The positive one is purgatorial, a crucible from which the redeemed emerge purified like metal in a smelting operation. Thus the Egypt from which Israel has been delivered is spoken of several times as a "furnace of iron," and the purity of the spiritual body is sometimes symbolized by metal (Revelation 1:15). Images of refinement and purification in a furnace recur in connection with language (Psalm 12:6) as well as in the afflictions of life (Proverbs 17:3; Isaiah 48:10). The best known of these purgatorial furnaces is the one constructed by Nebuchadnezzar for his attempted martyrdom of the three faithful Jews in the Book of Daniel. Their song in the Apocrypha is a highly concentrated praise to God for the beauty and glory of the original creation, which their purification in the furnace has evidently enabled them to see. Obviously, in this extension of furnace symbolism, we have modulated from the technological to the purgatorial, and the furnace has become the human body.

In the Septuagint the word "furnace" (*kaminos*) identifies a number of different words in Hebrew (we may compare [GC 177] the Septuagint *kibotos*, ark or chest, which identifies Noah's ark and the ark of the covenant). In Isaiah 31:9 "furnace" is a metaphor for the fire on the altar, and in Abraham's vision in Genesis 15 God puts a "furnace" (RSV "pot") between the pieces of the animals Abraham has cut in two. The use of furnace in this context suggested an apocalyptic prophecy to Christopher Smart in *Jubilate Agno:*

For the furnace shall come up at last according to Abraham's vision.

We have two aspects of all these furnace images and their relatives: an environment which is either evil and to be escaped from, or imperfect and to be transformed by an inward fire. The transforming inward fire is, we said, the energy of the human body, and the physical body is a metaphorical crucible for the spiritual body that arises from it. The phrase "candle of the Lord" in the Book of Proverbs (20:27), Jesus' adaptation of this image in urging us to let the inner lights of our bodies shine out and not cover them with inertia or deliberately darkened vision (Matthew 5:15), and the association of the apocalyptic revelation with fire and light at the end of the Biblical story all belong here. Closely linked is the parable of the talents, which in English has transformed a word meaning a certain weight of precious metal into a word meaning an inner creative power.

It is an easy metaphorical step from here to thinking of the poet's body as a purgatorial crucible in which his work is forged. Such images are, as we should expect, most frequent in the Romantic period, when we have Blake beginning *Milton* by invoking the inspiration that flows from the garden of Eden in his brain into his arm, Keats recreating the goddess Psyche and her cult in his own mind, Coleridge describing the poet as having fed on the milk and honey of paradise and as reviving within himself the song of the maiden in Abyssinia (supposed by some to be the site of Paradise, according to Milton).

The creative body may also be linked to two images in the *Odyssey:* the two entrances to the cave of the Nymphs, one for mortals and the other for immortals (xiii, 110 ff.), and the two gates of dreams, the gate of ivory for illusory dreams and the gate of horn for genuine ones (xix, 562 ff.: see also *Aeneid,* vi, 893 ff.). As a product of nature, the human psyche sucks in a vast body of raw data for the imagination through dreams, fantasies, sense impressions of the outer world, emotional reaction to other psyches, and so on. We call a good deal of this real, but from the point of view of human creation all of it is illusion. Its content may be creative or demonic, noble or vicious, tender or cruel: it brings with it both the evils and the virtues of its natural origin. This illusory material is processed by consciousness, and the consciousness lives in a world it considers real, though its whole central area is an artefact it has constructed itself.

Similar metaphorical thinking developed the later doctrine of purgatory as an after-death world of purification, normally symbolized by fire. In Dante, of course, *Purgatorio* is the middle section of the three parts of the total divine comedy, but there is a larger sense in which the visions of hell and heaven are a part of the purgatorial vision for Dante as narrator of the poem, and consequently for us as readers of it. The *Inferno* describes what is a purgatory for Dante rather than a hell, because he escapes from it, and the *Paradiso* completes an educating and refining process that the *Purgatorio* has begun.

The Biblical pattern for the purgatorial vision is the Exodus narrative, which is in three major parts. First is the sojourn in Egypt, the "furnace of iron," a world visited by plagues, where the Egyptian desire to exterminate the Hebrews goes into reverse with the slaughter of the Egyptian firstborn sons. This episode concludes with the crossing of the Red Sea, the separation of Israel from Egypt, and the drowning of the Egyptian host. The second episode is the wandering in the wilderness, a labyrinthine period of lost direction, where one generation has to die off before a new one can enter the Promised Land (Psalm 95:11). This is one of several features indicating that we are in a world transcending history, and that it is in the more poetic language of the prophets that the true or symbolic meaning of Egypt, wilderness and Promised Land emerges more clearly.

The third stage is the entry into the Promised Land, where Moses, personifying the older generation, died just outside it. In Christian typology (GC 172; *Paradise Lost* xii, 307 ff.) this means that the law, which Moses symbolizes, cannot redeem mankind: only his successor Joshua, who bears the same name as Jesus, can invade and conquer Canaan. And yet Canaan seems a rather shrunken and anticlimactic form of the paradisal land of promise flowing with milk and honey that was originally promised to Israel. Perhaps Moses was really the only person to see the Promised Land: perhaps the mountain outside it he climbed in his last hours was the only place from which it could be seen.

In Dante the *Inferno* corresponds to the confinement in Egypt, and the approach to Purgatory to the crossing of the Red Sea (those making the approach are singing the appropriate Psalm, 114). *Purgatorio* proper corresponds to the wandering in the wilderness, the labyrinthine element being conventionalized into a spiral climb up a mountain; and the giants and other enemies on the borders of the Promised Land correspond to the polarizing of good and evil visions at the end of the *Purgatorio*. We have the unveiling of Beatrice's face contrasted with the exposed "ventre" of the Siren; the chariot of the griffin of faith contrasted with the progression of the Beast and the Whore; Dante's achieving of free will, where he becomes his own Pope and Emperor, against his condemnation by Beatrice as one who has forgotten and abandoned the divine vision personified in her. Here the *Purgatorio* is following the structure of the Bible, which leads to a similar apocalyptic polarization, and also encapsulating the function of literature itself, as a historical product enabling us to see history from above and below.

In Spenser's *Faerie Queene* the world called "Faerie" represents a higher level of nature, a world of moral realization where virtues and vices separate from one another. The conception of human life as repeating the myth of the Exodus is clearest in the first book, where the Redcross Knight goes through a sequence of purgatorial visions up to his final battle with the dragon of death and hell on the boundary of the Promised Land or regained Eden, which he wins for the heroine Una. The phrase about the purpose of human life in one of Keats's letters, a "vale of soul-making," is also purgatorial, though neither of Keats's longer poems seems to have quite that shape. Strindberg's later plays, especially the "Damascus" series and *The Great Highway,* also assimilate human life to a purgatorial vision, usually with some imagery of ascent underlying it, although Strindberg reverts to the traditional penal conception of purgatory.

In any case the fall of the hierarchical chain-of-being cosmos enabled poets to treat Promethean symbolism and the emergence of titanic powers in man more freely. Goethe's Faust, at the end of the Second Part, is dragged off to heaven as arbitrarily as his prototype was to hell, because all is forgiven to the man who continually strives, as God explained to Mephistopheles back in the original Prologue. The First Part is called a tragedy, though it is very little of one for Faust himself, who manages to push the real suffering off on Gretchen. But still the imagery of an upward ascent is fairly well preserved at the beginning and end of the Second Part.

In Blake's later "Prophecies" the main theme is the fall and redemption of Albion, the giant human body in whom the totality and unity of human beings are the same thing. Albion's fall was the same thing as the appearance of the Genesis creation as we now see it, and his redemption is the work of Los, a blacksmith god whose pounding hammer is also the beating of the human heart and whose furnaces are the creative powers of a warm-blooded animal. That Los should be a worker in iron seems curious in view of Blake's strongly anti-technological attitude, but he thinks of his own time as an "iron age" which is revolutionary because it is a time in which there is nowhere to go but up. Los is also the spirit of prophecy, which is equated with the arts and with creative time. "The Tyger" is a powerful fusion of technological and purgatorial imagery associated with creation, and the Promethean aspect of it comes out in the line "What the hand dare seize the fire?"

In Eliot's more traditional mythical schema the purgatorial process does not simply arise from the lower depths of the human psyche, but is a human response to a divine Spirit descending in tongues of flame. The divine descent and the human response inform the two stanzas of the lyric in the fourth section of "Little Gidding," the latter being associated with Hercules' funeral pyre: Hercules, because he was one of the very few human beings to enter the community of gods in Greek mythology. Throughout "Little Gidding," which was written during the bombing of London, there runs also a demonic parody of bombs falling and fires breaking out in the streets. This forms the setting of a dialogue between the narrator and a "familiar compound ghost" representing the poetic tradition. The setting deliberately recalls a scene in Dante's *Inferno,* but when the ghost discusses the social function of the poet he gives a purgatorial twist to a phrase of Mallarmé: the poet's task, he says, is "to *purify* the dialect of the tribe."

Yeats's "Byzantium" also describes a mysterious technological-purgatorial-alchemical world in which "blood-begotten spirits" cross water at their death to be processed in "smithies," and go through a purgatorial operation which involves dance, fire and transformation into "glory of changeless metal." In Yeats, as in Eliot, a descending movement of the old chain-of-being type complements the purgatorial ascent. Eliot preserves its more traditional Christian features; but in Yeats's "Sailing to Byzantium," we get a more paradoxical vision of the divine, spiritual, human and natural elements in the chain—as, respectively, a "drowsy Emperor," sages in "God's holy fire," lords and ladies of Byzantium, and a toy bird in a golden tree representing nature transfigured into the "artifice of eternity." The vision is not one of authority or divine grace but of an order raised above time, where the poet sings of past, present and future in the final line. Both the Byzantium poems may cause us to wonder whether Yeats is talking about life after death or about the poet's imaginative transforming of reality. We soon realize that this is one of those either-or questions that have to be turned into both-and answers before it makes sense.

This last point indicates that the purgatorial processes already traced include the theme of the poet's self-education, the perfecting of his skill and the social function of his craft. We notice how prominent in Dante's *Purgatorio* is the figure of Statius, the poetic disciple of Virgil who had surpassed Virgil in the sense of accepting the Christian revelation, and so becomes a prototype, almost a kind of double, of Dante himself. Statius is one of many poets and painters in the *Purgatorio* who constitute a cultural tradition clarifying and improving itself as it goes on, the improvement being not so much in the quality of the work as in its effectiveness as a civilizing force. The implications of "civilizing" are not purely secular: as remarked earlier, there is no society so evil that it cannot produce something attractive in its culture, and the cultural achievement is the center of a vision of innocence, a lost but partially regained paradise.

At the end of the *Paradiso* Dante has reached the top of the *axis mundi,* and is in the presence of God, where the question "What happens next?" has no answer and no meaning. The goal of the creative ascent is the transcending of time and space as we know them, and the attaining of a present and a presence in another dimension altogether. The present is the expanded moment of awareness that is as long as recorded human history; the presence is the love that moves the sun and the other stars. But of course the journey takes place when Dante is still alive as we understand the word, and in that context "What happens next?" does have a meaning. With the next tick of the clock he resumes the horizontal journey of his fourteenth-century existence. There has to be a second coming for Dante, as traditionally for Jesus, and the final vision may include the suggestion that Dante is confident of his own salvation after his death. But primarily it means that he is confident of the salvation of his poetic vision, as an offering acceptable to God.

The image of an acceptable offering suggests some generic affinities between literature and prayer. Prayer is not directly addressed to anyone in this world, though others may overhear it, and though it is in part a talking to oneself, a way of achieving self-awareness without introversion. It is therefore related to the utterance of poets who praise without praising anything or anyone, who write in defiance of contemporary response, who claim a spiritual authority that nothing in nature or society seems to justify.

The primary concern of this fourth variation is property,

in the Aristotelian sense of what is proper to mankind, an extension of human power which is still a part of human identity. Possession, first of land, then of money, is the traditional form of property, and most of the great moral teachers, certainly including the Biblical ones, have been at pains to show that such possessions, which are so easily lost or are gained by the losses of others, are not a genuine concern in themselves, but, like sex and food, have to expand into other dimensions of existence before they become so. To clarify this we have to distinguish between social and individual property. Social property, whoever controls it, is based on what are usually called instruments of production, the technological advances that give human beings command over the environment. Individual property, when it is a genuine extension of human identity, consists of the verbal, mathematical, pictorial and other creative faculties of human beings.

The *fear* of technology is linked to the fear of something anti-creative in the mind, something that produces the mechanical act that repeats without knowing why, the clinging to set patterns of behavior however self-destructive or foolish. The creative opposite of this is the stabilizing repetition of practice, of what is called *habitus* in Latin and *hexis* in Greek, the repetition that gradually accumulates a skill. This contrast takes us back to Nature's distinction in Spenser's *Mutabilitie Cantos* between those over whom change rules and those who rule over change. Creative repetition is one of the central themes of the wisdom literature of the Old Testament, and reappears in such formulas as "without ceasing" (Romans 1:19, etc.) in the New.

The practice that develops a creative skill is also a descent journey, an assimilation of the conscious to the unconscious that is metaphorically underneath it. A stock example is a musician playing thousands of notes rapidly and accurately: he is not consciously attending to each note, though there must have been a time when he went through that phase. There is of course a mechanical element in this progress through practice, and machines can be constructed that have an efficiency far beyond the powers of human consciousness. But in the mind the two parts of the psyche are being assimilated on equal terms, a musician who plays mechanically being quite as much of a bore as a musician who has not developed enough mechanical skill. There can be no ascent of consciousness, however, without this preliminary sending of roots down into the unconscious by practice.

The two kinds of repetition, the automatic repetition and the repetition of habit or practice, are closely connected with two kinds of memory. There is a mechanical memory that simply extends the past into the present, and a cumulative memory that builds a present out of the past. Such an exhortation as Longfellow's "act in the living present" means very little if by present we mean an abstract present: a genuine present is always at the end of the past, when we have finished our narrative (up to that point) and are looking up and down. Similarly, the mechanical memory that broods on an unalterable past is in a state of bondage to it, whereas practice-repetition is a technique for setting oneself free. To practice the piano is to set oneself free to play it.

The theme of practice-repetition is, of course, involved in the metaphor of the ladder itself, with its image of step-by-step progression. The spiral form in which the ladder so often appears adds the image of cyclical movement to that of upward advance. The cycle in itself may symbolize either a constant frustration of energy, the "same dull round," in Blake's phrase, or its opposite, the self-contained energy at the apex of the spiral, where a symbol of further advance is no longer appropriate. We noted earlier the "cerchio" and "rota" at the end of the *Paradiso*.

The doctrine of purgatory is based on a conception of an "after" life, on the assumption that no human effort worth making can possibly be completed in one life, and has to be

finished in another, under more explicit divine guidance. But
metaphors of an after-life are apt to be confusing because they
suggest only an extension of our present experience into the
unknown. All after-life strictly relates to the future of the individual life or to that of humanity in history. In the New
Testament the Gospels present us with the first coming of the
Messiah, which takes place in time, and is therefore not the
apocalyptic second coming, or final separation of heaven and
hell. Such elements in Jesus' teaching as the parable of the wheat
and the tares (Matthew 13:24 ff.) warn us that life is still an
inseparable mixture of good and evil, or more accurately of
life and death. Everything in the first coming seems to be a
type of the second, and the very word second suggests a future.
But the future is still in time, and when we get to it we find
that there is nothing but more future. It seems to follow that
all revolutions in history powered by an apocalyptic vision directed toward a future are illusory, including the Christian
revolution.

So the purgatorial vision seems, so far as it is connected
with creative human effort, to point directly upward to the
paradisal world, as it does in Dante, to a world above time
where the poet "present, past and future sees" with Blake, or
sings with Yeats "Of what is past, or passing, or to come."
For Browning it was an unanswerable argument for the theis-
tic perspective that all human effort was so partial, it being the
role of God to complete what human beings could offer only
in part. In his poem "A Grammarian's Funeral" a pedant, as
many people would call him, who had spent his life on the
tiniest minutiae of Greek grammar, is borne in triumph by his
students up a purgatorial mountain to a city at the top "crowded
with culture," which is much closer to being the City of God
than any Renaissance town revitalized by the revival of learning, as the phrase at the end of the poem ("still loftier than the
world suspects") indicates. We may be reminded of Blake's
epigram: "Eternity is in love with the productions of time."

III

The technical, purgatorial and educational aspects of the Promethean vision lead up to a social one. The physical primary concerns of humanity, food, sex, possessions and freedom of movement, are elements in human life that we share with animals. It is the secondary concerns that are distinctly human, so if the twentieth century is an age in which primary concerns must again become primary, what this indicates is not an abolishing of secondary concerns but a renewed integration of humanity with nature. It is the emphasis on secondary concerns that has created law, with all its devices for postponing immediate gratification, and the arts, which are based on the distanced senses of sight and hearing, reducing the senses of direct contact, especially smell, to a very minor role. Such sublimations of sense have been the main agents in creating a new species of animal, one with a consciousness of community. The futility of trying to accomplish anything without a social context makes it obvious that human individuality is also a social product rooted in law, and is not antecedent to society.

It is traditional in Christianity to think of God as a trinity of power, wisdom and love, although of course the conception is not confined to Christianity, apart from the definitions associated with the word trinity. In this book we have been stressing particularly the wisdom and love that have always been linked in Christianity with the Word or Son of God and the Holy Spirit respectively. But the primitive basis of the idea of God is the human tendency to project anything that is mysterious or unexplored in human life, especially whatever has a power that seems to be independent of human power. The ultimate source of the sense of mysterious power is nature, with its earthquakes and floods, its droughts and thunderstorms, its predatory animals. The arbitrary and whimsical aspect of nature gradually retreats as we learn more about it, but human behavior, which is part of nature, still manifests it.

Throughout the Christian centuries there was an uneasy ambiguity between the conceptions of authority, which is always personal, and order, which is impersonal. The two meanings of the word law, in human life and in science, preserve this ambiguity in the language. God, being personal, tends to be associated with the moral and human meaning of law as authority, but in practice the authority is exercised by the human institutions of church, state and family, all of which suggest the metaphor of "Father," also applied to God. In this situation God becomes, in Blake's phrase, the ghost of the priest and king, to which we may add the head of the normally patriarchal family.

The title of this book, from Luke 4:32, alludes to many mysterious references to power by Jesus. "All power is given unto me in heaven and in earth," he tells his disciples (Matthew 28:18). This is the post-Easter Christ of the Resurrection, whose power is asserted in striking dramatic contrast with his refusal to exercise power of any kind, spiritual or physical, during the Passion. Divine power can act only in its own context of wisdom and love: in the midst of human folly its operations would have to be entirely inscrutable. Power outside that context operates only in hell. Nietzsche felt that he was completing the Promethean revolution against the sky-god by grounding human nature in a will-to-power. But Nietzsche's will-to-power does not distinguish demonic power, which uses words only to rationalize its brutality, from titanic or creative power, which is articulated in the arts and sciences and transforms the world through them. Being highly articulate himself, Nietzsche had little notion of what a will-to-power without words would lead to. Hence, though he himself was not anti-Semitic or racist, his social influence could produce only some kind of Nazism.

With the emergence of power-figures in this century for whom massacres, concentration camps and vast dislocations of people are necessary instruments of policy, the creative aspect of power disappears, and society starts on an anti-intellectual and anti-cultural course which is the road to hell on earth. This is not because intellectual or creative people are better than other people, but because such a policy is always the prelude to achieving the greatest misery for the greatest number. The degenerating of society begins with the sacrifice of primary concerns to the secondary concerns of an ideology. Once a society is at this point it finds that it cannot maintain a consistent ideology either, but breaks down into simple brutality and barbarism. The final stage is a genocide that eventually turns on itself.

Because no society in the world can afford to be complacent about such dangers, there is no more useful literary genre than the hell-fire sermon, as long as the hell is the real one that we make for ourselves, and as long as our response is genuinely concerned and not hysterical or counter-hysterical. One standard form of the hell-fire sermon is what is called the dystopia, the Utopian satire or ironic social vision, represented in this century by Orwell's *1984* and Solzhenitsyn's *First* Circle. The opposite of the dystopia, however, is hardly the Utopia itself, which is so often a contrived and anxiety-ridden form, one that apart from Plato and More has seldom achieved first-rate literary distinction.

The real opposite of the dystopia is rather the sense of a social norm already mentioned, the sense that enables irony to be ironic. An audience watching a comedy recognizes the absurdity and grotesqueness of the characters who usually dominate the action, because it already possesses a vision of a more sensible society, and many comedies move toward some visualization of such a society in their final moments. The same assumption of a social norm operates outside literature: one can hardly imagine, say, doctors or social workers unmotivated by some vision of a healthier or freer society than the one they see around them.

The norm we are speaking of has two levels. On the lower

level is a vision of fulfilled secondary concerns, the sense of a political ideology that has some connection with the processes actually going on in society, or a religious community that has some relation in practice to its theoretical goals. On the higher level is a vision of fulfilled primary concerns, freedom, health, equality, happiness, love. If this vision disappears or is replaced by the ideological one, then, however admirable the ideology may be in theory, it is subject to strong pressures to become obsessive, and so start on the downward path already indicated. If the primary vision remains there, we have the model of the earthly paradise that Dante, with his infallible insight in such matters, placed on the top of the mountain of purgatorial and creative effort.

Anyone interested in both the Bible and literature will eventually find himself revolving around the Book of Job like a satellite. Here I am trying to give a previous discussion of it a context fitting the present argument (GC 193 ff.). Job is struggling with a human situation so ironic as to leave him totally confused about its context. He assumes the context of a trial, with judge, prosecutor and counsel for the defense. He does not know, as the reader knows, about the prosecuting role of Satan and his "Does Job fear God for naught?" But naturally, like any other unfairly treated person, he wishes he could know the case against him (31:35). At the same time he is obliged to act as his own counsel for the defense, and for all his protests of confidence in his own case he feels intensely the inadequacy of having to speak for himself. He trusts however that sooner or later he will be provided with a "redeemer," as the AV calls him (19:25), a vindicator, avenger, or whatever, who will enable him, curiously, not to understand his situation, or even to get back its original form, but to attain a direct vision of God (19:27). This turns out in fact to be the primary thing that does happen (42:5), even though his property is also restored.

Job does not know either that there are two kinds of trial, the purgatorial trial which is a testing and refining operation, and which is directed toward what one can still be, and a trial of accusation like the "last Judgment," which pronounces on the past. It is the former that he is really involved in, not the latter as he thinks. Hence the sudden twist in the story that turns it from a tragedy into a comedy is a total reversal of expectation for Job, to say nothing of his friends. God himself answers Job out of the whirlwind: the judge himself comes down from the bench.

God ignores all questions of Job's guilt or innocence and of the justice or injustice of his own ways. We hear no more of wagers with Satan. God starts from the most obvious feature in the situation: the fact that Job does not understand it. He answers Job by recapitulating his original creation in the form of a vision which is held in front of Job in the present. Job is not allowed to look back to a chain of causation in the past, which would be a matter of relying on the wrong kind of memory. He has reached the end of his narrative in his present situation, and must now look up and down. What he sees is the good creation in its original unspoiled form: at one pole there is the intelligible harmony when the morning stars sang together; at the other is the leviathan who is king over all the children of pride (41:34). After this vision of a polarized cosmos Job can be restored to his original state because God has restored himself, so to speak, to *his* original state.

What is finally restored at the end of the story, however, is a society. Job may not be involved in a judgment type of trial, but his three friends are: they have been slandering God by calling him just. They are the ones to be convicted and pardoned, and Job is not restored until he prays for them (42:10). After this Job's family reappears; his friends troop back bringing money and gifts, symbols of a functioning society, and Job acquires the most beautiful women in the world for his daughters. The touch of fantasy in this last reminds us that Job's new society is held together by Job's revitalized vision, or renewed individuality, which is both its center and its circumference.

The great speech of Job that concludes Chapter 31 is not

really addressed to Job's friends, hardly even to God, nor is it simply a soliloquy. If taken as rhetoric, as an attempt to justify the ways of man to God, it is entirely futile. The friends consider the speech self-righteous (32:1), perhaps even blasphemous or atheistic, natural as such responses might be in Job's situation. But they are wrong: what the speech expresses is pure human primary concern, a concern for freedom against servitude, for happiness against misery, for health against disease. It is the voice of the poet whose imagination keeps insisting, in the teeth of all the virtues of resignation and obedience and even common sense, that most of the world it is in has no business to be there.

The answer of God, the reversing movement of the voice of prophecy or kerygma, does not really answer anything: as ordinary rhetoric it is eloquent but pointless. What it does is to put Job's primary concerns into a larger context of what Paul Tillich calls ultimate concern. The mysteries represented in metaphor by the first creation in Genesis, the mysteries of birth and death and "thrownness," can never be understood because they can never be objectified. But there is a creation that mystifies and a creation that reveals, and the latter is identical with the former. Except that the mysterious creation, the one infinitely far back in the past, is the one that Job has heard of but cannot directly see (42:5). When the infinitely remote creation is re-presented to him, he becomes a participant in it: that is, he becomes creative himself, as heaven and earth are made new for him. He is given no new discovery, but gains a deeper apprehension of what is already there. This deeper apprehension is not simply more wisdom, but an access of power.

Myths of a paradise lost in the past or a hell threatening us after death are myths corrupted by the anxieties of time. Hell is in front of us because we have put it there; paradise is missing because we have failed to put it there. The Biblical perspective of divine initiative and human response passes into its opposite, where the initiative is human, and where a divine response, symbolized by the answer to Job, is guaranteed. The union of these perspectives would be the next step, except that where it takes place there are no next steps.

Between the end of Job's speech and the beginning of God's answer we have Elihu, perhaps a later insertion by someone who shared Elihu's characteristics, bumptious, confident, proud of his close relation to the contemporary, sure of his ability to defend God and condemn Job. His credentials are very dubious, but he has his own place in the story. When we become intolerably oppressed by the mystery of human existence and by what seems the utter impotence of God to do or even care anything about human suffering, we enter the stage of Eliot's "word in the desert," and hear all the rhetoric of ideologues, expurgating, revising, setting straight, rationalizing, proclaiming the time of renovation. After that, perhaps, the terrifying and welcome voice may begin, annihilating everything we thought we knew, and restoring everything we have never lost.

Notes

INTRODUCTION

p.xii,   line 20   "misunderstanding." Fully documented in Robert D. Denham: *Northrop Frye: An Annotated Bibliography of Primary and Secondary Sources* (1987).

p.xii,   line 25   "repetitiveness." By this I mean that I have plundered various essays of mine written during the last decade or so, more particularly for the quotations.

p.xiii, line 3   "Graves." Robert Graves, *The White Goddess: A Historical Grammar of Poetic Myth* (1948).

p.xxiii, line 11   "Wallace Stevens." *The Necessary Angel* (1951), 84.

p.xxiii, line 19   "Norton lectures." Italo Calvino: *Six Memos for the Next Millennium* (1988), 112.

CHAPTER ONE

The running title of Part One is taken from Wallace Stevens, "Notes toward a Supreme Fiction," ix.

p.7,   line 11   "Derrida." See Jacques Derrida, *Of Grammatology*, tr. G. C. Spivak (1976).

p.58, line 23   "Tennyson." The lines conclude "To the Queen," the epilogue to *Idylls of the King*.

p.60, line 8   "Lawrence." Lawrence's phrase is "trust the tale."

                Logic (1938).

p.12, line 16   "Whitehead." *Science in the Modern World* (1926), ch. 1.

p.23, line 2	" 'I-Thou' relationship." Buber's *I and Thou* will be referred to later: I am not suggesting that Buber would consider that gods were a part of the "Thou" world.

CHAPTER TWO

p.32, line 23	"Anaxagoras." Of course Anaxagoras had other "impieties": Socrates in Plato's *Apology* seems anxious to dissociate himself from him. See Philip Wheelwright, *The Pre-Socratics* (1966), 154.
p.34, line 34	"Pastoral Epistles." Titus 3:9.
p.35, line 13	"Plato." "Probable tale" is Jowett; "likely story" is from H. D. P. Lee (Penguin Books, 1965).
p.39, line 21	"Petrarch's *Secretum*." Otherwise known as *De Contemptu Mundi*.
p.41, line 32	"Valéry." "Poetry and Abstract Thought," *Collected Works*, 7, tr. Denise Folliot (1958), 69 ff. Yeats's phrase is the concluding line of "Among School Children."
p.42, line 32	"platitudes." I am saying that all people need these things, not necessarily that they all want them or know what to do with them if they have them.
p.43, line 25	"*gaya scienza*." The phrase used by medieval Provençal poets about their poetry, translated by Nietzsche as "*fröhliche Wissenschaft*."
p.45, line 12	"physical roots." In other words, primary concerns have a spiritual dimension as well as a physical one. If we ask what the difference is between spiritual primary concerns and ideological secondary concerns, the answer is that the former are related to mature societies where the society is assumed to exist for the sake of the individuals within it, and the latter to hierarchical or authoritarian societies that subordinate the individual to the group as represented by its ascendant caste.
p.50, line 32	"recent book." Julian Jaynes, *The Origin of Consciousness in the Breakdown of the Bicameral Mind* (1976).
p.52, line 21	"Keats's phrase." Letter to Woodhouse, October 27, 1818.
p.54, line 1	"Puttenham." See *Elizabethan Critical Essays*, ed. Gregory Smith, II, 8. For Chapman see *op. cit*. I, 299.
p.57, line 14	"Hopkins." See *A Hopkins Reader*, ed. John Pick (1966), 29–30.

p.58, line 23   "Tennyson." The lines conclude "To the Queen," the epilogue to *Idylls of the King*.

p 60, line 8   "Lawrence." Lawrence's phrase is "trust the tale."

CHAPTER THREE

p.68, line 24   "Derrida." *Writing and Difference*, tr. Alan Bass (1978).

p.73, line 10   "Laforgue." I have taken this from the introduction to *Moral Tales*, tr. William Jay Smith (1956), xi.

p.74, line 9   "verbal icon." See W. K. Wimsatt and Monroe C. Beardsley, *The Verbal Icon* (1954).

p.74, line 32   "Roland Barthes." See *Writing Degree Zero*, tr. Annette Lavers and Colin Smith (1977).

p.81, line 29   "Montaigne." "Of Giving the Lie," *Essays*, Book II. I have used the Charles Cotton translation.

p.85, line 14   "Heraclitus." See Philip Wheelwright, *Heraclitus* (1959), 63; for Heidegger, see *Poetry, Language, Thought*, tr. Albert Hofstadter (1971), 163 ff.

p.87, line 18   "Laforgue." "Dimanches" in *Dernier Vers*.

CHAPTER FOUR

p.97, line 10   "Butler's phrase." Joseph Butler, *Analogy of Religion* (1736).

p.98, line 27   "Chesterton's phrase." G. K. Chesterton, *The Everlasting Man*, II, iv.

p.103, line 18   "difference." Another possibility is that he lifted an apocalypse from someone else, perhaps a Jewish one.

p.104, line 8   "earlier hymns." Walter Kasper, *Jesus the Christ*, tr. V. Green (1976), 126.

p.107, line 18   "Swedenborg." *True Christian Religion*, I, 8.

p.119, line 15   "early Christian father." Clement, according to Eusebius. See R. H. Lightfoot, *St. John's Gospel: A Commentary* (1956), 31.

p.123, line 33   "Yeats." "Anima Hominis," v, in *Per Amica Silentia Lunae*.

p.126, line 17   "Donne." *Devotions on Emergent Occasions*, Meditation 17.

p.127, line 4   "*puer aeternus*." C. G. Jung and C. Kerenyi, *Essays on a Science of Mythology*, tr. R. F. C. Hull (1949).

p.127, line 34   "Valéry." *Collected Works*, vol. 8, tr. Malcolm Cowley and James R. Lawler, 294 ff.

p.130, line 19   "Emily Dickinson." *The Poems of Emily Dickinson*, ed. Thomas H. Johnson (1958), III, 1283.

p.131, line 23   "shrewdly observed." Erich Heller, *The Disinherited Mind* (1952), 126.

p.133, line 7   "Michel Foucault." *The Order of Things* (1971), II, v.

p.135, line 15   "Buber." *I and Thou* (2nd ed.), tr. Ronald Gregor Smith (1958).

CHAPTER FIVE

p.145, line 12   "Cowley." "On the Death of Mr. Crashaw," 22.

p.145, line 21   "Giles Fletcher." *Christ's Triumph over Death*, st. 7.

p.150, line 10   "Bertrand Russell." *A History of Western Philosophy* (1945), ch. 23.

p.153, line 26   "Osiris." *The Book of the Dead*, tr. Sir E. A. Wallis Budge (1953), xxxv. For the "Egyptian ritual," below, see Theodor H. Gaster, *Thespis* (Anchor Books ed., 1961), 396.

p.154, line 27   "Glastonbury Tor." See Geoffrey Ashe, *Avalonian Quest* (1982).

p.155, line 18   "Donne." *Devotions on Emergent Occasions*, Meditation 2.

p.155, line 25   "Mithraism." See *The Labyrinth*, ed. S. H. Hooke (1935), 45 ff.

p.156, line 11   "*Sepher Yetzirah*." Quoted from *Origins: Creation Texts from the Ancient Mediterranean* (1976), tr. Charles Doria and Harris Lenowitz, 58. For the rendering of the title see Carlo Suares: *The Qabala Trilogy* (1985). For the Kabbalistic techniques of gematria, notarikon and temura see Gershom G. Scholem: *Major Trends in Jewish Mysticism* (1941), 100.

p.158, line 23   "further afield." See Apollodorus: *The Library*, tr. Sir J. G. Frazer (Loeb Classical Library), II, 318 ff. Also Mircea Eliade, *Shamanism* (1964), ch. 4.

p.159, line 30   "suggested influences." *Dante's Divina Commedia*, ed. C. H. Grandgent (1933), xxx.

p.162, line 32   "Yeats." Letter to Joseph Hone, September 24(?), 1927.

p.165, line 24   "outside the poets." G. W. F. Hegel, *Phenomenology of the Spirit*, tr. A. V. Miller (1977), 14; Ludwig Wittgenstein, *Tractatus Logico-Philosophicus*, tr. D. F. Pears and B. F. McGuiness (1961), 6.54.

p.165, line 30   "Donne." Satyre 3.

p.166, line 25   "Heraclitus." Philip Wheelwright, *op. cit.* 68, 147; the two early Christian writers are Hippolytus and Clement of Alexandria.

p.170, line 32   "Jonson." *Critical Essays of the Seventeenth Century*, ed. J. E. Spingarn, II, 210 ff.

p.171, line 23   "Donne." "Ecclogue 1613."

p.172, line 10   "Voltaire." *Dictionnaire philosophique:* "Chaîne des Êtres crées."

p.173, line 3   "Hölderlin." "Buonaparte" (1797).

p.173, line 33   "*Faust.*" Line 1117.

p.177, line 3   "irony." There is also the fact that *mnester* means both "suitor" and "calling to mind."

p.180, line 26   "Ovid." *Metamorphoses*, Book 12, 43 ff.

p.187, line 1   "Blake." "There is no Natural Religion," II, v.

CHAPTER SIX

p.189, line 16   "Graves." *The White Goddess*, ch. 19 ff.

p.190, line 19   "*natura naturans.*" I am aware that this distinction has other dimensions of meaning; but the simplified contrast is my concern here.

p.190, line 29   "*Paradise Lost.*" viii, 345–46.

p.191, line 33   "center of the J myth." This chapter is mainly devoted to what might be called the myth of the second Oedipal stage, where the son becomes the father and the mother rejuvenates into a bride. This theme appears in the background of Greek comedy also: see F. M. Cornford, *The Origin of Attic Comedy* (Anchor Books ed., 1961), 41, 162.

p.193, line 17   "Quaternity." C. G. Jung, *Psychology and Religion,* tr. R. F. C. Hull (1958). Jung describes "the problem of the fourth" as "an absolutely essential ingredient of totality" (127).

p.193, line 23   "Eckhart." Meister Eckhart, *The Essential Sermons (etc.),* tr. Edmund Colledge and Bernard McGinn, 177 ff.

p.198, line 2   "Rechabites." *The Old Testament Pseudepigrapha,* ed. James H. Charlesworth (1985), II, 443 ff.

p.199, line 30   "Blake." "The Mental Traveller," cited again below.

p.204, line 7   "muddled." *The Gnostic Scriptures,* tr. Bentley Layton (1987), 384.

p.205, line 21   "Hölderlin." "An die Madonna" (1803).

p.211, line 11   "Keats." Letter to Fanny Keats, July 2–4, 1818.

p.213, line 16   "pseudepigrapha." *The Old Testament Pseudepigrapha*, II, 177 ff.

p.216, line 34   "Blake." *Jerusalem*, 69.

p.220, line 15   "Keats." "Sonnet (to Homer)."

p.222, line 24   "Kierkegaard." *Either/Or*, tr. David F. and Lillian Marvin Swenson (1949), 35 ff.

p.226, line 9   "Chaucer." These are the opening lines of *The Parliament of Fowls*.

CHAPTER SEVEN

p.231, line 9   "standard work." Thorkild Jacobsen, *The Treasures of Darkness* (1976), ch. 2. The sacred marriage was the central theme of the previous chapter; the fertility that is supposed to spring from it follows the descent-and-return pattern of the present one.

p.233, line 27   "recognized." Stith Thompson, *The Folk Tale* (1946), 50 ff.

p.236, line 3   "type." *Coryat's Crudities* (reprint of 1905), II, 328.

p.247, line 8   "selfish gene." Richard Dawkins, *The Selfish Gene* (1978).

p.247, line 30   "elsewhere." Northrop Frye, ed., *Romanticism Reconsidered* (1963).

p.249, line 16   "usurping son." F. W. J. Schelling, *Philosophie der Mythologie* (*S.W.* xi).

p.253, line 6   "Some scholars think." Mircea Eliade, *Patterns in Comparative Religion*, tr. Rosemary Sheed (1958), ch. 4.

p.254, line 19   "*Beowulf.*" Lines 1605 ff.

p.255, line 10   "Yeats." See "A Dialogue of Self and Soul," where the self returns to the cycle and the soul ascends to a world of self-annihilation.

p.256, line 5   "strictly regulated." John N. Bleibtreu, *The Parable of the Beast* (1968), Part 2.

p.263, line 31   "excremental vision." Norman Brown, *Life against Death* (1959), ch. 13.

p.268, line 31   "Otto Rank." *Beyond Psychology* (1941), ch. 1. See also the "Zoroaster" passage in Shelley, *Prometheus Unbound*, I, i, 192 ff.

p.270, line 5   "interpolated verse." *Odyssey*, xi, 602–04. See the final paragraph of Yeats's *A Vision*.

p.271, line 11   "prison of Narcissus." I am indebted here to Jay Macpherson, *The Spirit of Solitude* (1982) for a comprehensive survey of Narcissus themes.

CHAPTER EIGHT

p.275, line 8   "overkill." The passage probably refers also to the prescriptions for chastity in the Israelite army in Deuteronomy 20:7.

p.275, line 22   "free with their women." Of course sexual reversal is very easy in myth: goddesses seducing male mortals appear in the stories of Gilgamesh and Ishtar, Odysseus and Calypso, Venus and Adonis, Phoebe and Endymion, etc.

p.276, line 31   "Wordsworth." *Prelude,* Book I, 398 (1850 edition).

p.282, line 5   "Gide's conception." See especially *Les Caves du Vatican.*

p.289, line 10   "Heidegger." See "What is Metaphysics?", in *Existence and Being,* ed. Werner Brock (1949), 336. For Bergson see *Creative Evolution,* tr. Arthur Mitchell (1911), 275 ff.

p.289, line 22   "Boehme." Jakob Boehme, *Six Theosophic Points,* tr. John Rolleston Earle (1958). See especially the introduction by Nicolas Berdyaev.

p.290, line 25   "*Faust.*" Part II, 6256. See Walter Arndt's translation, ed. Cyrus Hamlin (1976), 358.

p.291, line 18   "Donne." "A Valediction: Of Weeping."

p.292, line 4   "Yeats." *A Vision,* under phase 15.

p.292, line 9   "Mallarmé." Letter to Cazalis, May 14, 1867.

p.304, line 3   "Possession." I am indebted here to Lewis Hyde, *The Gift: Imagination and the Erotic Life of Property* (1979), for its demonstration that the social context of creativity is a gift economy, not a smash-and-grab one.

p.305, line 33   "doctrine of purgatory." See Hans Küng, *Eternal Life?,* tr. Edward Quinn (1985), 139 ("Purgatory is God Himself").

Index

Index of
Biblical Passages

OLD TESTAMENT

NEW TESTAMENT